Wittgenstein

Ludwig Wittgenstein (1889–1951) is considered by most philosophers – even those who do not share his views – to be the most influential philosopher of the twentieth century. His contributions to the philosophy of language and philosophy of mind – as well as to logic and epistemology – permanently altered the philosophical landscape, and his *Tractatus Logico Philosophicus* and *Philosophical Investigations* continue to be studied in philosophy departments around in the world. In this superb introduction and overview of Wittgenstein's life and work, William Child discusses:

- Wittgenstein's early work, *Tractatus Logico-Philosophicus*: its account of language, thought, and logic; its metaphysical remarks; and its view of the limits of language
- the transition from the *Tractatus* to *Philosophical Investigations*
- Wittgenstein's later philosophy of language
- intentionality and rule-following
- philosophy of mind and psychology
- knowledge and certainty
- philosophy of religion and anthropology
- the legacy and influence of Wittgenstein's ideas in philosophy, and beyond.

Including a chronology, glossary, and helpful conclusions to each chapter, *Wittgenstein* is essential reading for anyone coming to Wittgenstein's philosophy for the first time.

William Child is a Fellow in Philosophy at University College, Oxford, and University Lecturer at the University of Oxford. He is author of *Causality, Interpretation, and the Mind* (1994), and co-editor (with David Charles) of *Wittgensteinian Themes: Essays in Honour of David Pears* (2001).

GW00497957

Routledge Philosophers

Edited by Brian Leiter
University of Chicago

Routledge Philosophers is a major series of introductions to the great Western philosophers. Each book places a major philosopher or thinker in historical context, explains and assesses their key arguments, and considers their legacy. Additional features include a chronology of major dates and events, chapter summaries, annotated suggestions for further reading and a glossary of technical terms.

An ideal starting point for those new to philosophy, they are also essential reading for those interested in the subject at any level.

Hobbes	A. P. Martinich
Leibniz	Nicholas Jolley
Locke	E. J. Lowe
Hegel	Frederick Beiser
Rousseau	Nicholas Dent
Schopenhauer	Julian Young
Freud	Jonathan Lear
Kant	Paul Guyer
Husserl	David Woodruff Smith
Darwin	Tim Lewens
Aristotle	Christopher Shields
Rawls	Samuel Freeman
Spinoza	Michael Della Rocca
Merleau-Ponty	Taylor Carman
Russell	Gregory Landini

Forthcoming:

Adorno	Brian O'Connor
Habermas	Kenneth Baynes
Heidegger	John Richardson
Hume	Don Garrett

William Child

Wittgenstein

Routledge
Taylor & Francis Group

LONDON AND NEW YORK

This edition published 2011
by Routledge
2 Park Square, Milton Park, Abingdon, Oxon, OX14 4RN

Simultaneously published in the USA and Canada
by Routledge
270 Madison Ave, New York, NY 10016

Routledge is an imprint of the Taylor & Francis Group, an informa business

Typeset in Joanna MT and Din by Swales & Willis Ltd, Exeter, Devon
Printed and bound in Great Britain by
CPI Antony Rowe, Chippenham, Wiltshire

British Library Cataloguing in Publication Data
A catalogue record for this book is available from the British Library

Library of Congress Cataloging in Publication Data
Child, William (T. William)
  Wittgenstein / by William Child.
    p. cm.—(Routledge philosophers)
  Includes bibliographical references (p.) and index.
  1. Wittgenstein, Ludwig, 1889–1951. I. Title.
  B3376.W564C53 2010
  192—dc22   2010045108

ISBN 13: 978-0-415-31205-9 (hbk)
ISBN 13: 978-0-415-31206-6 (pbk)
ISBN 13: 978-0-203-81775-9 (ebk)

Printed and bound in Great Britain by
CPI Antony Rowe, Chippenham, Wiltshire

For Julia

Acknowledgements

Many people have helped me, in many ways, in the writing of this book.

I first learned about Wittgenstein from David Pears, who taught me as an undergraduate and graduate student in Oxford; from P. M. S. Hacker, who supervised my work on Wittgenstein as a BPhil student; and from John McDowell, with whom I studied the philosophy of logic and language for the BPhil. Their teaching and writings have had an enduring influence on my work.

I have learned an enormous amount from colleagues in Oxford and elsewhere with whom I have discussed Wittgenstein, and from written comments on my work. I am particularly grateful to Arif Ahmed, Anita Avramides, Tom Baldwin, Bill Brewer, John Campbell, David Charles, Naomi Eilan, Philippa Foot, Elizabeth Fricker, Jane Heal, Marie McGinn, Adrian Moore, Christopher Peacocke, Roger Squires, Peter Sullivan, Alberto Voltolini, and Tim Williamson.

A number of anonymous referees reviewed the proposal for this book and offered valuable advice and feedback. And four anonymous readers read the entire typescript for the publishers, making detailed comments and suggestions. Their advice has been extremely helpful and has led to many improvements.

I have discussed Wittgenstein's work with several generations of undergraduate and graduate students whom I have taught in Oxford. I have been lucky to have had such consistently clever and committed students and I am grateful to them all.

Over the last ten years or so, I have presented work on or relating to Wittgenstein at conferences and workshops in Lund, Beijing, Bertinoro, Washington DC, Murcia, Canterbury, Lisbon, Stirling, Reggio Emilia, Santa Cruz, Aberdeen, Stockholm, Kirchberg, Hatfield, and Southampton. And I have given talks on Wittgensteinian themes at the Universities of Bristol, East Anglia, Nottingham, Oxford, Reading, Southampton, Vercelli, Warwick and York; at Trinity College Dublin and University College Dublin; and at the Institute of the Czech Republic in Prague. I would like to thank the organizers of those events as well as the participants – whose questions, comments, and criticisms of my contributions have been very helpful.

I am grateful to Julia Drown, Dexter Drown, and Ottilie Drown for much help and encouragement while I have been working on this book.

I would like to thank the Series Editor, Brian Leiter, for inviting me to write the book; and Tony Bruce and Adam Johnson from Routledge.

In Chapter 6, I have used some material that first appeared in my article 'Memory, Expression, and Past-Tense Self-Knowledge', *Philosophy and Phenomenological Research*, 73, 2006, pp. 54–76. I am grateful to the editor and publishers for permission to do so.

Thanks are due to the UK Arts and Humanities Research Council for a Research Leave Scheme award, during the tenure of which I completed Chapter 6, on Wittgenstein's philosophy of mind and psychology.

Oxford, October 2010

A note on editions of Wittgenstein's work

A list of Wittgenstein's works appears in the References section at the end of the book. The abbreviations used in giving references in the text are listed in the next section.

There are two published translations of the *Tractatus*. The original English translation, produced by C. K. Ogden with the assistance of Frank Ramsey, was published in 1922 and is still in print. A new translation was produced in 1961 by D. F. Pears and B. F. McGuinness, and revised in 1971 in the light of Wittgenstein's correspondence with Ogden about the first translation. I have quoted from the Pears and McGuinness edition.

Philosophical Investigations was published in 1953, with a translation by G. E. M. Anscombe. The 2nd and 3rd editions appeared in 1958 and 2001, respectively. The 4th edition was published in 2009, with an English translation that has been comprehensively revised and modified by P. M. S. Hacker and Joachim Schulte. This is now the standard edition on sale and I have quoted throughout from the revised translation.

As well as revising the English translation, the 4th edition of *Philosophical Investigations* has renamed the two parts of the book. What was, in the previous editions, known as *Philosophical Investigations* Part I is now called simply *Philosophical Investigations*. Paragraph numbers for this part of the book are the same in all four editions. I follow the standard practice of using those numbers in references: e.g. 'PI §243' refers to *Philosophical Investigations* §243 (which appears in the 1st to 3rd editions as *Philosophical Investigations* Part I §243). What was previously called *Philosophical Investigations* Part II has been renamed *Philosophy of Psychology — A Fragment* (for the editors' rationale for this change, see PI pp. xxi–xxii), and paragraph numbers have for the first time been introduced into this part of the book; for ease of use, the editors have also indicated the page numbering of the 1st and 2nd editions, which has long been the standard method of referring to this material. I have followed the terminology adopted in the 4th edition. For the benefit of readers using earlier editions, references to passages in *Philosophy of Psychology – A Fragment* are given in two forms: one appropriate to the 4th edition (e.g. PPF §111 – referring to paragraph 111 in *Philosophy of Psychology – A Fragment*); the other appropriate to the 1st and 2nd editions (e.g. PI II xi p. 193 – referring to *Philosophical Investigations* Part II, section xi, page 193). (The pagination of the 3rd edition is different from that of the 1st and 2nd editions. A helpful scheme for translating between the paginations of the 1st and 2nd editions, the pagination of the 3rd edition, and the paragraph numbers in the 4th edition, can be found in Day and Krebs 2010: 357–72.)

Abbreviations

1889   Ludwig Wittgenstein born, 26 April, in Vienna.

1903–6   Having been educated at home to the age of 14, attends *Realschule* (technical school) in Linz, Upper Austria.

1906–8   Studies mechanical engineering at the *Technische Hochschule* (technical university) in Charlottenburg, Berlin.

1908–11   Conducts research in aeronautics in Manchester, working on kites and on the design of a jet engine and a propeller. Becomes interested in logic and the foundations of mathematics. Reads Bertrand Russell's *Principles of Mathematics*.

1911   Visits Gottlob Frege in Jena to discuss Frege's work on the foundations of mathematics. Advised by Frege to study with Russell.

1911   Arrives in Cambridge and meets Russell.

1912–13   Admitted as an undergraduate and then as an advanced student at Cambridge, with Russell as his supervisor.

1913   Death of Karl Wittgenstein, Ludwig's father. Wittgenstein inherits a large fortune.

1913–14   Spends most of the year in Skjolden, a small village in a remote part of Western Norway, working on logic and philosophy. Visited there by G. E. Moore in March 1914.

1914–18   War breaks out. Volunteers for Austro-Hungarian Army and joins an artillery regiment. Serves on a boat on the Vistula; then in an artillery workshop; and from 1916 to 1918 on the Eastern Front and finally the Southern Front. Receives a number of decorations for bravery. Promoted several times, reaching rank of *Leutnant* in 1918. Continues to work on philosophy throughout this time.

1918   Completes typescript of *Tractatus Logico-Philosophicus* while on leave during Summer 1918.

1918–19   Prisoner of War, held in Cassino, Italy.

1919   Returns to Vienna. Gives away his inheritance to his brother and sisters. Meets Russell in The Hague to discuss the *Tractatus*. Struggles to find a publisher for the *Tractatus*.

1919–20   Trains as a school teacher in Vienna. Works as a gardener at the monastery of Klosterneuburg in Summer 1920.

1920–6   Works as a teacher in a series of elementary schools in mountain villages (Trattenbach, Puchberg-am-Schneeberg, and Otterthal) in Lower Austria. Visited there by young Cambridge philosopher Frank Ramsey in 1923 for discussion of the *Tractatus*.

1921   Publication of the *Tractatus* (*Logisch-philosophische Abhandlung*) in Germany.

1922   Publication of the *Tractatus* in Britain, with English translation.

1926–8   Designs and supervises the building of a large house for his sister, Margarete, in the Kundmanngasse, Vienna.

1927   Meets Moritz Schlick, Professor of Philosophy at Vienna, who had earlier written to Wittgenstein expressing admiration for the *Tractatus*. Begins a series of philosophical meetings and conversations with Schlick and other philosophers of the Vienna Circle.

1929   Returns to Cambridge in January. Awarded PhD in July, having submitted the *Tractatus* as his doctoral thesis, and been examined by Russell and G. E. Moore.

1930–6   Faculty Lecturer in Philosophy at Cambridge, and Fellow of Trinity College. In connection with his consideration for the Fellowship, produces in 1930 the typescript published as *Philosophical Remarks*.

1933   Produces 'The Big Typescript', which he continues to revise for several years. (His revised version is now published as *The Big Typescript*. A selection from versions of the typescript had earlier been published as *Philosophical Grammar*.)

1933–4   Dictates *The Blue Book* to his class in Cambridge.

1935–6   Dictates *The Brown Book* to two students.

1936–7   Lives in the small house he had designed and had built in 1914 in Skjolden, Norway. Continues to work on a book intended for publication.

1938   Austria annexed by Germany in March 1938. Applies for British Citizenship, which is granted in June 1939. Returns to work in Cambridge. Completes typescript of an early version of *Philosophical Investigations*. Cambridge University Press accepts proposal to publish this work; Wittgenstein abandons the plan.

1939   Elected Professor of Philosophy at Cambridge, successor to G. E. Moore; becomes a Professorial Fellow of Trinity College. Remains Professor until 1947.

1941–3   Works as a porter at Guy's Hospital in London. Continues to lecture at Cambridge on alternate weekends, and to write on the foundations of mathematics.

1943–4   Works as a technician in medical research unit in Newcastle.

1944   Lives in Swansea, February to October, writing on rule-following and sensation language. Returns to Cambridge in October and resumes professorial duties. Continues work on *Philosophical Investigations*. Cambridge University Press accepts new proposal to publish this work together with the *Tractatus*; Wittgenstein again abandons publication plans.

1946   Completes his final version of *Philosophical Investigations*.

1947   Resigns Cambridge Professorship.

1948–9   Lives in Ireland, first on a farm in County Wicklow, then in a remote cottage in Galway, then in a hotel in Dublin. Writes on philosophy of psychology. His typescripts and notes from the period 1946–9 have been published as *Remarks on the Philosophy of Psychology* volumes I and II, and *Last Writings on Philosophy of Psychology* volume I. Completes typescript of *Philosophy of Psychology – A Fragment* (also known as *Philosophical Investigations* Part II).

1949–51   Lives with friends in Oxford, USA, and Cambridge. Is increasingly unwell, and is diagnosed with cancer in autumn 1949. Continues to work on philosophy, writing the notes now published as *On Certainty*, *Remarks on Colour*, and *Last Writings on the Philosophy of Psychology* volume II.

1951   Dies in Cambridge, 29 April. Buried at St Giles Cemetery, Cambridge.

One

Life and works

1. INTRODUCTION

Ludwig Wittgenstein was born in Vienna in 1889, and died in Cambridge in 1951. His *Tractatus Logico-Philosophicus*, a 70-page classic of twentieth-century philosophy, was completed in 1918, when Wittgenstein was 29. He then abandoned philosophy for 10 years, working first as a primary school teacher in rural Austria, and then as an architect, building a house for his sister in Vienna. Soon after his return to philosophy in 1929 he published a short conference paper; but he disliked the paper and spoke on a different subject at the conference for which it was intended. He published nothing more in his lifetime. But from 1929 until his death in 1951 he worked almost continuously on philosophy, writing thousands of pages in manuscript and typescript and, for much of this time, teaching in Cambridge, where he was a Lecturer and later Professor of Philosophy. He made a number of attempts to produce a book that properly expressed the thoughts he had developed since writing the *Tractatus*. But he was dissatisfied with each attempt, and never published these thoughts himself, leaving it to his literary executors to bring his work to publication after he died.

Wittgenstein's second major work, *Philosophical Investigations*, was published posthumously in 1953. The standard editions of this work contain two parts. In the first three editions (published in 1953, 1958, and 2001) these are labelled *Philosophical Investigations* Part I and Part II. The 4th edition (published in 2009) calls them, respectively, *Philosophical Investigations* and *Philosophy of Psychology — A Fragment*. I shall use the terminology of the 4th edition. The published text of *Philosophical Investigations* is the last of a series of versions of his projected book that Wittgenstein produced in the period from 1937 to 1946. *Philosophy of Psychology — A Fragment* is a selection by Wittgenstein from the work he did in the three years to 1949.

The years since 1953 have seen the publication of a large body of other work by, or originating from, Wittgenstein. Some of Wittgenstein's typescripts and notebooks have been published as books; there are texts he dictated to students; notes taken by students at his lectures; and so on. And all of Wittgenstein's manuscripts and typescripts are now available in an electronic edition. None of this material was intended by Wittgenstein for general publication, and most of what are, nowadays, treated as works by Wittgenstein were regarded by him as being, at very best, work in progress. But these writings are important in their own right; they cast light on the ideas expressed in Philosophical Investigations and they show Wittgenstein's thinking on topics that are not directly discussed in Philosophical Investigations.

In the period following the publication of Philosophical Investigations it was common to regard Wittgenstein as the originator of two quite different and diametrically opposed philosophies: the early philosophy of the Tractatus, and the later philosophy of Philosophical Investigations. With the publication of more of Wittgenstein's writing, and with the critical distance afforded by time, the relation between Wittgenstein's early and later work seems more complicated, in at least two ways. In the first place, it is clear that there are significant continuities between the Tractatus and Philosophical Investigations as well as significant discontinuities. There is a lively and continuing debate among commentators about the nature, extent, and relative importance of these continuities and discontinuities. Second, Wittgenstein's writings between 1929 and 1951 do not represent a unified and homogeneous 'later philosophy'. The ideas presented in Philosophical Investigations developed gradually after Wittgenstein's return to philosophy, with significant changes along the way. Some writers identify a distinct 'middle period' in Wittgenstein's philosophical work, represented by his writings from the early 1930s. Others see Wittgenstein's last writings – the work he did after the composition of Philosophical Investigations – as embodying distinctive new ideas. My own view is that we do best simply to read each work in the context of its place in the development of Wittgenstein's ideas, without trying to count a number of distinct phases in his philosophy.

2. BACKGROUND AND EARLY LIFE

Wittgenstein was the youngest of eight children; he had four brothers and three sisters. His father, Karl Wittgenstein, was a leading figure in the iron and steel industry; one of the richest men in the

Austro-Hungarian Empire. His mother, Leopoldine, was a talented musician. Musical evenings at the family's mansion in Vienna were attended by Brahms and Mahler, among others. The family had a collection of art that included works by Klimt (who painted a portrait of Wittgenstein's sister, Margaret Stonborough) and Rodin. Wittgenstein's brother, Paul, was a concert pianist: he lost his right arm in the First World War but continued to perform; it was for him that Ravel and Prokofiev each composed a piano concerto for the left hand. And Wittgenstein shared the passion for music that was common to most of the family. 'It is impossible for me to say one word in my book about all that music has meant in my life', he once said to a friend; 'How then can I hope to be understood?' (Drury 1981: 173).

In his early years Wittgenstein, like his siblings, was educated at home. That changed when he was in his early teens. Their father had subjected Ludwig's older brothers to a rigorous educational regime, designed to prepare them for a life in commerce and industry. But the consequences were disastrous for two of Ludwig's brothers, who had very different talents and interests from their father. Hans, a musical genius, ran away to the USA and disappeared in 1902, apparently having killed himself. Rudolf, an actor, committed suicide in Berlin in 1904. Partly as a result of Hans's death, the younger brothers, Ludwig and Paul, subsequently received a more orthodox education, and were sent away to school in 1903. For three years, to 1906, Ludwig attended a technical school in Linz. From 1906 to 1908 he studied at the technical university at Charlottenburg, Berlin. He later told a friend that, though 'he had been brought up to engineering . . . he had neither taste nor talent' for the subject (McGuinness 1988: 93). But, though he clearly suffered from the weight of his father's desire that at least one of his sons should succeed in a technical profession, his fascination with machinery was genuine and enduring. In childhood, he built a working sewing machine. And 'even in his last years he would spend a whole day with his beloved steam-engines' at the Science Museum in London (von Wright 1955: 4–5). Having gained a diploma from Berlin, Wittgenstein moved to Manchester, where he stayed from 1908 to 1911, registered as a research student at the University of Manchester. He was first occupied in building and experimenting with kites at a meteorological research station at Glossop. He subsequently worked on the design of a jet engine, and later on a propeller, the design of which he patented in 1911.

In these early years, Wittgenstein made no formal study of philosophy. He remarked later that 'he had read Schopenhauer's *Die Welt als Wille und Vorstellung* (*The World as Will and Representation*) in his youth and that his first philosophy was a Schopenhauerian epistemological idealism' (von Wright 1955: 6) – a view that distinguishes between the world as it appears to us (the 'empirical world' or world 'as representation') and the world as it is in itself (the 'noumenal world' or world 'as will'), regarding the world as it is in itself as accessible to us via our own experience of willing. Other early intellectual influences included the physicists Ludwig Boltzmann and Heinrich Hertz, both of whom wrote on philosophy as well as science. Their views about the relation between thought and reality are echoed in parts of Wittgenstein's *Tractatus*. And Wittgenstein was sympathetic to Hertz's conception of philosophy, quoting with approval Hertz's remark that the task of philosophy is not to advance positive theories of its own but 'to shape expression in such a way that certain worries disappear' (BT: 310).

While working as a research student in Manchester, Wittgenstein became increasingly interested in mathematics and the foundations of mathematics. He attended lectures and seminars on these topics. And he made a close study of Bertrand Russell's *The Principles of Mathematics* and Gottlob Frege's *Grundgesetze der Arithmetik* (*The Basic Laws of Arithmetic*), both of which are concerned with the project of deriving mathematics from basic, self-evident logical principles. In 1909 he formulated an attempted solution to one of the problems Frege and Russell were addressing, which he sent to a friend of Russell's, and in 1911 he visited Frege at Jena, in Germany. Frege advised him to go to Cambridge to study the foundations of mathematics with Russell. The next two years proved to be pivotal in the intellectual lives of both Wittgenstein and Russell.

3. 1911–19: CAMBRIDGE, THE FIRST WORLD WAR, AND THE *TRACTATUS*

Wittgenstein arrived in Cambridge in October 1911. He went straight to see Russell, on whom he made an immediate impression. Russell wrote:

an unknown German appeared, speaking very little English but refusing to speak German. He turned out to be a man who had learned engineering at Charlottenburg, but during his course had acquired, by

himself, a passion for the philosophy of mathematics & has now come
to Cambridge on purpose to hear me.

(Russell, Letter to Ottoline Morrell, 18 October 1911, quoted in
Monk 1990: 38–9; though Russell writes of 'an unknown German',
Wittgenstein was actually Austrian)

The next day he wrote: 'My German friend threatens to be an
infliction, he came back with me after my lecture & argued till
dinner-time – obstinate & perverse, but I think not stupid' (Russell,
19 October 1911, in Monk 1990: 39). And four weeks later, 'My
ferocious German came and argued at me after my lecture. He is
armour-plated against all assaults of reasoning. It is really rather a
waste of time talking with him' (Russell, 16 November 1911, in Monk
1990: 40).

By the end of the Cambridge term Wittgenstein was unsure whether
to pursue philosophy or to continue his work in aeronautics. He asked
Russell's advice:

My German is hesitating between philosophy and aviation; he asked
me today whether I thought he was utterly hopeless at philosophy,
and I told him I didn't know but I thought not. I asked him to bring me
something written to help me judge.

(Russell, 27 November 1911, in Monk 1990: 40)

It was when Wittgenstein presented him with what he had written
during the Christmas vacation that Russell saw the true extent of his
ability. It was, he wrote, 'very good, much better than my English
pupils do. I shall certainly encourage him. Perhaps he will do great
things' (Russell, 23 January 1912, in Monk 1990: 41).

Soon after, Wittgenstein was enrolled as an undergraduate and then
as an advanced student at Cambridge, with Russell as his supervisor. He
spent the next five terms, until summer 1913, working in Cambridge
in close intellectual collaboration with Russell. During this time, he
also formed lasting friendships with the philosopher G. E. Moore and
the economist J. M. Keynes, among others. On the death of his father,
in January 1913, he inherited a great fortune.

For most of the academic year 1913–14 Wittgenstein lived by himself in a remote village in Western Norway, working on philosophy
and developing the views he had begun to form in Cambridge. Moore

visited him in Norway in the spring of 1914; and Wittgenstein dictated to Moore some notes reporting his new ideas, which he hoped would be a means of communicating them to Russell.

War broke out in August 1914. Wittgenstein was exempted from military service on grounds of health: he had had more than one operation on a hernia. But his intense sense of duty, and his conviction that he should undergo the same hardships as others, led him to volunteer for the Austro-Hungarian army. As his sister Hermine put it, 'he was not only concerned with defending his fatherland, but . . . he also felt an intense desire to take some difficult task upon himself, and to perform something other than purely intellectual labour' (Hermine Wittgenstein 1981: 3). Having enlisted in an artillery regiment at the start of the war, he served initially on a boat on the Vistula, and then in an artillery workshop in Krakow. There, his technical aptitude was recognized and he was given the status of officer. In the years 1916–18 he served on the Eastern Front, and later the Southern Front, in conditions of great hardship and danger, first as an artillery observer and subsequently as an officer. He won a number of decorations for bravery, and was eventually promoted to the rank of *Leutnant*.

During the war years, Wittgenstein kept working on philosophy; the philosophical notebooks he maintained in the first two years of the war have been published as *Notebooks 1914–1916*. They show him continuing to wrestle with the problems about logic and language that he had worked on in Cambridge and then in Norway. And his remarks on those topics are increasingly interspersed with thoughts about good and evil, life and death, the meaning of life, the mystical, and so on. The last surviving remark from Wittgenstein's notebooks in these years concerns ethics and suicide: 'If suicide is allowed then everything is allowed. . . . Or is even suicide in itself neither good nor evil? (NB: 91, 10 January 1917). He had often thought of suicide before, telling a friend in 1912 that he had 'felt ashamed of never daring to kill himself' (McGuinness 1988: 93). On one occasion during the war he was saved from suicide by a chance encounter with his uncle (McGuinness 1988: 264). And he wrote to a friend in 1920 that 'I have continually thought of taking my own life, and the idea still haunts me sometimes' (Engelmann 1967: 33).

Wittgenstein completed the text of the *Tractatus* while on leave in August 1918. He had the typescript of the book with him when he was taken prisoner at the end of the war, and managed to send it to Russell while in detention. He remained a prisoner of war, at Cassino in Italy, until August 1919.

4. 1919–28: RETREAT

On his release from captivity after the war, Wittgenstein returned to Vienna. He had three immediate preoccupations: to have the *Tractatus* published; to get rid of his fortune; and to find an occupation that he regarded as honest and worthwhile. He had no desire to continue with philosophical work. In the *Tractatus*, he thought, he had said all there was to say; there was nothing left for him to do in philosophy. As he wrote in the preface to the book: 'I believe myself to have found, on all essential points, the final solution of the problems' (TLP: Introduction p. 4). He made the same point in a letter to Russell: 'I believe I've solved our problems finally. This may sound arrogant but I can't help believing it' (13 March 1919, WIC: 89). And five years later, in 1924, he wrote to Keynes:

> You ask me in your letter whether you could do anything to make it possible for me to return to scientific work. The answer is, No: there's nothing that can be done in that way, because I myself no longer have any strong inner drive towards that sort of activity. Everything that I really *had* to say, I have said, and so the spring has run dry. That sounds queer, but it's how things are.
>
> (4 July 1924, WIC: 153)

Finding a publisher for the *Tractatus* proved to be difficult and frustrating. That was hardly surprising, since the book was written in a terse and highly idiosyncratic style that made few concessions to the reader. Wittgenstein himself warned Russell that even he 'would not understand it without a previous explanation as it's written in quite short remarks' (13 July 1919, WIC: 89). And, as he realized: 'This of course means that *nobody* will understand it; although I believe, it's all as clear as crystal' (ibid.). The *Tractatus* was rejected by a number of publishers before one was found who was willing to produce the book with an introduction by Russell, explaining the fundamental ideas and the importance of Wittgenstein's work. But that arrangement fell through when Wittgenstein read what Russell had written: 'When I actually saw the German translation of the Introduction', he wrote to

Russell, 'I couldn't bring myself to let it be printed with my work. All the refinement of your English style was, obviously, lost in the translation and what remained was superficiality and misunderstanding' (6 May 1920, WIC: 119). At that point, Wittgenstein gave up his attempts to have the book published:

> Either my piece is a work of the highest rank, or it is not a work of the highest rank. In the latter (and more probable) case I myself am in favour of its not being printed. And in the former case it's a matter of indifference whether it's printed twenty or a hundred years sooner or later.
>
> (6 May 1920, WIC: 120)

In the event, the *Tractatus* was published in Germany in 1921 (in what proved to be the final number of the journal *Annalen der Naturphilosophie*), and in Britain – with an English translation and Russell's Introduction – in 1922. The book had an immediate impact. Keynes reported to Wittgenstein in 1924 that the *Tractatus* 'dominates all fundamental discussions at Cambridge since it was written' (29 March 1924, WIC: 151). And in the same year, the German philosopher Moritz Schlick wrote to Wittgenstein from Vienna:

> there are a number of people here – I am one myself – who are convinced of the importance and correctness of your fundamental ideas and who feel a strong desire to play some part in making your views more widely known.
>
> (WVC: 13)

Wittgenstein returned from the war determined to give up the fortune he had inherited from his father six years earlier. He had survived the war, but he continued to feel that it was wrong for him to live a life of luxury and plenty; he believed he should share the hardships experienced by other people, and that he should earn his own living. He arranged for the whole of his inheritance to be given to his sisters and his surviving brother, Paul (his fourth brother, Kurt, a cavalry officer, had shot himself at the end of the war) – insisting that the money should be irrevocably transferred to them and that no part of it should be kept in trust for him.

In 1919–20 Wittgenstein trained as a schoolteacher. He needed a source of income. He was attracted to teaching as an honest occupation, which he approached with a degree of idealism and a desire to improve the minds of his pupils. And he saw in the life of a teacher in rural Austria a way of testing himself and his character. Having qualified in 1920, he spent the next six years as an elementary school teacher in three mountain villages in Lower Austria. He achieved excellent results with the best of his students, with whom he formed good and happy relationships. But he was much less successful with those who were less bright or who were intimidated by him; he found them intensely frustrating. And he found it hard to tolerate the villagers. He wrote to Russell in 1921:

> I am still at Trattenbach, surrounded, as ever, by odiousness and baseness. I know that human beings on the average are not worth much anywhere, but here they are much more good-for-nothing and irresponsible than elsewhere . . . I don't get on well here even with the other teachers.
>
> (23 October 1921, WIC: 126)

And in 1922:

> I have been very depressed in recent times . . . Not that I find teaching in the elementary school distasteful: quite the contrary. But what's HARD is that I have to be a teacher in this country where people are so completely and utterly hopeless. In this place I have not a single soul with whom I could talk in a really sensible way.
>
> (undated 1922, WIC: 132)

He remained a teacher until 1926, when he resigned his job and returned to Vienna.

From 1926 to 1928, Wittgenstein lived in Vienna, where he was occupied with the design and construction of a mansion for his sister Margaret – a project on which he collaborated with the architect Paul Engelmann, whom he had met in Olmütz in 1916, and with whom he had formed a close friendship. The house, which now serves as the Cultural Department of the Bulgarian Embassy, is striking for its complete lack of ornament and decoration. And Wittgenstein exhibited his characteristic perfectionism and attention to detail in every aspect of the work. His sister Hermine reports:

Ludwig designed every window, door, window-bar and radiator in
the noblest proportions and with such exactitude that they might
have been precision instruments. Then he forged ahead with his
uncompromising energy, so that everything was actually manufactured
with the same exactness. I can still hear the locksmith, who asked him
with regard to a keyhole, 'Tell me, Herr Ingenieur, is a millimetre here
really that important for you?' and even before he had finished the
sentence, the loud, energetic 'Ja', that almost made him recoil.
Yes, Ludwig had such a sensitive feeling for proportions that half a
millimetre really did matter. Time and money were not allowed to be
of any consequence in such a case.

(Hermine Wittgenstein 1981: 7)

And:

The strongest proof of Ludwig's relentlessness with regard to precise
measurements is perhaps the fact that he decided to have the ceiling
of a hall-like room raised by three centimetres just as the cleaning of
the completed house was to commence. His instinct was absolutely
right and his instinct had to be followed.

(ibid.: 9)

These years in Vienna are notable for the gradual rekindling of
Wittgenstein's involvement in philosophy. Schlick had written to
him in December 1924, keen to meet the author of the *Tractatus*. They
eventually met in Vienna in early 1927, and Wittgenstein began
to meet Schlick and other philosophers of the group that was to
become the Vienna Circle of logical positivists, including Friedrich
Waismann, Rudolf Carnap, Herbert Feigl, and Maria Kasper. Those
meetings and conversations went on until the end of 1928, when
Wittgenstein returned to Cambridge. But Wittgenstein continued to
meet members of the Circle for several years after that, during vaca-
tions. Waismann's notes of these later conversations have been published in the volume *Wittgenstein and the Vienna Circle* and provide an interesting record of the development of Wittgenstein's ideas in the years
1929–32.

5. 1929–47: RETURN TO PHILOSOPHY – CAMBRIDGE, THE SECOND WORLD WAR, AND *PHILOSOPHICAL INVESTIGATIONS*

Wittgenstein returned to Cambridge in January 1929. He had come to miss the excitement and stimulation of doing philosophy. He had realized that the *Tractatus* was not the last word in philosophy. And he felt that he did now have something more to contribute. He was registered for the degree of PhD, and submitted the *Tractatus* as his PhD thesis. He was examined by Moore and Russell, and was awarded his doctorate in July 1929.

The following year, Wittgenstein was appointed to a Faculty Lectureship in the Faculty of Philosophy at Cambridge; the post continued until 1936. With the backing of Russell, Moore, and Keynes, he was elected to a Fellowship at Trinity College. Russell had to write a report on Wittgenstein's work for the Council of Trinity College and, for that purpose, Wittgenstein gave him a typescript he had completed in April 1930: a work that is now published as *Philosophical Remarks*. It is partly concerned, as was the *Tractatus*, with the topics of representation and meaning. But it differs from the *Tractatus* in a number of important respects – to be discussed in Chapter 4. And more than half of *Philosophical Remarks* deals with questions in the philosophy of mathematics: the sense of mathematical propositions, and the nature of proof, generality, and infinity in mathematics. Such questions remained an important ingredient in Wittgenstein's work over the coming years. Russell reported on this work in glowing terms:

> The theories contained in this new work of Wittgenstein are novel, very original, and indubitably important. Whether they are true, I do not know. As a logician who likes simplicity, I should wish to think that they are not, but from what I have read of them I am quite sure that he ought to have an opportunity to work them out, since when completed they may easily prove to constitute a whole new philosophy.
>
> (WIC: 183)

Wittgenstein quickly established a pattern of lecturing that he maintained throughout his time in Cambridge. Lectures were held from 5 p.m. to 7 p.m., normally in his own rooms in Trinity. His rooms, we are told:

> were austerely furnished. There were no ornaments, paintings, or photographs. The walls were bare. In his living-room were two canvas

chairs and a plain wooden chair, and in his bedroom a canvas cot. An
old-fashioned iron heating stove was in the centre of the living-room.
There were some flowers in a window-box, and one or two flower pots
in the room. There was a metal safe in which he kept his manuscripts,
and a card table on which he did his writing. The rooms were always
scrupulously clean.

(Malcolm 1984: 24–5)

And the character of the lectures themselves was quite distinctive:

Wittgenstein sat in a plain wooden chair in the centre of the room.
Here he carried on a visible struggle with his thoughts. . . . It is hardly
correct to speak of these meetings as 'lectures', although this is what
Wittgenstein called them. For one thing, he was carrying on original
research in these meetings. He was thinking about certain problems
in a way that he could have done had he been alone. For another thing,
the meetings were largely conversation. Wittgenstein commonly
directed questions at various people present and reacted to their
replies. Often the meetings consisted mainly of dialogue. Sometimes,
however, when he was trying to draw a thought out of himself, he
would prohibit, with a peremptory motion of the hand, any questions or
remarks. There were frequent and prolonged periods of silence, with
only an occasional mutter from Wittgenstein, and the stillest attention
from the others . . . One knew that one was in the presence of extreme
seriousness, absorption, and force of intellect.

(Malcolm 1984: 25)

From the time he returned to Cambridge in 1929 until his death
in 1951, Wittgenstein was almost continuously engaged in philosophical writing. He kept a manuscript notebook in which he wrote
philosophical remarks. And in other manuscript volumes he wrote out
more finished versions of his thoughts. From time to time he dictated
selections from these manuscript volumes to a typist. He would then
continue to work on these typescripts, often cutting a typescript into
small remarks which were then rearranged, revised, and supplemented
with further manuscript remarks. A further typescript would be dictated from the resultant version. The catalogue of Wittgenstein's *Nachlass* – the work left behind after his death – lists some 80 manuscripts
and 40 typescripts: most of them written in the period after 1929 (for
full details, see von Wright 1993).

A number of Wittgenstein's posthumously published writings date from the period of his Faculty Lectureship in 1930–36. An important typescript, published as *The Big Typescript*, was originally produced in 1933 and gradually revised until 1937: it deals with topics including language, thought and intention; the nature of experience; the philosophy of mathematics; and the character of philosophy itself. A version of some of this material has also been published as *Philosophical Grammar*. In addition, there are two works that Wittgenstein dictated to his students: *The Blue Book* and *The Brown Book*, dictated in 1933–34 and 1934–35, respectively. *The Brown Book* includes what is recognizably an early version of the first 180 or so sections of *Philosophical Investigations*. *The Blue Book* – which Wittgenstein described to Russell as a set of notes 'dictated . . . to my pupils so that they might have something to carry home with them, in their hands if not in their brains' (BB: v) – deals in part with the same topics, but also with questions about experience and subjectivity.

In 1936, Wittgenstein's Lectureship at Cambridge came to an end and he retreated again to Norway, where he lived in a house that he had had built in 1914; he worked there – with a few short breaks – until the end of 1937. The work done during 1936–37 was the basis for a typescript prepared the following year, which became sections 1–188 of the final version of *Philosophical Investigations*. In 1938, Cambridge University Press accepted a proposal to publish a book by Wittgenstein – for which this material was intended. At this stage, Wittgenstein was planning a book that would start with a discussion of language, meaning, and understanding and then proceed, via a discussion of the topic of following a rule, to a treatment of questions in the philosophy of mathematics. But he soon gave up that plan, dissatisfied with the arrangement of the material and, particularly, with what he had written on philosophy of mathematics.

Austria was annexed by Germany in March 1938. Soon afterwards, Wittgenstein applied for British citizenship, which was granted in June 1939. He became increasingly anxious about the situation of his brother Paul and sisters Helene and Hermine; the family's Jewish ancestry placed them in considerable danger from the Nazi regime. He played a part in the discussions that led to the family agreeing to transfer money to the Reichsbank in return for a declaration that the Wittgensteins' 'racial classification under the Reich Citizenship Law presents no further difficulties' (quoted in Monk 1990: 400).

In 1939, Wittgenstein was elected to the Professorship of Philosophy in Cambridge – previously held by G. E. Moore – and to a Professorial Fellowship at Trinity College. With the exception of the brief 1929 paper, 'Some Remarks on Logical Form', he had published nothing since his return to philosophy 10 years previously, but he was recognized as one of the leading philosophers of his time and, as the Cambridge philosopher C. D. Broad said, 'to refuse the chair to Wittgenstein would be like refusing Einstein a chair of physics' (quoted in Rhees 1981: 156). He lectured that year on the foundations of mathematics, to an audience that included the mathematician Alan Turing, and much of his writing in this and subsequent years was concerned with topics in the philosophy of mathematics. A selection of these writings, dating from 1937 to 1944, has been published as *Remarks on the Foundations of Mathematics*.

Wittgenstein took no pleasure at all in the institutional life of his College and University. And he had an extremely low opinion of academic philosophy in general: indeed, he actively discouraged his pupils from becoming professional philosophers. His friend Norman Malcolm quotes a letter Wittgenstein wrote him in response to the news that he had received his PhD:

> Congratulations to your PhD! And now: may you make good use of it! By that I mean: may you not cheat either yourself or your students. Because, unless I'm very much mistaken, *that's* what will be expected from you. And it will be *very* difficult not to do it, & perhaps impossible; & in this case: may you have the strength to *quit*.
>
> (22 June 1940, Malcolm 1984: 88)

And a few months later:

> I wish you good luck; in particular with your work at the university. The temptation for you to cheat yourself will be OVERWHELMING (though I don't mean more for you than for anyone else in your position). *Only by a miracle* will you be able to do decent work in teaching philosophy. Please remember these words, even if you forget everything I've ever said to you; &, if you can help it, don't think that I'm a crank because nobody else will say this to you.
>
> (3 October 1940, Malcolm 1984: 89)

Wittgenstein's general distaste for academic life became even more intense after the outbreak of the Second World War in 1939. As in

1914, he felt a keen need to do something useful, and to share the hardship and danger of war on the same footing as other people. After making several attempts to find some suitable war work, he arranged to become a porter in the dispensary at Guy's Hospital in London. That arrangement was facilitated by John Ryle, Regius Professor of Physic at Cambridge, and brother of the Oxford philosopher Gilbert Ryle. After meeting Wittgenstein, John Ryle wrote in a letter:

> I was so interested that after years as a Trinity don, so far from getting tarred with the same brush as the others, he is overcome by the deadness of the place. He said to me 'I feel I will die slowly if I stay there. I would rather take a chance of dying quickly.' And so he wants to work at some humble manual job in a hospital as his war-work and will resign his chair if necessary, but doesn't want it talked about at all. And he wants the job to be in a blitzed area.
>
> (quoted in Monk 1990: 431)

While working as a porter at Guy's — for which he was paid 28 shillings a week — Wittgenstein continued to write on philosophy of mathematics in his manuscript notebooks. On alternate weekends he travelled to Cambridge to give lectures. He also became interested in a research project at Guy's into 'wound shock' — a frequent diagnosis in victims of trauma, but whose existence as a genuine condition was doubted by the Guy's researchers. In 1942 the project moved to Newcastle, and Wittgenstein followed as the project technician, working in that capacity from 1943 to 1944.

At the start of Michaelmas Term 1944, Wittgenstein returned to Cambridge and resumed his professorial duties. Over the next two years, he produced the final version of *Philosophical Investigations* as we now have it. It begins in the same way as the typescript he had prepared in 1938, with a discussion of language and meaning. But its second half is completely new, dealing with sensation-language and other topics in philosophy of mind. In 1944 Cambridge University Press again accepted a proposal to publish Wittgenstein's work: the plan was for a book that would reproduce the *Tractatus* alongside Wittgenstein's later thoughts. But, as before, Wittgenstein became dissatisfied with his efforts and he abandoned the attempt to publish his work himself.

Three years after his return from war work, in 1947, Wittgenstein resigned his Professorship. He increasingly disliked life in Cambridge.

And he found it impossible to combine his duties as Professor with the philosophical work he wanted to do. As he wrote to Norman Malcolm in August of that year:

> I'd like to be alone somewhere & try to write & to make at least one part of my book publishable. I'll never be able to do it while I'm teaching at Cambridge. Also I think that, quite apart from writing, I need a longish spell of thinking *alone*, without having to talk to anybody.
>
> (27 August 1947, Malcolm 1984: 103)

He tendered his resignation in the summer of 1947 and stood down from his Professorship at the end of the year.

6. 1947–51: FINAL YEARS

From late 1947 to early 1949, Wittgenstein lived in Ireland: first on a farm in County Wicklow, then in a remote cottage in Galway, and finally in a hotel in Dublin. His health was increasingly fragile, but he continued to work on the topics that had occupied him since 1946: the concepts of thinking, intention, belief, imagination, mental imagery, perceptual experience, memory, the emotions, bodily awareness, and so on. The work he did in these years was the basis for two typescripts and a manuscript – published as *Remarks on the Philosophy of Psychology* volumes I and II, and *Last Writings on the Philosophy of Psychology* volume I. In 1949, he dictated a further typescript, containing a selection of remarks drawn mostly from those three sources. That typescript is published as *Philosophy of Psychology – A Fragment* (or *Philosophical Investigations* part II, as it was called in the 1st, 2nd, and 3rd editions of *Philosophical Investigations*).

Had Wittgenstein been in better health, it seems likely that he would have continued to develop and revise this work on philosophy of psychology. And he would have liked to have found a way to juxtapose his treatment of topics in the philosophy of psychology with a discussion of topics in the philosophy of mathematics. As he writes in the final paragraph of *Philosophy of Psychology – A Fragment*: 'An investigation is possible in connection with mathematics which is entirely analogous to our investigation of psychology. . . . It might deserve the name of an investigation of the "foundations of mathematics"' (PPF §372 (PI II xiv p. 232)). But by this time, he was resigned to the fact that his book would not be published in his lifetime, and that he would never pull together all the different elements of his work in a satisfyingly unified whole.

Wittgenstein spent the last two years of his life staying with friends in the USA, in Cambridge, and in Oxford. He visited his family in Vienna, and he undertook a last brief trip to Norway. He was increasingly unwell and, in autumn 1949, was diagnosed with cancer. But he continued to work on philosophy and, though he complained at various points of finding it impossible to think properly, he wrote extensive notebook remarks which have been published in three books that represent his final work. *On Certainty* deals with knowledge, certainty, and scepticism. Half of that work was written in Wittgenstein's last six weeks; the final remark is dated just two days before he died. *Remarks on Colour* is concerned with the nature of colour and is stimulated in particular by Goethe's Theory of Colour. *Last Writings on Philosophy of Psychology* volume II continues the reflections on the philosophy of psychology that had occupied Wittgenstein in 1946–49; the last of these remarks comes from two weeks before Wittgenstein's death.

When Wittgenstein learned that he had cancer, he 'expressed an extreme aversion and even fear of spending his last days in a hospital' (Malcolm 1984: 80). His doctor, Dr Edward Bevan, had generously invited him to come to his own house to die. Accordingly, Wittgenstein spent the last two months of his life as a guest at Dr Bevan's home in Cambridge. On his last night, before losing consciousness, he was told that his friends were on their way to see him. 'Tell them I've had a wonderful life!' he said. He died on 29 April 1951.

7. PLAN FOR THE BOOK

An introduction to the work of a great philosopher is bound to be selective. And it must skate over many matters of scholarly controversy. I have aimed to describe the most significant and most influential elements of Wittgenstein's philosophy, and to discuss writings from every period of his life. I have not attempted to give a comprehensive guide to the scholarly debate about his work; but I have indicated key points at which there are significantly divergent interpretations of Wittgenstein. The suggestions for further reading at the end of each chapter allow the interested reader to pursue those debates. The following brief description gives a guide to the contents of each chapter.

Chapters 2 and 3 deal with Wittgenstein's early work, *Tractatus Logico-Philosophicus*. Chapter 2 describes the account of language and thought advanced in the *Tractatus* – the celebrated Picture Theory of Representation – and the account of logic and analysis that go hand in hand with it. Chapter 3 considers the metaphysical remarks at the beginning of the *Tractatus*. And it discusses Wittgenstein's idea that 'there are . . . things that cannot be put into words' but that '*make themselves manifest*' (TLP: 6.522).

Chapter 4 deals with the transition from the *Tractatus* to *Philosophical Investigations*. It covers Wittgenstein's repudiation of the project of philosophical analysis that informs the *Tractatus* and his rejection, in the first 100 or so sections of *Philosophical Investigations*, of the *Tractatus*'s central doctrines about language and meaning. There are important continuities between the *Tractatus* and Wittgenstein's later work. But, as he wrote in the preface to *Philosophical Investigations*: 'since beginning to occupy myself with philosophy again, sixteen years ago, I have been forced to recognize grave mistakes in what I wrote in that first book' (PI p. viii). And Malcolm records that:

> Wittgenstein frequently said to me disparaging things about the *Tractatus* [though] he still regarded it as an important work . . . He told me once that he really thought that in the *Tractatus* he had provided a perfected account of a view that is the *only* alternative to the viewpoint of his later work.
>
> (Malcolm 1984: 58)

Chapters 5 to 8 deal with Wittgenstein's later philosophy: the work he did after his return to philosophy in 1929. Chapters 5 and 6 focus on ideas contained in *Philosophical Investigations* – though they draw significantly on other work of Wittgenstein's as well. Chapters 7 and 8 focus on aspects of Wittgenstein's thinking that are not explored at any length in *Philosophical Investigations*.

Chapter 5 concerns intentionality and rule-following. The intentionality of thought – its property of representing objects and states of affairs – is a central preoccupation in Wittgenstein's writings from the early 1930s: When I want an apple, he asks, what makes it the case that it is *an apple* that I want? When I expect Jones to arrive at 3 p.m., what makes it the case that the person I am expecting is *Jones*, and that what I am expecting him to do is *to arrive at 3 p.m.*? The same questions feature in *Philosophical Investigations* and beyond. Wittgenstein's discussion of following a rule has a central place in *Philosophical Investigations*. It occupies §§143–242 of the book, and provides a bridge between the discussion of language, meaning, and understanding in the first half of *Philosophical Investigations* and the treatment of topics in philosophy of mind in the second half. These passages have been a central topic of interpretative and philosophical debate over the last 30 years. And they are noteworthy as the area in which Wittgenstein's reflections on the philosophy of mathematics are most visible in the work that he himself prepared for publication. I do not explore the details of Wittgenstein's work on philosophy of mathematics in this book, but the discussion of following a rule includes themes that have an important place in that work.

Chapter 6 deals with the philosophy of mind and psychology, focusing largely on *Philosophical Investigations* and *Philosophy of Psychology – A Fragment* (or *Philosophical Investigations* Part II), but drawing also on early writings and conversations from 1929 to 1930, and on other material from 1946 to 1949. The first part of the chapter deals with Wittgenstein's discussion of sensations and sensation language and considers, among other topics, the famous private language argument of *Philosophical Investigations*: the argument that there could not be a 'private sensation language' – a language whose words 'refer to what only the speaker can know – to his immediate private sensations' (PI §243). The second part discusses Wittgenstein's response to some central ideas of two psychologists whose writings were particularly influential at the time: William James and Wolfgang Köhler.

Chapter 7 discusses *On Certainty*: the collection of remarks about knowledge and certainty that Wittgenstein wrote in the few months before his death. There has been a flourishing of interest in *On Certainty* in recent years. That is partly explained by a revival of interest in questions about knowledge and scepticism in contemporary philosophy. It also reflects a more general increase in the attention scholars have given to Wittgenstein's final work.

Chapter 8 deals with two linked topics: Wittgenstein's philosophy of religion and his views on the understanding of rituals and ceremonies – views that bear on anthropology and social science. Neither of these topics is very prominent in Wittgenstein's writings. But what he does say about them has attracted a great deal of interest, from scholars in other disciplines as well as from philosophers. I include them here because Wittgenstein's ideas on these topics have had a particular influence outside academic philosophy, and are particularly likely to have attracted the attention of general readers.

Chapter 9 reflects on the influence of Wittgenstein's ideas in philosophy and beyond.

SUMMARY

Wittgenstein was born into an exceptionally wealthy and very talented family. In early life he showed no special interest in philosophy; nor was he particularly successful at school. And his late teens and early twenties were a period of restlessness and unhappiness as he sought an occupation that would really engage him. His involvement in philosophy was stimulated by an interest in the foundations of mathematics, which he studied through the writings of Frege and Russell. His early years in Cambridge, from 1911 to 1913, were a crucial stage in his life, during which he worked intensively with Russell on problems of logic and language. Wittgenstein's early masterpiece, Tractatus Logico-Philosophicus, which developed from the work he began in Cambridge, was completed while he was a soldier fighting in the First World War and was published in 1921. It made an instant impact in Cambridge and Vienna, and established Wittgenstein's reputation as one of philosophy's deepest and most brilliant thinkers. Having completed the Tractatus, Wittgenstein withdrew from philosophy for 10 years: he no longer had a 'strong inner drive' towards philosophy; his 'spring ha[d] run dry'. He returned to philosophy in 1929, and for the next 18 years his philosophical life was largely based in Cambridge, where he was first a Lecturer and then, from 1939, Professor – with a break from 1941 to 1944, during which he was engaged in war work. In these later years he abandoned many of the doctrines of the Tractatus. He developed new views about language and meaning, and a new conception of the way in which philosophical understanding is to be achieved. And he wrote extensively on the philosophy of mind and the philosophy of mathematics. However, none of this work was published in his lifetime. He finished work on Philosophical Investigations in 1947, the year in which he resigned his Professorship at Cambridge. The typescript published as Philosophy of Psychology – A Fragment (in earlier editions, Philosophical Investigations Part II) was completed in 1949. Wittgenstein's final years were dogged by ill-health. But he continued to work on philosophy right up to his death in 1951. Philosophical Investigations was published posthumously in 1953 and, like the *Tractatus* more than 30 years earlier, was immediately recognized as a philosophical masterpiece. Many of Wittgenstein's typescripts and notebooks have been published as books since then. All of them are now available electronically.

FURTHER READING

There are two excellent biographies of Wittgenstein; I have relied heavily on them in writing this chapter. One deals just with the period up to the publication of the *Tractatus*:

McGuinness, B. (1988) *Wittgenstein: A Life − Young Ludwig 1889–1921*, London: Duckworth; reprinted, Harmondsworth: Penguin Books, 1990.

The other leading biography covers the whole of Wittgenstein's life:

Monk, R. (1990) *Wittgenstein: The Duty of Genius*, London: Jonathan Cape.

There are a number of memoirs of Wittgenstein written by friends who knew him at various stages of his life. They give a vivid impression of him, and make clear the forceful effect he had on those around him. See particularly:

Malcolm, N. (1984) *Ludwig Wittgenstein: A Memoir*, 2nd edition, Oxford: Oxford University Press.
Engelmann, P. (1967) *Letters from Ludwig Wittgenstein with a Memoir*, ed. B. McGuinness, trans. L. Furtmüller, Oxford: Blackwell.

Malcolm's memoir also contains a brief biography by another of Wittgenstein's friends:

von Wright, G. H. (1955) 'Ludwig Wittgenstein: A Biographical Sketch', *Philosophical Review* 64: 527–45.

Several other personal memoirs, including recollections by Wittgenstein's sister Hermine, are contained in:

Rhees, R. (ed.) (1981) *Ludwig Wittgenstein: Personal Recollections*, Oxford: Blackwell.

For a very helpful account of the intellectual and cultural environment of early-twentieth-century Vienna, and its influence on Wittgenstein's thought, see:

Janik, A. and Toulmin, S. (1973) *Wittgenstein's Vienna*, London: Weidenfeld and Nicolson.

Many of Wittgenstein's letters survive. They are a helpful source of historical information. They also give a good sense of Wittgenstein's character and emotions, his relationships with his friends, and his view of his own work. InteLex publish a complete electronic edition of Wittgenstein's correspondence in their Past Masters series. For a comprehensive collection of letters from Wittgenstein to Russell, Moore, Keynes, and other friends and colleagues from Cambridge, together with some of their letters to him, see:

B. McGuinness (ed.) (2008)*Wittgenstein in Cambridge: Letters and Documents 1911–51*, Oxford: Blackwell.

Engelmann's and Malcolm's memoirs (see above) contain the letters that each of them received from Wittgenstein. And Wittgenstein's letters to G. H. von Wright are printed in:

Klagge, J. and Nordmann, A. (eds) (1993) *Ludwig Wittgenstein*, Philosophical Occasions 1912–1951, Indianapolis: Hackett Publishing Company.

Most of the letters to Malcolm and von Wright are also reproduced in McGuinness's *Wittgenstein in Cambridge*.

For a complete catalogue of Wittgenstein's writings, see:

von Wright, G. H. (1993) 'The Wittgenstein Papers', in Wittgenstein, *Philosophical Occasions*.

Other one-volume introductions to Wittgenstein's work, which readers might like to consult, include:

Fogelin, R. (1995) *Wittgenstein*, 2nd edition, London: Routledge.
Kenny, A. (2006) *Wittgenstein*, revised edition, Oxford: Blackwell.
Schroeder, S. (2006) *Wittgenstein: The Way Out of the Fly-Bottle*, Cambridge: Polity.
Schulte, J. (1992) *Wittgenstein*, trans. W. Brenner and J. Holley, Albany, NY: SUNY Press.

Two

The *Tractatus*: language and logic

The *Tractatus* deals with familiar philosophical topics: the nature of reality; how we represent the world in language and thought; logic; and so on. What it says about those topics is related at many points to the views of other philosophers: most notably Frege and Russell. But the *Tractatus* is unlike any other work of philosophy: not so much because of the views it contains, but because of its style and presentation. Its statements are terse and oracular, with minimal explanation or supporting argument. It is written not in continuous prose but in brief paragraphs, arranged in a decimal numbering system that 'indicate[s] the logical importance of the propositions, the stress laid on them in [Wittgenstein's] exposition' (TLP: p. 5, note). But despite the *Tractatus*'s forbidding appearance, its content is less alien than it first seems.

The seven main propositions of the *Tractatus* – the propositions assigned the integers 1 to 7 – read as follows:

1 The world is all that is the case.
2 What is the case – a fact – is the existence of states of affairs.
3 A logical picture of facts is a thought.
4 A thought is a proposition with a sense.
5 A proposition is a truth-function of elementary propositions.
   (An elementary proposition is a truth-function of itself.)
6 The general form of a truth-function is $[\bar{p}, \bar{\xi}, N(\bar{\xi})]$.
   This is the general form of a proposition.
7 What we cannot speak about we must pass over in silence.

That list of propositions – in which each remark picks up and expands on a concept introduced in the previous proposition – illustrates the careful crafting of Wittgenstein's presentation. It also provides an immediate indication of the four main themes of the *Tractatus*:

- Reality
- Thought and language
- Logic and the analysis of complex propositions into elementary propositions
- The limits of what can be expressed in language.

This chapter deals with the *Tractatus*'s account of representation, logic, and analysis. Chapter 3 will consider Wittgenstein's discussion of reality and the limits of language.

1. REPRESENTATION

'A proposition', Wittgenstein says, 'is a picture of reality' (TLP: 4.01). 'At first sight', he admits, 'a proposition – one set out on the printed page, for example – does not seem to be a picture of the reality with which it is concerned' (4.011). Nonetheless, he insists, when we understand how propositions represent reality we will see that a proposition is a picture: that the way in which propositions represent reality is essentially the same as the way in which pictures represent reality. That is the fundamental intuition behind the *Tractatus* account of linguistic meaning. To understand the account, therefore, we must first understand Wittgenstein's general account of picturing; then we can see how he applies that account to the case of language.

Wittgenstein's theory of pictorial representation is succinctly stated:

2.12 A picture is a model of reality.

2.13 In a picture objects have the elements of the picture corresponding to them.

2.131 In a picture the elements of the picture are the representatives of objects.

2.14 What constitutes a picture is that its elements are related to one another in a determinate way.

2.141 A picture is a fact.

2.15 The fact that the elements of a picture are related to one another in a determinate way represents that things are related to one another in the same way.

We can highlight three essential features of this account. First, each element of a picture corresponds to an element of the scene it depicts.

So, for example, a given patch on the surface of the painting on my wall corresponds to one man; another patch corresponds to a second man. Second, the fact that the elements of the picture are arranged in a particular way represents that the corresponding elements of the world are arranged in the same way. If the elements in the world really are arranged in that way, then the picture is correct, or true; if the elements in the world are not arranged that way, then the picture is incorrect, or false. For example, the fact that the patch of paint that corresponds to the first man is to the left of the patch that corresponds to the second man represents that the first man is standing to the left of the second man. If the first man really was standing to the left of the second man on the occasion the painting represents, then the picture is correct – in that respect, at least. The third crucial feature is that, as Wittgenstein puts it, 'a picture contains the possibility of the situation it represents' (2.203); if some situation is represented in a picture, then it is possible for that situation to obtain. A picture can represent a situation that *does not* obtain; but it cannot represent a situation that *could not* obtain – an impossible situation.

Wittgenstein thinks this account of pictorial representation captures what is essential to *all* representation. It applies to pictures in the ordinary sense. But, he thinks, it also applies to three-dimensional models, to maps, to musical scores, and to every other kind of representation. In a musical score, for instance, the marks on the stave correspond to the individual notes in the piece of music; the arrangement of the written notes represents the same arrangement of notes in the piece of music; and a score cannot represent an impossible arrangement or combination of notes. Exactly the same account of representation, Wittgenstein thinks, applies to propositions. Thus, each feature in his general account of pictorial representation is exactly mirrored in his account of propositions:

4.01   A proposition is a picture of reality.
       A proposition is a model of reality as we imagine it.
3.22   In a proposition a name is the representative of an object.
3.14   What constitutes a propositional sign is that in it its elements
       (the words) stand in a determinate relation to one another.
       A propositional sign is a fact.
3.21   The configuration of objects in a situation corresponds to the
       configuration of simple signs in the propositional sign.

The three essentials of picturing, Wittgenstein thinks, apply directly to propositions. First, each element in a proposition – each word – corresponds to an element in the situation that is represented by the proposition – an object. Second, the fact that the words are arranged in a particular way represents that the corresponding objects are arranged in the same way: the proposition is true if the objects are arranged in that way; it is false if they are not. Third, a proposition cannot represent an impossible situation:

> It is as impossible to represent in language anything that 'contradicts logic' as it is in geometry to represent by its coordinates a figure that contradicts the laws of space, or to give the coordinates of a point that does not exist.
>
> (3.032)

When the idea that a proposition is a picture is stated as briefly as that, it is easy to wonder what is interesting or contentious about it; how far does it really take us in understanding how language functions? To get a clearer sense of the content and significance of the picture theory, we need to understand the problems it is meant to address; how it differs from other accounts of meaning that were on offer at the time; and how exactly the analogy between pictures and propositions is supposed to work. We can examine each of those points in turn.

i. The problem of propositional representation

'A proposition', writes Wittgenstein, 'communicates a situation to us' (4.03). But *how* does it communicate a situation; what is the connection between a proposition and the situation it communicates?

In thinking about the relation between language and reality, it is natural to start with the relation between a name and the thing it names. For that relation seems relatively easy to understand: a name functions by standing for an object; and it seems relatively easy to see what that involves. But the connection between a proposition and the situation it communicates is fundamentally different from the connection between a name and the object it names. In the first place, in order to understand a new or unfamiliar name we must have its meaning explained; we must learn which object it stands for. But we can understand a new proposition without needing to have its meaning explained. As Wittgenstein puts it: 'We understand the sense of a propositional sign without its having been explained to us' (4.02); 'It belongs to the essence of a proposition that it should be able to communicate a new sense to us' (4.027). But if propositions were connected to reality in the same way as names — by being individually attached to elements in reality — that would be impossible. In the second place, a proposition can be perfectly meaningful even if it is false. But again, if propositions were connected to reality in the same way as names, that would be hard to understand. The meaningfulness of a name consists in its standing for an object. So a name that stands for no object at all — an empty name — has no meaning. (That, at any rate, was Wittgenstein's view, which he shared with Russell.) Now suppose a proposition functioned like a name, by standing for an item in the world. And consider the proposition 'Desdemona loves Cassio'. If the proposition is true — if Desdemona does love Cassio — then there is a state of affairs in the world that corresponds to that proposition: the state of affairs of Desdemona loving Cassio. So, we might think, the proposition 'Desdemona loves Cassio' means what it does by virtue of standing for that state of affairs. But what if the proposition is false? In that case, there is no state of affairs of Desdemona loving Cassio; there is nothing in the world for the proposition to stand for. So if the meaningfulness of a proposition consisted in its standing for an item in the world, the proposition 'Desdemona loves Cassio' would have no meaning. But that conclusion is absurd; it is obvious that a proposition can be meaningful without being true. For both these reasons, then — the fact that we can understand new propositions without having their meanings explained, and the fact that a proposition can be false yet meaningful — the connection between a proposition and reality cannot work in the same way as the connection between a name and reality. How, then, does it work?

In 1912, when Wittgenstein arrived in Cambridge, Russell had worked out what he thought was a solution to these problems: the 'multiple relation theory of judgement' (Russell 1910; Russell 1912: ch. 12). (Russell presents his view as an account of judgement or belief rather than an account of linguistic meaning. For present purposes, we can gloss over the difference.) Suppose Othello believes that Desdemona loves Cassio. That belief is false; Desdemona does not love Cassio. So, as we have seen, Othello's belief cannot involve the obtaining of a relation between Othello and the state of affairs of Desdemona loving Cassio; there is no such state of affairs. Russell proposes, instead, that

Othello's belief involves a relation between him and the entities his belief is about: Desdemona, the relation of loving, and Cassio. The relation of believing, says Russell, 'knits together' the person who has the belief (Othello) and the objects of the belief (Desdemona, loving, and Cassio). And it can knit Othello together with those objects whether or not the objects actually are related in the way he believes them to be. Othello's belief is true if Desdemona really is related to Cassio by the relation of loving; otherwise it is false. But even if the belief is false, it still has a definite content.

Russell's account is an attempt to answer the question, how a proposition or belief can be meaningful but false. But, Wittgenstein thinks, it is itself unacceptable. A first objection is that Russell treats a judgement as 'a complex whole' (Russell 1912: 73), a 'complex object', or a 'complex unity' (Russell 1912: 74); it is a complex object made up of the subject of the judgement (say, Othello) and the objects of his belief (say, Desdemona, loving, and Cassio). But a complex object, Wittgenstein thinks, has no *significance*: it does not *say* or *represent* that something is the case. After all, we can combine any words at all to make a complex object – the complex object 'Othello Desdemona Cassio believes loves', for example – but that object does not say anything. So a proposition must be different from a complex object like that. But nothing in Russell's theory tells us how it differs. So Russell's theory does not explain how a proposition communicates a situation: how it succeeds in *saying* something.

Wittgenstein raises a second objection to Russell, which he puts like this: 'The correct explanation of the form of the proposition, "*A* makes the judgement p", must show that it is impossible for a judgement to be a piece of nonsense. (Russell's theory does not satisfy this requirement.)' (TLP: 5.5422). Russell conceives a judgement as a complex made up of the person doing the judgement and the objects of her judgement. But what ensures that the judgement 'knits together' those objects in a way that is really possible for the objects? What prevents me judging that loving Desdemona's Cassio, or that this table penholders the book (see NL: 103)? It is evidently impossible, Wittgenstein thinks, to judge a piece of nonsense like that. But, he thinks, Russell's theory does not explain why it is impossible.

In 1913, partly in response to these objections, Russell amended his theory. He proposed that someone who judges that Desdemona loves

Cassio must be acquainted not only with the objects of the judgement (Desdemona, loving, and Cassio) but also with the 'form' of the complex 'Desdemona loves Cassio' – 'the way in which the constituents are combined in the complex' (Russell 1913: 98). In order to understand the proposition 'Desdemona loves Cassio', Russell proposed, we must know 'what is supposed to be done with' the component objects: Desdemona, Cassio, and the relation of loving (Russell 1913: 116). If we are acquainted with the form of the complex, then we have the general idea of one object being related to another. Taken together with the knowledge that Desdemona and Cassio are objects, and that loving is a relation, that allows us to understand the proposition 'Desdemona loves Cassio' regardless of whether or not it is true. What makes it impossible to understand the 'proposition' 'loving Desdemona's Cassio' is that that combination of elements does not 'fit' the form of one object being related to another: for loving is not an object; and Desdemona is not a relation.

In Wittgenstein's view, however, this amendment of Russell's theory was no more successful than the original version. In the first place, the amended view still treats a proposition as a complex. So, Wittgenstein thinks, it remains vulnerable to the point that a complex object does not say that something is the case. In the second place, Russell's new theory involves the idea of acquaintance with logical forms and logical objects – the idea of 'logical intuition' (Russell 1913: 101). In order to understand a proposition, Russell thought, we must be acquainted with the pure logical form of the complex it represents. And in order to understand the words 'or', 'not', 'all', 'some', and so on, we must be acquainted with the logical objects they denote (ibid.). But in Wittgenstein's view, there are no logical objects (we will see in section 2.ii below how that principle informs his treatment of logical propositions). There is no realm of logical forms and logical objects, analogous to the empirical world, but lying somewhere beyond it. And there is no logical experience necessary in order to understand either logic or ordinary propositions. Concerning logic, Wittgenstein says this:

> The 'experience' that we need in order to understand logic is not that something or other is the state of things, but that something *is*: that, however, is *not* an experience.
>
> Logic is *prior* to every experience – that something *is so*.
>
> (TLP: 5.552)

Concerning ordinary propositions, he says that a proposition 'is understood by anyone who understands its constituents' (TLP: 4.024). To understand the proposition 'Desdemona loves Cassio', we need to understand the words 'Desdemona', 'loves', and 'Cassio'; but we do not also need acquaintance with a logical form. Russell's amended theory depends on a world of logical forms and logical objects, and a faculty of logical intuition, that Wittgenstein completely rejects.

ii. Propositions as pictures

How did the picture theory address the problems faced by Russell's account? The first problem was that Russell's theory treated propositions as complex objects, and that a mere complex – 'a blend of words' (TLP: 3.141) or 'a set of words' (3.142) – does not say anything. Wittgenstein's response to that problem is the idea that 'a propositional sign is a fact' (TLP: 3.14). It is the fact that the elements in a proposition are arranged in the way they are, he thinks, that represents that objects are arranged in the corresponding way. In that way, Wittgenstein stresses the fundamental difference between the way that a name has meaning and the way that a proposition has meaning – a difference which, he says, 'is obscured by the usual form of expression in writing or print. For in a printed proposition, for example, no essential difference is apparent between a propositional sign and a word' (3.143).

But the difference, he insists, is crucial. A name, or a set of names, or a composite name, does not *communicate* anything; it does not *say that something is the case* (see 3.142–3.143). What does that is a fact: the fact that the elements of the proposition are related in a certain way. In the proposition 'Desdemona loves Cassio', it is the fact that the name 'Desdemona' is related to the name 'Cassio' in the way it is that says that Desdemona loves Cassio. (How, in Wittgenstein's view, is the name 'Desdemona' related to the name 'Cassio' in the proposition 'Desdemona loves Cassio'? Different commentators offer different answers to that question. But a plausible suggestion is this: it is the fact that 'Desdemona' stands to the left of the word 'loves' and 'Cassio' stands to the right of the word 'loves' that says that Desdemona loves Cassio.)

A second problem with Russell's account, according to Wittgenstein, was its failure to explain why it is impossible to judge a piece of nonsense. How did his own theory explain it? If a proposition is a picture, what prevents it picturing something impossible? In the case of a three-dimensional model, it is easy to see why we cannot represent an impossible state of affairs. Suppose we use model cars to represent the relative positions of real cars in a road accident. (Wittgenstein said that the idea that a proposition is a picture of reality came to him when he read a newspaper report of a Paris lawsuit concerning a traffic accident. The accident was represented by means of model cars, dolls, and so on (see NB: 7; von Wright 1955: 8).) The elements of the represented state of affairs, the cars, are physical objects. The elements of the model, the model cars, are also physical objects. It is this fact – that the elements of the model are things of the same kind as the objects they represent – that ensures that the representational elements cannot be arranged in a way that is impossible for the objects they represent. We cannot, for instance, use model cars to represent the impossible state of affairs of two cars being in exactly the same place at the same time. To do that, we would have to put two model cars in the same place at the same time. And that is impossible, for the same reason that it is impossible for two real cars to occupy the same place at the same time: their physical nature. With linguistic representation, however, it is less easy to see what rules out combining words in ways that are impossible for the things to which they correspond. We cannot make a 3-D model that shows two cars in the same place at the same time. But we can *say* 'Car A and Car B were in exactly the same place at the same time'. And isn't that a picture of an impossible state of affairs? Wittgenstein insists that it is not. We need to understand what rules it out.

In the *Notebooks*, Wittgenstein writes: 'One name is representative of one thing, another of another thing, and they themselves are connected; in this way – like a *tableau vivant* – the whole images the situation' (NB: 26; compare TLP: 4.0311). That is a succinct statement of the picture theory. The passage continues:

> The logical connection [between the names] must, of course, be one that is possible as between the things that the names are representatives of, *and this will always be the case if the names really are representatives of the things.*
>
> (NB 26, emphasis added)

If names 'really are representatives of the things', Wittgenstein thinks, they cannot be combined in ways that are not possible 'as between the things the names are representatives of'. So in order for a word to function as the name of an object – to be a representative of that object – it is not sufficient that the word should be associated with the object; it must also be used in a way that respects the combinatorial possibilities of the object. If we combined words in a way that was not possible for the objects those words putatively stood for, we would not be using the words as names of the objects at all. But what ensures that our use of a name does respect the combinatorial possibilities of the corresponding object? What prevents us combining names in ways that are not possible for the objects they name?

We can distinguish two general approaches one might take in answering that question: a 'bottom-up' approach and a 'top-down' approach. On the bottom-up approach, we start by identifying an object that is to be named. Then we determine its nature: its possibilities of combining with other objects in states of affairs. That allows us to make sure that we combine the name of the object with other names only in ways that respect the object's combinatorial possibilities. We thereby satisfy Wittgenstein's condition for using a word as a representative of the object. On the top-down approach, by contrast, the relation between names and objects is more like the relation between the terms in a scientific theory and the things the theory is about. Consider the term 'quark', which refers to a kind of fundamental physical particle. The word 'quark' is introduced as part of a whole theory about the ultimate constitution of matter. The theory contains words for various kind of particle; it contains generalizations about the behaviour of those particles, about their relations to one another and to other phenomena, and so on. The theory as a whole defines what a quark is; it is a particle that has the characteristics set out in the theory. So it is in virtue of its place in the theory as a whole that the word 'quark' names the kinds of particle it does. The top-down model sees the relation between names and objects in the *Tractatus* in a similar way. Our everyday language is a kind of 'theory' about the world. The totality of true propositions implicitly defines the nature and identity of the objects we are talking about when we use our everyday language. It is in virtue of its place in this overall 'theory' that a given name picks out the object it does. If we take this view, the question 'What ensures that we combine names only in ways that are possible for the corresponding objects?' is misplaced. In the case of a scientific theory, it would be idle to ask what ensures that the words 'quark', 'lepton', 'proton', and 'neutron' are combined only in ways that are possible for the corresponding particles. It is *because* the words are combined in the ways they are – ways that *are* possible for the corresponding particles – that the words serve to pick out those particles; that is part of what makes the theory a theory about quarks, leptons, and the rest. Similarly, on the top-down view of Tractarian names, it is *because* words are combined in the ways they are that they function as names of the objects they do: objects whose combinatorial possibilities are mirrored by the combinatorial possibilities of the names. There is, on this view, no question of first identifying an object and then needing to ensure that we use its name only in ways that respect its combinatorial possibilities.

Which approach does Wittgenstein take in the *Tractatus*? Does he think that names are correlated with objects in a bottom-up or a top-down way? Wittgenstein does not say what kind of entity he takes an object to be; he gives no examples of objects, and no examples of names. It would require a process of logical analysis, he thinks, to get from sentences of our ordinary language to elementary propositions composed of names of simple objects. And he does not know what the end-point of that process of analysis will be. As he put it later, commenting on the *Tractatus*: 'I used to believe . . . that it is the task of logical analysis to discover the elementary propositions . . . I [thought] that the elementary propositions could be specified at a later date' (WVC: 182). It might seem, then, that Wittgenstein simply says too little for us to tell whether he takes a bottom-up or a top-down approach. But in fact there are good reasons for thinking that Wittgenstein does not conceive of the relation of names to objects in a bottom-up way.

The bottom-up model works best if Tractarian objects are objects of acquaintance: things we encounter in perception. We perceive an object; we give it a name; we go on to use the name in ways that respect the object's combinatorial possibilities. But Wittgenstein does not think of Tractarian objects as things that we know by perceptual acquaintance. He says that 'If objects are given, then at the same time we are given *all* objects' (5.524). But if Tractarian objects were objects of perceptual acquaintance, it would be hard to make sense of that remark. For it is certainly not true that if one is perceptually acquainted with some objects then one is at the same time perceptually acquainted with *all* objects. The remark makes better sense on the top-down approach. On that view, one knows an object by mastering a language that contains a name for the object – just as one knows what a quark is by mastering the theory that contains the term 'quark'. And just as, in grasping a scientific theory, one learns simultaneously of all the kinds of entity it mentions, so there is a sense in which, when one masters a whole language, one thereby comes to know simultaneously all the objects that are named in that language.

Another consideration in favour of a top-down reading of the *Tractatus* is that the picture theory is a general theory of representation; the account it offers is supposed to apply not just to language but also to thought. A sentence is a picture of a state of affairs; it is made up of names that are correlated with objects. In the same way, Wittgenstein thinks, a thought is a picture of a state of affairs; it is made up of simple psychical elements which, like names, are correlated with simple objects. So the question, how the elements of a picture are attached to the objects they represent, arises for the psychical components of thoughts just as much as it arises for names. But it is hard to see how the bottom-up model of the attachment of names to objects could be transferred to the case of thought. On Wittgenstein's view, thinking of an object, a, involves the presence in one's mind of some psychical element, α, which functions as a representative of a. How does α come to represent a? The bottom-up model suggests that we must first identify a, and then use the psychical element α in a way that respects a's combinatorial possibilities. But in order to identify a, we must already have some way of thinking of it; our mind must already contain some psychical element, β, that functions as a representative of a. And how was the relation between β and a established? If that relation was established in the bottom-up way, we must already have had some other way of thinking of a. And so on, without end. So the bottom-up model seems unable to explain the connection of psychical elements with the objects they represent. Once more, then, we make better sense of the *Tractatus* if we understand the relation between the elements of a picture and objects on the top-down rather than the bottom-up model.

Finally, how plausible is the idea that a proposition functions by picturing a state of affairs? As we shall see in Chapter 4, Wittgenstein himself came to reject the picture theory. One of his objections was that the picture theory focused exclusively on the use of language to make statements that are true or false. But, he came to see, we use language to do lots of other things: to give expression to sensations and emotions, to lay down rules and conventions, to express moral attitudes and religious commitments, and so on. The *Tractatus* account of meaning ignored those kinds of use; it took one use of language and treated it as the paradigm for all meaningful language.

But Wittgenstein did not just come to think that the picture theory focused on too limited a sub-set of the uses of language. He also came to reject the theory even as an account of those propositions that do make statements that are true or false. For the picture theory was simply too abstract and programmatic to provide any genuine illumination. That is a criticism that Wittgenstein himself expressed in the early 1930s:

> Anything can be a picture of anything, if we extend the concept of picture sufficiently. If not, we have to explain what we call a picture of something, and what we want to call the agreement of the pictorial character, the agreement of forms.
>
> For what I said really boils down to this: that every projection must have something in common with what is projected no matter what is the method of projection.
>
> (PG: 163)

The *Tractatus* says too little about what it takes for a proposition to be a picture of a given state of affairs to give a substantive content to the idea that a proposition is a picture. It says that 'the possibility of propositions is based on the principle that objects have signs as their representatives' (4.0312). But without an account of exactly how a sign comes to be the representative of a particular object, it is hard to know how to apply the theory to our actual language. We have seen that Wittgenstein favours a 'top-down' view, on which the correlations between words and objects are effected by the 'theory' that is built into our use of the language as a whole. But what is it about the way we actually use our language that makes it embody the 'theory' it does? The *Tractatus* gives no detailed answer to that question. It gives the framework of an account of meaning. But it tells us too little about how to apply that framework to give anything like a satisfying account of the meanings of propositions in our actual language.

2 ANALYSIS AND LOGIC

i. Elementary propositions and complex propositions

According to the *Tractatus*, a proposition is a picture of reality. That is a claim about all meaningful propositions: from very simple propositions such as 'Desdemona loves Cassio' or 'Fido is on the mat' to highly complex propositions of economics, biology, physics, and so on. But the account of propositions as pictures that we have given so far applies directly only to the very simplest propositions of all: what Wittgenstein calls 'elementary propositions' (TLP: 4.21–4.22). An elementary proposition, Wittgenstein thinks, is a picture in the most direct way possible: it consists of names that stand for simple objects; the fact that those names are arranged in a given way represents that the corresponding objects are arranged in the same way. But the propositions of ordinary language are not made up of names that stand for simple objects. For one thing, the objects whose names occur in ordinary propositions – people, animals, countries, and so on – are complex objects, not simples. For another thing, many words that occur in everyday propositions are not, on the face of it, names of objects at all: there are verbs, adjectives, and adverbs; connectives such as 'and', 'or', and 'but'; numerals; and so on. So how does the picture theory apply to the propositions of our ordinary, everyday language?

Wittgenstein's answer is that our everyday propositions are constructed from elementary propositions: 'Suppose that I am given *all* elementary propositions: then I can simply ask what propositions I can construct out of them. And there I have *all* propositions . . .' (4.51). Correspondingly, to explain or reveal the meaning of an everyday proposition we must analyse it into its component elementary propositions. 'It is obvious', he writes, 'that the analysis of propositions must bring us to elementary propositions which consist of names in immediate combination' (4.221). Wittgenstein has no idea how in detail the analysis of any actual proposition of ordinary language will proceed. But, he thinks, he does know what the general form of that analysis must be. 'A proposition', he writes, 'is a truth-function of elementary propositions' (5, emphasis added). So the analysis of any proposition whatsoever will display that proposition as a truth-function of elementary propositions. What does that mean?

A truth-function of elementary propositions is a proposition built up from elementary propositions in such a way that its truth or falsity depends only on the truth or falsity of those elementary propositions. For example, the proposition 'p and q' is a truth-function of the elementary propositions p and q. Whether or not 'p and q' is true depends only on whether the component propositions p and q are true or false: it is true if the component propositions are both true; it is false if one or both of the component propositions is false. Similarly, the proposition 'not-p and not-q and not-r' is a truth-function of the elementary propositions p, q, and r: it is true if and only if all three of the component elementary propositions are false. And, according to Wittgenstein, *every* proposition is constructed from elementary propositions in this way: by combining them in different ways with the logical connectives 'and', 'not', 'or', and, 'if . . . then . . .'

Wittgenstein devised an elegant way to represent truth-functions of elementary propositions – known now as the *truth-table* notation (see TLP: 4.31ff.). For example, he represents the complex proposition 'p and q' by means of the following truth-table.

	p	q	
1	T	T	T
2	T	F	F
3	F	T	F
4	F	F	F

Each line in the truth-table (numbered 1 to 4) represents a possible situation – a possible combination of truth and falsity of the elementary propositions p and q. The truth-table tells us (by the T or F in the right-hand column) whether, in that situation, the complex proposition it represents is true or false. Thus:

- Line 1 represents the situation in which the propositions p and q are both true; in that situation, the truth-table tells us, the complex proposition is true.
- Line 2 represents the situation in which p is true and q is false; in that situation, the complex proposition is false.
- Line 3 represents the situation in which p is false and q is true; in that situation, the complex proposition is false.
- Line 4 represents the situation in which both p and q are false; in that situation, the complex proposition is false.

The truth-table as a whole represents a complex proposition by specifying the circumstances under which it is true and false. In the example just given, the truth-table represents the complex proposition that is true if p and q are both true, and false if one or both of p and q are false; that is to say, the proposition 'p and q'.

In saying that 'a proposition is a truth-function of elementary propositions', Wittgenstein's claim is that *every* proposition is constructed
from elementary propositions in the same kind of way; the sense of
every complex proposition can be exactly expressed by breaking the
proposition down into its component elementary propositions and
saying which combinations of truth and falsity of those elementary
propositions make the complex proposition true and which combinations make it false.

He then makes a further claim:

6.   The general form of a truth-function is $[\bar{p}, \bar{\xi}, N(\bar{\xi})]$
        This is the general form of a proposition.
6.001 What this says is just that every proposition is a result of succes-
        sive applications to elementary propositions of the operation
        $N(\bar{\xi})$.

To see the point of that claim, consider the following truth-table,
which represents a complex proposition constructed from three elementary propositions – p, q, and r.

	p	q	r	
1	T	T	T	F
2	T	T	F	F
3	T	F	T	F
4	T	F	F	F
5	F	T	T	F
6	F	T	F	F
7	F	F	T	F
8	F	F	F	T

The complex proposition represented by this truth-table is true in the
situation where each of the component propositions p, q and r is false
(line 8). It is false in every other situation (lines 1–7). In ordinary
English, we would express that as the proposition 'not-p and not-q and
not-r', or equivalently, 'neither p nor q nor r'. Now we can produce this
proposition from the elementary propositions p, q, and r by applying
the operation of *joint negation* – which Wittgenstein represents by the
sign $N(\bar{\xi})$ (see TLP: 5.502ff.). (The sign 'ξ' (pronounced *ksy*) represents one or more propositions; the sign '$N(\bar{\xi})$' represents the negation

of all the propositions that are represented by 'ξ'.) And the operation N($\bar{\xi}$) − the operation of joint negation − has a special place in the *Tractatus*. For it turns out that, using only the single operation of joint negation, we can construct any truth-function of elementary propositions at all. (This result was proved by the American logician H. M. Sheffer in 1913 (Sheffer 1913).) For example, we can construct the proposition '*p* or *q*' in two stages: first we apply the N($\bar{\xi}$) operation to the elementary propositions *p* and *q*, to produce the proposition 'not-*p* and not-*q*'; then we apply the N($\bar{\xi}$) operation a second time, to this proposition, 'not-*p* and not-*q*', to produce the proposition 'not (not-*p* and not-*q*)', which is equivalent to '*p* or *q*'. What Sheffer proved was that *every* truth-function of a given set of propositions can be constructed in the same way, by successive applications of the operation of joint negation. That is the point Wittgenstein is making in TLP 6–6.001. But we need not worry about the details. The key point for our purposes is simply the idea that every proposition is a truth-function of elementary propositions; every proposition is constructed from elementary propositions in such a way that its truth or falsity depends only on the truth or falsity of its component elementary propositions.

Now in ordinary language there are many complex propositions that, on the face of it, are not truth-functions of the simpler propositions they contain: propositions that are constructed from simpler propositions in ways that mean that the truth or falsity of the complex proposition is not determined by the truth or falsity of the component propositions alone. Take the proposition 'The tyre burst *because* it was overinflated'. For that proposition to be true, it must be true that the tyre burst, and it must be true that it was overinflated. But it must also be true that the tyre's being overinflated was *the cause* of its bursting. And whether or not the overinflation did cause the bursting is not determined by the truth of the component propositions alone. So '*p* because *q*' is not a truth-function of *p* and *q*. Similarly, the truth or falsity of the proposition 'Russell *believes that* Bismarck was an astute diplomatist' is not determined by the truth or falsity of the component proposition, 'Bismarck was an astute diplomatist'. For the proposition might be true without Russell believing it; and Russell might believe the proposition even if it was false. So 'A believes that *p*' is not a truth-function of *p*. The same is true for many other propositions of ordinary language − or so it seems. But such examples do not lead Wittgenstein to give up the principle that every proposition is a truth-function of elementary propositions. His view is that a closer examination of any apparent counter-example to the principle will reveal one of two things: either the proposition can in fact be analysed as a truth-function of elementary propositions; or it is not a meaningful proposition at all. It is not always clear exactly how Wittgenstein envisages treating particular kinds of proposition. For example, commentators differ about how to understand his treatment of the proposition 'A believes that p'. (For Wittgenstein's account, see TLP: 5.541–5.542. For differing interpretations, see Anscombe 1959: 87–90, and Kenny 1981: 144–6). But Wittgenstein's overall strategy certainly is clear: to show that, when completely analysed, any significant proposition will be revealed to be a truth-function of elementary propositions.

ii. Logical propositions and logical entailment

The *Tractatus*'s idea that every proposition is a truth-function of elementary propositions leads directly to its conception of logic: of the nature and status of logical propositions, logical relations between propositions, and logical inference. Logical propositions, Wittgenstein stresses, function in a completely different way from propositions that describe matters of empirical fact. Logical propositions 'are not pictures of reality' (4.462). And logical words are not names of objects: 'My fundamental idea', he writes, 'is that the "logical constants" are not representatives; that there can be no representatives of the logic of facts' (4.0312). (The 'logical constants' are the logical connectives 'and', 'not', 'or', and 'if . . . then . . .'.) We can start with this last claim: that the logical constants do not name objects.

On the *Tractatus* account, the function of words such as 'not', 'and', and 'or' is to combine elementary propositions into complex propositions. They tell us which combinations of truth and falsity of its component elementary propositions make a complex proposition true and false. But they do not pick out 'logical objects'; in Wittgenstein's view, and in contrast to Frege's and Russell's, there *are* no logical objects (see 4.441, 5.4). For example, the word 'not' in the proposition 'not-p' (in symbols: the sign '¬' in the proposition '¬p') does not pick out an item in the world: 'If there were an object called "¬", it would follow that "¬¬p" said something different from what "p" said, just because the one proposition would then be about ¬ and the other would not' (5.44). But it is obvious, Wittgenstein thinks, that '¬¬p' ('not-not-p') says exactly the same as 'p'. So the symbol '¬' (or the word 'not') cannot stand for an object. For similar reasons, he argues, the words 'and', 'or', and 'if . . . then . . .' do not stand for objects either (see TLP: 5.42).

Just as logical words do not function by naming 'logical objects', so logical propositions do not function by picturing 'logical states of affairs'. Logical propositions, Wittgenstein says, are *tautologies*: complex propositions that are constructed from elementary propositions in such a way that they are true for *every* combination of truth and falsity of their component elementary propositions. The simplest case of a tautology is the proposition 'p or not-p'. That proposition can be represented by the following truth-table.

	p	not-p	
1	T	F	T
2	F	T	T

In this truth-table, line 1 represents the situation in which p is true and not-p is false. Line 2 represents the situation in which p is false and not-p is true. The truth-table tells us that the complex proposition 'p or not-p' is true in both situations: 'the proposition is true for all the truth-possibilities of the elementary propositions' (4.46); it is a tautology. Similarly, the proposition 'if (p and (if p then q)) then q' is a tautology: it is true for every possible combination of truth and falsity of the component elementary propositions p and q. The same is true, Wittgenstein thinks, for every logical proposition.

A tautology, according to Wittgenstein, is not a picture of reality; it 'does not stand in any representational relation to reality' (4.462). A picture says that something is the case: that a particular state of affairs, or combination of states of affairs, exists. But a tautology does not represent the world as being one way rather than another; it is true whatever states of affairs exist. So a tautology 'says nothing'; it 'lacks sense'. Accordingly, the propositions of logic, being tautologies, 'say nothing' (6.11). Nonetheless, Wittgenstein says, logical propositions are not *nonsensical* (4.4611); they are made up of significant symbols arranged in legitimate ways. And they do 'indicate something about the world':

> The propositions of logic describe the scaffolding of the world, or rather they represent it. They have no 'subject-matter'. They presuppose that names have meaning and elementary propositions sense;

and that is their connection with the world. It is clear that something about the world must be indicated by the fact that certain combinations of symbols – whose essence involves the possession of a determinate character – are tautologies. This contains the decisive point. We have said that some things are arbitrary in the symbols that we use and that some things are not. In logic it is only the latter that express: but that means that logic is not a field in which *we* express what we wish with the help of signs, but rather one in which the nature of the absolutely necessary signs speaks for itself. If we know the logical syntax of any sign-language, then we have already been given all the propositions of logic.

(6.124)

But *what is* it about the world that is indicated by the fact that the proposition 'p or not-p', say, is a tautology? One way of answering that question would be this: 'The world has a logical form. Part of that form is that every possible state of affairs must either obtain or not obtain: that there is no third possibility. And it is *because* the world has that form that the proposition "p or not-p" is a tautology.' A view of that kind is suggested by the claim that '*something about the world* [is] indicated by the fact that certain combinations of symbols . . . are tautologies' (emphasis added). But the penultimate sentence of 6.124 gives a different impression. Logic, it says, is a field in which '*the nature of the absolutely necessary signs* speaks for itself' (emphasis added). That might suggest that the principle that every proposition is either true or false is a requirement imposed by the nature of *language* or *representation* rather than the nature of the world. On this view, any system of representation must respect the principle that every proposition is either true or false. But that principle is not imposed on language by anything else; it is simply a basic, necessary requirement of language or representation. The question of how to interpret Wittgenstein's remark in 6.124 reflects a broader question: how to understand the metaphysics of the *Tractatus* as a whole. We will return to that question in Chapter 3 section 1.ii below.

We have been discussing the *Tractatus*'s treatment of logical propositions. Its treatment of the logical relations between propositions is closely related – also stemming from the doctrine that every proposition is a truth-function of elementary propositions. Wittgenstein's idea is that all logical relations between propositions result from the ways

in which those propositions are constructed from elementary propositions. Suppose p follows from r. The reason for that, Wittgenstein thinks,
is that any combination of truth and falsity of elementary propositions
that makes r true also makes p true: in Wittgenstein's terminology, the
'truth-grounds' of p are 'contained in' the 'truth-grounds' of r (5.121).
So there is no way for r to be true without p also being true; if r is true,
p must be true. Consider the table below.

	p	q	p and q	p or q
1	T	T	T	T
2	T	F	F	T
3	F	T	F	T
4	F	F	F	F

Wittgenstein's idea is that one proposition entails another when every
combination of truth and falsity of elementary propositions that makes
the first proposition true also makes the second proposition true. For
example:

'p and q' entails p

There is one situation that makes 'p
and q' true: the situation represented
by line 1. That situation also makes p
true. So every situation that makes 'p
and q' true also makes p true. Thus,
'p and q' entails p.

p entails 'p or q'

There are two situations that make p
true (lines 1 and 2). Each of those situations also makes 'p or q' true. So every
situation that makes p true makes 'p or
q' true. Hence, p entails 'p or q'.

'p or q' does not entail 'p and q'

There are three situations that make
'p or q' true (lines 1, 2, and 3). One
of those situations (line 1) also makes
'p and q' true. But the two other situations (lines 2 and 3) make 'p and q'
false. So it is not true that every situation that makes 'p or q' true also makes
'p and q' true. Hence, 'p or q' does not
entail 'p and q'.

The cases illustrated here are very simple. But Wittgenstein's idea is that the same procedure can, in principle, be applied in every case. We analyse a given proposition into its component elementary propositions. That shows what combinations of truth and falsity of elementary propositions make the proposition true. If every such combination that makes the proposition true also makes some other proposition true, then the first proposition entails the second.

According to Wittgenstein, 'the only necessity that exists is *logical* necessity' (6.37, 6.375). And logical necessity, he thinks, is *truth-functional* necessity: necessity that results from the way in which elementary propositions are combined into complex propositions by the logical operators 'and', 'not', 'or', and 'if . . . then . . .'. So whenever there is a genuine entailment between two propositions, it is, in principle, possible to analyse the propositions in the way just illustrated, so as to reveal the source of the entailment. Take the relation between the propositions '*a* is red' and '*a* is green'. The two propositions are incompatible; the truth of '*a* is red' implies the falsity of '*a* is green', and vice versa. And Wittgenstein takes this incompatibility to be *logical* incompatibility. It is not simply a law of nature that nothing is both red and green all over; it is logically impossible for there to be such a thing (see 6.3751). So, on the *Tractatus* view, it must be possible to analyse the propositions '*a* is red' and '*a* is green' as truth-functions of elementary propositions in such a way that the source of their incompatibility is revealed. Wittgenstein's assumption was that '*a* is red' would be analysed as the conjunction of, say, '*a* is F' and '*a* is H', while '*a* is green' would be analysed as the conjunction of, say, '*a* is J' and 'not (*a* is H)'. So the incompatibility between '*a* is red' and '*a* is green' would be traced to the fact that the analysis of '*a* is red' contains an elementary proposition ('*a* is H') whose negation ('not (*a* is H)') is contained in the analysis of '*a* is green'. The logical incompatibility of '*a* is H' and 'not (*a* is H)' explains the logical incompatibility of '*a* is red' and '*a* is green' are logically incompatible. In that way, Wittgenstein thought, the incompatibility of '*a* is red' and '*a* is green' would be shown to be of essentially the same kind as the incompatibility of p and not-p. After completing the *Tractatus*, Wittgenstein realized that this explanation would not work: the logical impossibility of something's being simultaneously red and green, he came to think, is a basic, unanalysable feature of the system of colour propositions; it cannot be assimilated to truth-functional impossibility. As we shall see in Chapter 4 section 1 below, that was one of Wittgenstein's own earliest criticisms of the *Tractatus*.

SUMMARY

The *Tractatus*, completed in 1918 when Wittgenstein was 29, is a concise masterpiece of twentieth-century philosophy. At its heart is a theory of language and logic. A proposition, according to the *Tractatus*, is a picture of reality. The most basic kind of proposition – an elementary proposition – is composed entirely of names, each of which stands for a simple object. The fact that the names are arranged in the particular way they are represents that the corresponding objects are arranged in the same way. That is the driving intuition behind the *Tractatus*'s picture theory of language – a theory that was designed to explain how propositions function: stressing the fundamental difference between propositions and names and avoiding the problems Wittgenstein saw in Russell's theory of meaning. Wittgenstein says very little about how the correlation between names and objects is actually established or maintained. However, it seems clear that he conceives of the correlation in a 'top-down' rather than a 'bottom-up' way: we do not start by being acquainted with objects and then giving them names; rather, we know objects by grasping a language that contains names for them.

Every proposition, according to the *Tractatus*, is a truth-function of elementary propositions. That is to say, every proposition is built up from elementary propositions in such a way that the truth or falsity of the whole proposition is determined by the truth or falsity of its component elementary propositions. On the face of it, many propositions of ordinary language – propositions such as 'p because q' or 'A believes that p' – are not truth-functions of the simpler propositions they contain. But Wittgenstein held that, when fully analysed, every meaningful proposition would be revealed as a truth-function of elementary propositions.

A fundamental principle of the *Tractatus* is that logical words and logical propositions function quite differently from other words and propositions. Logical words – such as 'and', 'or', and 'not' – do not name objects. Instead, they tell us how elementary propositions are combined in complex propositions. And logical propositions – such as 'if p and (if p then q), then q' – are not pictures; they do not represent 'logical states of affairs'. Instead, they are tautologies: complex propositions that are true for every possible combination of truth and falsity of their component elementary propositions. Tautologies do not *say* anything about the world; rather, they *show* the logical properties of reality.

FURTHER READING

For good, recent introductions to the Tractatus, offering more detail than there has been space for here, see:

Morris, M. (2008) *Wittgenstein and the* Tractatus Logico-Philosophicus, London: Routledge.

White, R. (2006) *Wittgenstein's* Tractatus Logico-Philosophicus: *A Reader's Guide*, London: Continuum.

An earlier introductory book is:

Mounce, H. (1981) *An Introduction to Wittgenstein's* Tractatus, Oxford: Blackwell.

And there is a famous introduction, written by a friend and student of Wittgenstein's:

Anscombe, G. E. M. (1959) *An Introduction to Wittgenstein's* Tractatus, London: Hutchinson University Library.

A helpful line-by-line commentary on the text is contained in:

Black, M. (1964) *A Companion to Wittgenstein's* Tractatus, Cambridge: Cambridge University Press.

For a detailed discussion of the picture theory, see:

Pears, D. (1987) *The False Prison* vol. 1, Oxford: Oxford University Press, ch. 6.

There is a helpful discussion of the Tractatus's account of representation and logic, with particular emphasis on the latter, in:

Ricketts, T. (1996) 'Pictures, logic, and the limits of sense in Wittgenstein's *Tractatus*', in H. Sluga and D. Stern (eds), *The Cambridge Companion to Wittgenstein*, Cambridge: Cambridge University Press.

Three

The *Tractatus*: reality and the limits of language

The previous chapter dealt with the *Tractatus*'s accounts of language and of logic. Our discussion of those topics has pointed to questions about the nature of reality, and about the limits of what can be expressed in language. The *Tractatus* says that all language is analysable down to a level of elementary propositions, which are composed of names that are correlated with simple objects. But what kinds of things are these objects supposed to be? And what status are they supposed to have? Is the division of reality into simple objects a feature of the world as it is in itself? Or is it in some way determined by our system of representation? And do such questions even make sense? Similarly, we have seen that, according to the *Tractatus*, logical propositions do not 'stand in any representational relation to reality' (TLP: 4.462), but that they do 'indicate something about the world' (6.124). But how does Wittgenstein think that propositions can *show* something – the logical form of reality – that cannot be *said* (see 4.121, 4.1212)? These are the topics of the current chapter: the nature of reality; and Wittgenstein's 'theory of what can be expressed by propositions . . . and what cannot be expressed by propositions but only shown' – which, he wrote to Russell, 'is the cardinal problem of philosophy' (19 August 1919, WIC: 98).

1. REALITY

The *Tractatus* begins with a series of remarks about the nature of reality. The role of these remarks in the overall scheme of the *Tractatus* is controversial. The fact that Wittgenstein starts the book by describing the most general features of the world, and proceeds from there to an account of the necessary features of language, might make it seem that he thinks that the nature of reality is basic, and that the form of language is determined by the form of the reality it represents. But perhaps that appearance is misleading. Maybe Wittgenstein sees the relation between language and world in the opposite way: the form of language is basic; the form of reality is a projection of the language we use to describe it. Or perhaps he dismisses both views: language and reality have a common form; but that form is not imposed on language by the world; nor is it imposed on the world by language; it is simply a basic feature of language and world. We will discuss that issue in section 1.ii below. But we can start by considering, on its own terms, the picture of reality that Wittgenstein offers in these early sections.

i. Objects, states of affairs, and the world

The *Tractatus*'s vision of reality is neatly summarized in the following remarks:

1.   The world is all that is the case.
2.   What is the case – a fact – is the existence of states of affairs.
2.01 A state of affairs (a state of things) is a combination of objects (of things).
2.02 Objects are simple.

This metaphysical vision has four basic categories: objects, states of affairs, facts, and the world. *Objects* are simple: they have no parts or components; so they cannot be taken apart or decomposed. They are common to every imaginable or describable world and thus (Wittgenstein thinks) to every possible world:

> It is obvious that an imagined world, however different it may be from the real one, must have *something* – a form – in common with it.
>   Objects are just what constitute this unalterable form.
>   [. . .]
>   Objects are what is unalterable and subsistent; their configuration is what is changing and unstable.
>
> (2.022–3, 2.0271)

A *state of affairs* is a possible combination or configuration of objects. And, according to Wittgenstein, each state of affairs is independent of every other: 'From the existence or non-existence of one state of affairs it is impossible to infer the existence or non-existence of another'

(2.062). A given state of affairs either exists or does not exist; that is to say, objects either are combined in a given way or they are not combined in that way. A *fact* is the existence of a state of affairs (or, as Wittgenstein also sometimes puts it (e.g. 2.05), a fact is an existing state of affairs). And the world is the totality of facts (2.04, 1.1).

It is traditional to view Wittgenstein's system as a form of atomism: *logical atomism*, in Russell's terminology, to make the point that the atoms concerned are 'the atom[s] of logical analysis, not the atom[s] of physical analysis' (Russell 1918: 179). That is not a term that Wittgenstein used himself. But it seems an appropriate label. In fact, the metaphysics of the *Tractatus* involves two kinds, or levels, of atomism: *objects* are one kind of atom; *facts* are another. Tractarian objects are, in one sense, the fundamental atoms of reality: 'the substance of the world', as Wittgenstein puts it (2.021). But in Wittgenstein's way of thinking, the atoms from which the world is composed are not objects; they are facts, or truths. In his words: 'The world is the totality of facts, not of things' (1.1). Or again: 'The world divides into facts' (1.2), rather than dividing into objects. He spelled out this conception in a conversation with a student in 1930–31:

> 'The world is everything that is the case.' This is intended to recall and correct the statement 'The world is everything that there is'; the world does not consist of a catalogue of things and facts about them (like the catalogue of a show). For, 1.1, 'The world is the totality of facts and not of things'. What the world is is given by description and not by a list of objects.
>
> (WLC i: 119)

As Wittgenstein says, this conception of the world contrasts sharply with the conventional conception of the world as an object – or a vast collection of objects. On that conception of the world, we will talk of there being facts *about* the world: the fact that Paris is south of London, for instance, or that gold is less dense than lead. On Wittgenstein's conception, by contrast, a fact is not a truth *about* the world; it is *part of* the world – one of the atoms that collectively make up the world. And the world is the totality of facts.

When one reads these early sections of the *Tractatus*, one is immediately struck by two questions. First, what are simple objects supposed to be? What are these simple, unalterable elements that are common to every possible world? Second, what reason is there for believing that there are such things?

Wittgenstein gives no examples of simple objects. He is certain that there are simple objects. But the reason for his certainty is not that he has actually analysed any proposition down to its component elementary propositions and identified simple objects that are picked out by the simple, unanalysable names; it is, rather, that he has an argument that convinces him that there must be simples. So the most direct answer to the question 'What are Tractarian objects supposed to be?' is that Wittgenstein himself does not know. But can we nonetheless identify the kinds of thing Wittgenstein might have in mind when he talks about objects: the kinds of thing he might regard as candidates for being objects?

One issue is whether Wittgenstein thought that objects would be the kinds of thing we call 'objects' in ordinary English (or 'Gegenstanden' in ordinary German): particular, individual things such as chairs or tables (though presumably much smaller than chairs or tables, since chairs and tables are composite things and Tractarian objects are supposed to be simple). Or did he think that the category of objects would include properties and relations: the property of redness, for example, or the relation of being heavier than? Or did he perhaps think of objects in some other way? Wittgenstein certainly took different attitudes to this issue at different times in the development of the *Tractatus*. In January 1913, he wrote in a letter to Russell that qualities, relations, and so on are not objects. 'The reason for this', he wrote, 'is a very fundamental one: I think that there cannot be different Types of things! In other words, whatever can be symbolized by a simple proper name must belong to one type' (WIC: 38). But a notebook entry two years later, in June 1915, takes the opposite view: 'Relations and properties, etc. are *objects* too' (NB: 61). So it is clear that Wittgenstein explored both views. But it is not clear that the *Tractatus* itself favours one view over the other.

On the assumption that some Tractarian objects, at least, are individual things, a second issue concerns the kinds of thing they might be. In early readings of the *Tractatus*, objects were often assumed to be sense-data: immediate objects of sensory awareness. That maximized the similarity between Wittgenstein and Russell, who, in the period leading up to the *Tractatus*, held that the physical world is a construction from actual and possible sense-data (see Russell 1914). We know that Wittgenstein expressed interest in Russell's view, and that Russell sent Wittgenstein a copy of one of the papers in which he developed it (WIC: 38, 77). Wittgenstein's notebooks consider the suggestion that sense-data are simple objects: 'It seems to me perfectly possible', he writes, 'that patches in our visual field are simple objects' (NB: 64). And the *Tractatus*, too, mentions 'speck[s] in the visual field' in a discussion of objects (2.0131). So it might seem tempting to read Wittgenstein's metaphysics as essentially the same as Russell's. On this interpretation, Tractarian objects are actual or possible sense-data; the world is made up of the existence of configurations of such sense-data.

However, there is little justification for reading the *Tractatus* this way. In the first place, the scattered remarks about points in the visual field are matched by opposing remarks about the possibility that minute physical particles – material points – are simple objects. For example: 'The division of the body into *material points*, as we have it in physics, is nothing more than analysis into *simple components*' (NB: 67; see also NB: 69). And the *Tractatus*, too, mentions material points and physical particles in discussing objects and analysis (6.3432, 6.3751). So the most we can say is that Wittgenstein allowed both that objects could turn out to be sense-data and that they could turn out to be physical particles. But in the *Tractatus* he is clearly not advocating either view of objects. The *Tractatus*, in sharp contrast to Russell's writings, contains no theory of perception and no theory of knowledge. But if Wittgenstein were advancing a view that was anything like Russell's, one would expect him to deal with precisely those matters: for Russell's whole idea of constructing the physical world from actual and possible sense-data is motivated by his view of perception – specifically, by the idea that the only things we know by direct observation are the 'immediate data of sense: certain patches of colour, sounds, tastes, smells, etc.' (Russell 1914: 140). Wittgenstein's fundamental concern in the *Tractatus* is with logic and representation. His theory of how language functions leads him to views about the general form of reality: if language is to be possible, there must be simple objects that combine in states of affairs. But all that the theory of language requires is that reality has that general atomistic form; it does not require the truth of one particular version of atomism rather than any other. So Wittgenstein does not interest himself in the merits or demerits of particular views about what simple objects might be. For his purposes, that is not necessary.

I said that Wittgenstein has an argument to show that, if language is to be possible, there must be simple objects. What exactly is the argument? It is stated very succinctly, near the start of the *Tractatus*:

2.021   Objects make up the substance of the world. That is why they cannot be composite.

2.0211   If the world had no substance, then whether a proposition had sense would depend on whether another proposition was true.

2.0212   In that case we could not sketch any picture of the world (true or false).

But (spelling out Wittgenstein's line of thought) we obviously *can* 'sketch pictures of the world'; we *can* use language to say things that are true or false. So the world *does* have substance. That is to say, there *are* objects that are simple and are common to any describable world.

To see how the argument is supposed to work, we need to address two questions. First, if there were no simple objects, why would that mean that the sense of one proposition depended on the truth of another proposition? Second, if the sense of one proposition did depend on the truth of another proposition, why would that make language impossible? We can take those questions in order.

Suppose there were no simple objects: that every object was complex. Then every object would be made up of simpler components; each of those simpler components would itself be made up of even simpler components; and so on, *ad infinitum*. Now consider the proposition Fa, which says that a is F. By hypothesis, the object a will be a complex object. Let us suppose that it is made up of two simpler components, α and β, standing to one another in the relation R. Now Wittgenstein, following Russell, takes it for granted that if a given word has the function of standing for an object, and there is no object that it stands for, then any proposition containing that word will make no sense. Applying that principle to the present case, it is a condition for the proposition Fa to have a sense that the complex object a exists; otherwise, the name 'a' would be empty and the proposition Fa would be nonsense. But the requirement that a exists is just the requirement that its component parts, α and β, stand to each other in the relation R. And that, in turn, is just the requirement that the proposition $\alpha R \beta$ ('α stands in the relation R to β') is true. So, Wittgenstein concludes, if every object was complex, then the sense of the proposition Fa would depend on the truth of another proposition – the proposition $\alpha R\beta$, which says that the complex mentioned in the first proposition exists.

But why would that matter? Suppose the sense of the proposition Fa *does* depend on the truth of the proposition $\alpha R\beta$ – and similarly for every other proposition. Why is that supposed to make language impossible? After all, if the proposition $\alpha R\beta$ is true, then the complex object *a does* exist; so the name 'a' *does* have a meaning and the proposition Fa *does* have a sense. Admittedly, it will be a contingent fact that $\alpha R\beta$ is true. So it will be a contingent fact that the name 'a' has a meaning and that the proposition Fa has a sense. If things were other than they actually are – if the proposition $\alpha R\beta$ were false, and the object a did not exist – then the proposition Fa would have no sense. But, on the face of it, that does nothing to undermine or impugn the fact that, as things are, the proposition Fa does have a sense. That, at any rate, seems a reasonable view. But Wittgenstein disagrees. Whether a proposition has a sense, he thinks, cannot depend on matters of contingent fact: 'A proposition has a sense that is independent of the facts' (4.061). One reason why Wittgenstein says this is that he thinks that, whatever situation we find ourselves in, it must be possible to understand what is said by any proposition without first needing to determine any matter of contingent fact. Another reason is that he thinks that, if a proposition makes sense at all, then when we use it to describe some possible world – some way things might have been – the proposition must be either true or false with respect to that world; it must not simply lack a sense. A proposition that made sense with respect to some possible worlds but not others would have a sense that was not 'determinate' (see 3.23) or 'complete' (see 5.156); and that would not be a genuine sense at all (see Proops 2004: 117–19). But that is how things would be if the sense of the proposition Fa depended on the contingent fact that the proposition $\alpha R\beta$ is true (i.e. the contingent fact that the complex object a exists). In that case, Fa would have a sense in the actual world and it would have a sense with respect to any other situation in which the complex object a existed; but, Wittgenstein thinks, it would have no sense with respect to any situation in which a did not exist.

Wittgenstein's argument is ingenious. But few readers find it persuasive. And some of the main reasons for doubting the force of the argument are articulated by Wittgenstein himself, when he comments in *Philosophical Investigations* on versions of his own *Tractatus* argument. (PI

§39 discusses the argument that names must refer to simples. PI §55 discusses the argument that names must signify things that are indestructible.) We can highlight three points. First, the *Tractatus* argument assumes that a name functions simply by standing for an object, and that a proposition will be meaningless if it contains a name to which no object corresponds. But we might reject those assumptions – as Wittgenstein does in *Philosophical Investigations* (see PI §§40–4). A name, he argues there, may have a meaning when its bearer no longer exists: we can still use the name 'Mr NN' when Mr NN has died; and we can still use the name 'Nothung' (the name of Siegfried's sword in Wagner's Ring cycle) even when the sword it names has been broken apart. Second, the *Tractatus* argument assumes that a proposition only has a sense if it has an absolutely determinate sense. A meaningful proposition, it assumes, must be either true or false with respect to every possible situation: there must be no 'truth-value gaps' – no possible situations in which it would be neither true nor false. But Wittgenstein came to reject that assumption, too (see e.g. PI §§71, 88, 99). A concept, he argued, may have 'blurred edges'; its boundaries may be indefinite. But it is a mistake to think that 'an indefinite boundary is not really a boundary at all' (PI §99). For example, the boundary between what counts as a game and what does not is indefinite. But the indefiniteness of the boundary does not make the concept *game* unusable; nor does it mean that there are no cases in which something clearly is or is not a game. Similarly, even if the proposition Fa would be neither true nor false in a situation in which the complex object *a* did not exist, that does not make it meaningless; nor does it mean that there are no cases in which the proposition is clearly true or clearly false. Third, the *Tractatus* assumes that a proposition's having a sense cannot depend on any matters of contingent fact. But the repudiation of that assumption is a major theme in *Philosophical Investigations*. Wittgenstein came to think that the meanings of our words depend at many points on contingent empirical truths (see e.g. PPF §365 [PI II xii]; PI §142). We will explore that theme in later chapters. For now, the point to note is that the *Tractatus* argument for simples depends on a very strong assumption to the effect that a proposition's having a sense cannot depend on any contingent facts; that that assumption is eminently disputable; and that Wittgenstein himself later came to reject it.

ii. Realism, idealism, and deflationism

We can turn now to the issues raised at the start of this section. What is the status of the metaphysical picture that Wittgenstein sets out in opening sections of the *Tractatus*? What role does it have in the overall scheme of the book? And, in particular, what is the status of Tractarian objects? We can distinguish three ways of answering this last question, corresponding to a *realist* interpretation of the *Tractatus*, an *idealist* interpretation, and a *quietist* or *deflationary* interpretation. We can begin with the contrast between the realist and idealist interpretations.

Objects are 'the simple constituent parts of which reality is composed' (that phrase comes from PI §47, where Wittgenstein is discussing Tractarian objects). But what are these simple constituent parts? The realist thinks there is an absolute fact of the matter about what the simple parts of reality are: it is not up to us what to count as a simple part of reality; it is an intrinsic feature of reality itself. The idealist, by contrast, holds that what the simple constituent parts of reality are is in some way dependent on our system of thought or language: the simple parts of reality are not *absolutely* simple; they are just the parts into which our system of thought or language divides it. We can illustrate the contrast with an analogy (see PI §§47–8). Consider the question, what are the simple constituent parts of which a chessboard is composed? On one view, the answer to that question is determined by the nature of reality itself: the chessboard is 'composed of 32 white and 32 black squares'; those are, absolutely, its simple constituent parts. That is like the realist view of objects. On a different view, analogous to the idealist view of objects, what count as the simple constituents of the chessboard is a matter of the system of representation we use to describe it. We *can* represent the chessboard as composed of 32 black and 32 white squares. But we could equally well say 'that it was composed of the colours black and white and the schema of squares' (PI §47); or that it was composed of 32 rectangles, each containing one white and one black square; and so on. On this view, the division of the chessboard into simple constituent parts is not an absolute matter – something determined by the intrinsic nature of the chessboard; it is, rather, a matter of our system of representation and the way in which it segments the chessboard into parts.

The debate between the realist and the idealist interpretations of the *Tractatus* is broadly analogous. The two interpretations agree that language and reality are isomorphic: reality is divisible into simple objects; language is analysable into simple names; there is a 1:1 correlation between names and objects. But they disagree about the relative priority of the elements of this isomorphism. On the realist reading of the *Tractatus*, the division of reality into simple objects is an intrinsic feature of reality – a feature of reality *as it is in itself*. It is *because* reality has the structure it does that any language adequate to represent reality must have the same structure. And it is *because* reality is composed of the simple objects it is that any possible language must be made up of names that stand for those objects. The idealist interpretation of the *Tractatus* reverses that order of explanation: it takes the structure of language as basic, and sees the structure of reality as a reflection of the language we use to describe it. On this view of the *Tractatus*, Wittgenstein's thought proceeds along the following lines. It is a basic requirement on any language that it can be analysed to the point where we reach simple names: words that cannot be analysed in terms of other words. These names must get their significance by being correlated with something in reality. And those elements of reality, the worldly correlates of simple names, will count as simple elements of reality. That is to say: because language must be divisible into simple representational elements, any description that uses language (which is to say, any description at all) must represent the world as being divided into simple objects. But the division of reality into simple objects is not a feature of reality *as it is in itself*: it is a feature of reality *as it appears to us* – reality *as we represent it*. Putting this in the terminology of the idealist philosopher Immanuel Kant, we might say that the division of reality into Tractarian objects is a feature of *empirical reality* (reality as it appears to us), rather than a feature of *noumenal reality* (reality as it is in itself). And in one remark Wittgenstein himself employs exactly that terminology: 'Empirical reality', he says, 'is limited by the totality of objects' (5.5561, emphasis added).

A third way of seeing Wittgenstein's talk of objects in the *Tractatus* rejects both the realist and the idealist interpretations. It takes a *quietist* or *deflationary* view of objects. The point at issue between the realist and the idealist is whether the division of reality into Tractarian objects is an intrinsic feature of reality; or whether, rather, it is a product of the language we use to describe the world. But the deflationist rejects both interpretations. For in Wittgenstein's view, she thinks, the question to which realism and idealism offer competing answers – the question,

'Are simple objects *intrinsically* and *absolutely* simple?' – is unintelligible. There is a straightforward standard of simplicity: something is a simple object if, at the level of complete analysis, it is picked out by a simple name. But once it is settled that something is simple by that standard, there is no room for a further question, 'Is the object intrinsically simple?' The question makes no sense. And if the question makes no sense, then neither does any theory that purports to answer it. The truth, according to the deflationist, is this. There are simple elements of language. There are simple elements of reality. And they are correlated with each other. But that is all there is to say. The structure of language and the structure of reality are on a par; neither is more basic than the other. So, in particular, the isomorphism of language and reality is not to be explained by any theory – whether realism or idealism – that takes one side of the isomorphism as basic and appeals to its general features to explain the general features of the other side of the isomorphism. Such theories make no sense.

Which of these views is right? When he wrote the *Tractatus*, was Wittgenstein a realist about objects; or an idealist; or did he take the deflationary view? In 1929, when Wittgenstein was explaining and developing the ideas of the *Tractatus* in discussion with the philosophers of the Vienna Circle, he offered an account of objects that does seem to reject the realist approach. At that stage, he still held the Tractarian view that 'in analysing propositions we must eventually reach [elementary] propositions that are immediate connections of objects' (WVC: 74). But he insisted that these 'objects' would be nothing like what we might ordinarily think of as objects: elementary propositions, he said, will not mention 'single "objects", chairs, books, tables, and their spatial relations' (WVC: 42); they will not have the subject-predicate structure of ordinary language. 'Just think of the equations of physics – how tremendously complex their structure is. Elementary propositions, too, will have this degree of complexity' (WVC: 42). Now if objects are not to be conceived as individual things, what will they be like? Wittgenstein offers a model:

> Whatever colour I see, I can represent each of them by mentioning the four elementary colours red, yellow, blue, green, and adding how this particular colour is to be generated from the elementary colours .... Every statement about colours can be represented by means of such symbols. If we say that four elementary colours would suffice,

> I call such symbols of equal status *elements of representation*. These
> elements of representation are the 'objects' . . . . It is simply where
> we have elements of representation of equal status that we speak of
> objects.
>
> (WVC: 42–3; see also WVC: 251)

The four elementary colours – red, yellow, blue, green – can be used
to represent any colour; they are the basic elements of representation
(see also WVC: 45). And where there are basic elements of representation like this, Wittgenstein says, we can speak of objects. So we can
regard red, yellow, blue, and green as *objects*. The implication is that
something's counting as an object is entirely a matter of its having a
basic role in our system of representation; it is not a matter of its having any kind of absolute, metaphysical simplicity. As Wittgenstein puts
it in *Philosophical Investigations*, in a passage where he is commenting on a
Tractatus-like view of objects:

> What looks as if it *had* to exist is part of the language. It is a paradigm
> in our game; something with which comparisons are made. And this
> may be an important observation; but it is none the less an observation
> about our language-game – our mode of representation.
>
> (PI §50)

In 1929, then, Wittgenstein seems definitely to reject the realist conception of objects. But that does not tell us how he conceived
of objects when he wrote the *Tractatus*. Maybe the account he offered
in 1929 articulates what he thought when he wrote the *Tractatus*.
But perhaps it is a different view: expressed in the framework and
vocabulary of the *Tractatus*, but embodying an alternative view of
objects.

There is nothing we can point to in the text of the *Tractatus* as conclusive evidence in favour of one of the three interpretations of its
metaphysical remarks: realism, idealism, or deflationism. One reason
for that is that Wittgenstein expresses himself so briefly and offers so
little supporting explanation. A second reason is that all three views
agree that objects are simple elements of reality, that names are simple
elements of language, that the combinatorial possibilities of names
match the combinatorial possibilities of objects, and so on. So the
explicit statements set out in the relevant sections of the *Tractatus* do

not discriminate between these different views. Third, as we shall see in section 2 below, the Tractatus explicitly maintains that it is impossible intelligibly to articulate any claim about the nature and status of objects. Even such apparently innocuous propositions as 'There are 2 objects', 'The name "a" refers to an object', or 'Objects are simple' are, strictly speaking, nonsensical. What such apparent propositions try to say cannot be said at all; it is shown by features of the language. So it is part of the realist and the idealist interpretations of the Tractatus that, on Wittgenstein's view, we cannot intelligibly state those views of the relation between language and reality. We cannot, therefore, expect to base our interpretation of the metaphysics of the Tractatus on any explicit statement of the form 'Objects have so-and-so features', for it is acknowledged on all sides that, according to the Tractatus, no such statement would be intelligible.

That might seem to establish the correctness of the deflationary interpretation. For if the position of the Tractatus is that neither realism nor idealism can intelligibly be stated, how could Wittgenstein possibly be advocating either of those positions? Commentators who argue for a deflationary reading of the Tractatus's metaphysical remarks press precisely that point. But the realist and idealist readings have something to say in response to the point. As I have just said, and as we shall explore in section 2, Wittgenstein holds that there are things that cannot be said but that are shown by language. For example, what we want to express when we say 'There are 2 objects' cannot properly be said at all; instead, it is shown by there being two names that have different meanings (see WIC: 99, quoted in section 2.i below). On the realist and idealist readings of the Tractatus, we should in the same way see the Tractatus as embodying a metaphysical vision – a vision of the relation between language and reality – that cannot intelligibly be articulated in language, but which is nonetheless shown in language.

Which interpretation makes best sense of Wittgenstein's thinking? Is Wittgenstein best seen as belonging to the realist tradition of Moore and Russell, of William James, and of Ernst Mach? Should we locate him, rather, in the idealist tradition of Kant and Schopenhauer? Or had he, in the Tractatus, already developed the kind of deflationary approach to metaphysical questions that is prominent in his later philosophy? These are intensely debated issues in the interpretation of the Tractatus, and I shall not attempt to resolve them here. But the discussion in section 2 will cast light on an issue that is central to the debate: how we should understand the Tractatus's claim that there are things that cannot be said but that can be shown.

2. THE LIMITS OF LANGUAGE

Wittgenstein writes, in the Preface to the Tractatus:

> The whole sense of the book might be summed up in the following words: what can be said at all can be said clearly, and what we cannot talk about we must pass over in silence.
>
> Thus the aim of the book is to draw a limit to thought, or rather – not to thought, but to the expression of thoughts: for in order to be able to draw a limit to thought, we should have to find both sides of the limit thinkable (i.e. we should have to be able to think what cannot be thought).
>
> It will therefore only be in language that the limit can be drawn, and what lies on the other side of the limit will simply be nonsense.
>
> (TLP: Preface p. 3)

Charting the limits of intelligible thought is not like charting the boundaries of a country on a map. In charting the boundaries of a country, we can draw a line on the map and identify this area as lying inside the boundary and that area as lying outside it. But in charting the limits of what can be thought, we cannot draw a line and identify these thoughts as lying within the limit and those thoughts as lying outside it. For there are no thoughts lying beyond the limit of intelligible thought. So, Wittgenstein says, we have to draw the limits of thought in language. We do that by identifying this combination of signs as a genuine proposition, which expresses a thought, and that combination of signs as a mere pseudo-proposition, which expresses nothing at all.

Wittgenstein says that what lies beyond the limit of language – 'what we cannot talk about' – must be 'pass[ed] over in silence'. He repeats the point virtually word for word in the final proposition of the Tractatus: 'What we cannot speak about we must pass over in silence' (TLP: 7). But he certainly does not regard what we cannot talk about as unimportant. As he says in a 1919 letter to Ludwig Ficker (whom he hoped might publish the Tractatus):

> The book's point is an ethical one. I once meant to include in the preface a sentence which is not in fact there now but which I will write

out for you here, because it will perhaps be a key to the work for you. What I meant to write, then, was this: My work consists of two parts: the one presented here plus all that I have *not* written. And it is precisely this second part that is the important one. My book draws limits to the sphere of the ethical from the inside as it were, and I am convinced that this is the ONLY *rigorous* way of drawing those limits. . . . I would recommend you to read the *preface* and the *conclusion*, because they contain the most direct expression of the point of the book.

(Engelmann 1967: 143–4)

And in a letter to Russell, Wittgenstein says again that 'the main point' of the *Tractatus*:

is the theory of what can be expressed (*gesagt*) by propositions – i.e. by language – (and, which comes to the same, what can be *thought*) and what can not be expressed by propositions, but only shown (*gezeigt*); which, I believe, is the cardinal problem of philosophy

(19 August 1919, WIC: 98)

But where is the boundary between what can be expressed by propositions and what cannot? As we shall see, Wittgenstein relegates to the category of nonsense many uses of language that we ordinarily take to be perfectly intelligible: for example, the propositions (or, as he sees them, apparent propositions) of ethics and of philosophy itself. But why does he think such propositions are nonsensical, and what does he mean when he says that there are things that cannot be *said* but that can be *shown* (e.g. 4.1212, 6.522)? What are these things? And how exactly are they shown?

The distinction between intelligible language and nonsensical pseudo-propositions flows directly from Wittgenstein's account of representation. A proposition, he thinks, represents the existence and non-existence of states of affairs; it says that objects are combined in certain ways and not combined in other ways. On that account, the only genuine propositions are those that state matters of empirical fact. For those are the only propositions that represent the existence and non-existence of states of affairs. So, according to Wittgenstein, intelligible language – 'what can be said' – is limited to the 'propositions of natural science' (6.53). That is an extremely radical view of where the limits of language lie. It rules out as nonsensical whole classes of apparent propositions that we ordinarily think we understand; and it entails the impossibility of saying anything at all about many matters that we ordinarily regard as topics of intelligible debate.

We can loosely classify into three groups the kinds of subject matter that, in Wittgenstein's view, lie beyond the limits of language. First, there are the logical properties of language and the world; the essential features of representation and reality. Second, there are ethics and aesthetics, the meaning of life, and the mystical. Third, there is philosophy – including the propositions of the *Tractatus* itself, which Wittgenstein notoriously describes as 'nonsensical' (6.54). We can consider each of these areas in turn.

i. The logical properties of language and world

Wittgenstein says that language cannot represent the logical form of reality:

> Propositions can represent the whole of reality, but they cannot represent what they must have in common with reality in order to be able to represent it – logical form.
>
> In order to be able to represent logical form, we should have to be able to station ourselves with propositions somewhere outside logic, that is to say outside the world.
>
> Propositions cannot represent logical form: it is mirrored in them.
> What finds its reflection in language, language cannot represent.
> What expresses *itself* in language, *we* cannot express by means of language.
> Propositions *show* the logical form of reality.
> They display it.
>
> (4.12–4.121)

In the same way, he thinks, we cannot intelligibly *say* that one proposition contradicts or follows from another. The logical relation between two propositions is *shown* by their structure – by the way they are made up from elementary propositions (4.1211); and 'what *can* be shown, *cannot* be said' (4.1212). Similarly, we cannot use language to say that things have the essential properties – in Wittgenstein's terminology, the 'formal' or 'internal' properties – they do. 'A property is internal', he explains, 'if it is unthinkable that its object should not possess it'

(4.123) − if it is essential to the object's being the object it is. For example, if *a* is an object, the property of *being an object* is a formal property of *a*; *a* could not be what it is if it were not an object. Similarly, it is a formal or internal property of the state of affairs *aRb* that it includes the object *a*: *aRb* could not be the state of affairs it is if it did not include *a*. And, according to Wittgenstein:

> It is impossible . . . to assert by means of propositions that such internal properties and relations obtain: rather, this makes itself manifest in the propositions that represent the relevant states of affairs and are concerned with the relevant objects.
>
> (4.122)

For example, *a* is an object. But we cannot *say* that *a* is an object; the apparent proposition '*a* is an object' is a nonsensical pseudo-proposition (4.1272). What we are trying to say when we utter this pseudo-proposition is *shown* by the behaviour of the sign '*a*' in propositions that mention *a*. Thus, the fact that '*a*' functions as a name, which cannot be analysed, shows that '*a*' stands for a simple object. Similarly, according to Wittgenstein, we cannot say that there are two objects (or any other number of objects): 'what you want to say by the apparent proposition "There are 2 things" is *shown* by there being two names which have different meanings' (19 August 1919, WIC: 99).

Why does Wittgenstein maintain that it is impossible to state the logical properties of propositions, or the formal properties of objects and states of affairs? A short answer is that the meaninglessness of such apparent propositions as '*a* is an object' or '*p* is equivalent to *not-not-p*' is a direct consequence of his account of representation. A proposition, on Wittgenstein's account, states the existence of a contingent state of affairs. It 'must restrict reality to two alternatives: yes or no'. And both alternatives must be possible: it must be possible for the proposition to be true; and it must be possible for it to be false. That is why 'one can understand [a proposition] without knowing whether it is true' (4.024). But '*a* is an object' does not meet these conditions. If it were a meaningful proposition, it would be necessarily true; for being an object is an essential property of *a*. So it would not restrict reality to two alternatives: yes or no. And we could not understand it without knowing that it was true. Similarly for the apparent proposition '*p* is equivalent to *not-not-p*'. Given Wittgenstein's view of what it is for something to be a meaningful proposition, the meaninglessness of such apparent propositions follows directly.

But that immediately raises a further question: why does Wittgenstein accept such a restrictive view of what makes sense? He seems to offer an explanation in notes he dictated to Moore in April 1914:

> Logical so-called propositions *show* [the] logical properties of language and therefore of [the] universe, but *say* nothing.
>
> [. . .]
>
> It is impossible to *say* what these properties are, because in order to do so, you would need a language, which hadn't got the properties in question, and it is impossible that this should be a *proper* language. Impossible to construct [an] illogical language.
>
> > (NB: 108. For a later occurrence of essentially the
> > same argument, see PR: 53, 55)

Suppose we want to state a logical property of language and reality – a necessary truth: for example, the necessary truth that not-not-p entails p. In order to say that, Wittgenstein thinks, we would need a language in which it is not a necessary truth that not-not-p entails p. His reasoning is this: (i) The proposition 'not-not-p entails p' only makes sense if the proposition 'not-not-p does not entail p' also makes sense. (ii) The proposition 'not-not-p does not entail p' only makes sense if it describes a possible state of affairs – if it is possible for the proposition to be true. (iii) It is only possible for the proposition 'not-not-p does not entail p' to be true if it is not a necessary truth that not-not-p entails p. So: (iv) In order to say that it is a necessary truth that not-not-p entails p we need a language in which it is not a necessary truth that not-not-p entails p. But: (v) There is no such language. For it is a necessary truth that not-not-p entails p; that was our starting point.

What should we make of this argument? It depends on two crucial premises. First, that the proposition 'not-not-p entails p' makes sense only if the proposition 'not-not-p does not entail p' also makes sense. Second, that the proposition 'not-not-p does not entail p' makes sense only if it describes a possible state of affairs: only if it could be true. But those premises are simply an application to this case of Wittgenstein's general condition for something's being a meaningful proposition: that a proposition must restrict reality to two alternatives – yes or no; that it must be capable both of being true and of being false. So the argument does nothing to justify that condition; it simply takes it for granted. Wittgenstein is right that, if we accept this condition on something's being a meaningful proposition, we cannot meaningfully describe the logical form of language and reality. But we are left without a convincing explanation of why we should accept it.

ii. Value, the meaning of life, and the mystical

We can turn now to the second area in which Wittgenstein says we can say nothing: questions of value, the meaning of life, and the mystical. Wittgenstein writes:

> The sense of the world must lie outside the world. In the world, everything is as it is, and everything happens as it does happen: *in* it no value exists – and if it did exist, it would have no value.
>
> If there is any value that does have value, it must lie outside the whole sphere of what happens and is the case. For all that happens and is the case is accidental.
>
> (6.41)

If the world has meaning or value at all, its meaning or value cannot depend on anything that happens in the world. For anything that happens will be 'accidental': a matter of contingent fact. And Wittgenstein takes it for granted that, if the world has value, it cannot be a contingent fact that it has value. Given that assumption, it is a short step to the conclusion that we cannot state the sense or value of the world in language. For on Wittgenstein's view, as we have seen, all that can be stated in propositions are contingent matters of fact. And the sense of the world, he thinks, does not lie in any matter of fact.

For similar reasons, Wittgenstein thinks that the sense of life, 'the solution of the problem of life' (6.521), cannot be stated in language: 'The solution of the riddle of life in space and time lies *outside* space and time. (It is certainly not the solution of any problems of natural science that is required.)' (6.4312). But all that can be stated in language are the facts of natural science; facts that 'lie in space and time'. So we cannot *say* what the sense of life is.

> We feel that even when all *possible* scientific questions have been answered, the problems of life remain completely untouched.

> Of course there are then no questions left, and this itself is the
> answer.
>   The solution of the problem of life is seen in the vanishing of the
> problem. (Is not this the reason why those who have found after a long
> period of doubt that the sense of life became clear to them have then
> been unable to say what constituted that sense?)
>
> (6.52–6.521)

The suggestion that we cannot say what the meaning of life is is not at
all unnatural. For it is plausible to think that understanding the meaning of life is a matter of *seeing the point* of life, and that seeing the point
of life is a matter not of learning certain facts about life but, rather, of
seeing the existing facts in a particular light, or from a particular point
of view. Indeed, Wittgenstein employs exactly that metaphor – of seeing things in a particular way, from a particular point of view – in connection with ethical and aesthetic value. He writes:

> The work of art is the object seen *sub specie aeternitatis*; and the good
> life is the world seen *sub specie aeternitatis*. This is the connection
> between art and ethics.
>   The usual way of looking at things sees objects as it were from the
> midst of them, the view *sub specie aeternitatis* from outside.
>
> (NB: 83)

To see things *sub specie aeternitatis* is, literally, to see them 'under the aspect
of eternity'. Figuratively, it is to see things from an objective point
of view, a point of view that abstracts from one's own interests and
involvement. And if Wittgenstein thinks that appreciating the ethical or
aesthetic value of an action, an object, a character, or a state of affairs,
is a matter of seeing it in a particular way – a way that puts aside one's
own interests and involvement – we can see why he says that:

> It is impossible for there to be propositions of ethics.
> Propositions can express nothing that is higher.
> It is clear that ethics cannot be put into words.
> Ethics is transcendental.
>
> (6.42–6.421)

Propositions can only state facts. And if facts are what Wittgenstein takes them to be – the existence of states of affairs, which are

configurations of objects – then seeing the world from a disinterested or objective point of view is not a matter of seeing different facts; it is a matter of seeing the old facts in a new light.

In the case of logical and formal properties, Wittgenstein accompanies the negative claim that we cannot *say* that something has a given logical or formal property with the positive claim that a thing's logical or formal properties are *shown* in language. The parallel positive claim is less prominent in his remarks about value. But it does appear: 'There are, indeed, things that cannot be put into words. They *make themselves manifest*. They are what is mystical' (6.522). (The German word that is here translated 'make manifest' – *zeigen* – is the same word that is elsewhere translated as 'show'.) However, it is less clear for the case of value than for the case of logical or formal properties exactly how this process of showing is supposed to work. One can see how Wittgenstein thinks that the use of the sign '*a*' can show that it is the name of an object. But how, in his view, does 'what is mystical' show itself? In features of our use of language? But if so, then what are those features and how do they show 'what is mystical'? Or does 'what is mystical' show itself in some other way? But in that case, what is that way? Wittgenstein leaves those questions hanging.

If we accept Wittgenstein's idea that the only genuine propositions are statements of contingent fact – 'propositions of natural science' – then he is right that 'it is impossible for there to be propositions of ethics'. For propositions of ethics would obviously not be propositions of natural science. But most readers of the *Tractatus* have found it more plausible to allow that there are propositions of ethics and thus to reject Wittgenstein's restriction on what counts as a genuine proposition. One possibility is to argue that Wittgenstein is wrong to think that a genuine proposition must say something that is true or false. Ethical propositions, we might say, are genuine propositions. But they do not purport to state facts. They function in a different way: for example, as expressions of approval or disapproval of an action or a person; or as injunctions about how to behave. A different possibility is to agree with Wittgenstein that a proposition must say something that is true or false, but to broaden our conception of what can count as saying something true or false. So, we might think, propositions such as 'He should have kept his promise' or 'She shouldn't have been so unkind' do state facts. The facts they state will be ethical facts, of course, not facts of natural science. But, we might think, there is no good reason to accept Wittgenstein's assumption that the facts of natural science are the only facts there are.

iii. Philosophy and the *Tractatus*

The third area in which Wittgenstein argues that it is impossible to say anything is philosophy itself. He writes:

> The correct method in philosophy would really be the following: to say nothing except what can be said, i.e. propositions of natural science – i.e. something that has nothing to do with philosophy – and then, whenever someone else wanted to say something metaphysical, to demonstrate to him that he had failed to give a meaning to certain signs in his propositions. Although it would not be satisfying to the other person – he would not have the feeling that we were teaching him philosophy – *this* method would be the only strictly correct one.
>
> (6.53)

Wittgenstein thinks that 'most of the propositions and questions to be found in philosophical works are . . . nonsensical' (4.003). Examples of the kinds of philosophical proposition that he would regard as nonsensical would include the following: Russell's claim that 'a physical thing is the class of its appearances' (see Russell 1914: 149); propositions about the a priori form of reality, such as Kant's claim that space and time are a priori forms of intuition – features that are imposed by our minds as conditions for perceiving the world; the claim that human beings have free will of a kind that is incompatible with causal determinism; and so on. Though we may have the illusion of understanding such claims, Wittgenstein thinks, they say nothing at all; they are nonsense. But he does not restrict this criticism to the propositions advanced by other philosophers. He thinks the propositions of the *Tractatus* are nonsense too:

> My propositions serve as elucidations in the following way: anyone who understands me eventually recognizes them as nonsensical, when he has used them – as steps – to climb up beyond them. (He must, so to speak, throw away the ladder after he has climbed up it.)
>
> He must transcend these propositions, and then he will see the world aright.
>
> (6.54)

From the outset, readers of the *Tractatus* have found Wittgenstein's view of the propositions of his own book paradoxical. On the one hand, Wittgenstein says in the Preface that 'thoughts are expressed' in the book; and, he says, 'the truth of the thoughts that are here communicated seems to me unassailable and definitive' (TLP: Preface pp. 3–4). On the other hand, *Tractatus* 6.54, the penultimate remark in the book, says that Wittgenstein's own propositions are nonsensical. There is an obvious tension between those two claims. For how are true thoughts supposed to be communicated by a work that is made up of nonsensical propositions? As Russell puts it in his 'Introduction' to the *Tractatus*:

> What causes hesitation [in accepting Wittgenstein's position] is that, after all, Mr Wittgenstein manages to say a good deal about what cannot be said, thus suggesting to the sceptical reader that possibly there may be some loophole . . . . The whole subject of ethics, for example, is placed by Mr Wittgenstein in the mystical, inexpressible region. Nevertheless he is capable of conveying his ethical opinions. His defence would be that what he calls the mystical can be shown, although it cannot be said. It may be that this defence is adequate, but, for my part, I confess that it leaves me with a certain sense of intellectual discomfort.
>
> (Russell 1922: xxi)

Many readers have shared Russell's sense of discomfort.

What are we to make of the *Tractatus*, given Wittgenstein's avowal that its propositions are nonsensical? The most straightforward interpretation goes as follows. The *Tractatus* propounds a theory of meaning and logic. That theory is controversial, but it is certainly worth taking seriously. And it is a paradoxical consequence of this theory of meaning that most of the propositions in the *Tractatus* are nonsensical pseudo-propositions: they are attempts to *say* things that, by the lights of the *Tractatus* itself, are *shown* in language. For example, the *Tractatus* contains the remarks, 'A propositional sign is a fact' (3.14) and 'In a proposition a name is the representative of an object' (3.22). As we saw in Chapter 2, those remarks are crucial parts of Wittgenstein's account of how language functions. But, by Wittgenstein's own standards, they are nonsense. For they are attempts to state formal, or logical, properties of propositions and of names; and according to the *Tractatus* it is

impossible to state a thing's formal properties by means of propositions (4.122). The same goes for most of the other propositions in the
Tractatus. On this interpretation, the point of *Tractatus* 6.54 – which compares Wittgenstein's propositions to a ladder that must be thrown away
after it has been climbed – is this. The propositions of the *Tractatus* are
needed for communicating Wittgenstein's theory of meaning, and for
communicating the crucial corollary of that theory – that what matters
in life is not susceptible of linguistic expression. But having grasped
Wittgenstein's theory of language, and its crucial corollary, we come
to see that the theory itself cannot be meaningfully stated. If we see
Wittgenstein's position in this way, we must acknowledge that it contains a real tension. For, on this view, the propositions of the *Tractatus* are
supposed to succeed in communicating a definite theory of meaning.
But if they are nonsensical pseudo-propositions, as Wittgenstein says,
how can they communicate anything at all? Isn't Wittgenstein's position simply incoherent?

Some scholars have responded to this tension by proposing a different way of reading the *Tractatus* – sometimes called the 'new' or 'resolute' reading (see particularly Diamond 1991a, 1991b; Conant 1989).
The guiding principle of this interpretation is that we must apply with
total rigour the verdict of *Tractatus* 6.54 – that the propositions of the
Tractatus are nonsensical. So, it is argued, we must not see the *Tractatus*'s
propositions as attempts to articulate something that, if only we could
succeed in saying it, would be true. Rather, we should accept that they
are quite literally nonsensical: as nonsensical as a string of nonsense
words like 'piggly wiggle tiggle' (see Diamond 1991b: section 1). And
since the propositions of the *Tractatus* are literally nonsense, the book
does not advance any theory at all: about language, logic, the nature
of reality, or anything else. What, then, does it do? On the 'new' reading, the point of the *Tractatus* is essentially therapeutic. Wittgenstein's
aim is to reveal as empty the kinds of theory that philosophers have
traditionally advanced: theories of meaning, such as those of Russell
and Frege; metaphysical theories about the relation between language
and reality, such as realism or idealism; and so on. And he pursues
that aim by first presenting himself as advancing a definite theory of
meaning, and a positive philosophical theory of the relation between
language and reality, and then leading us to see that those theories, like
all philosophical theories, are unintelligible. His idea, then, is not to
endorse a theory of meaning; nor is it to *endorse* the picture of the relation

between language and reality that he presents for our consideration. His ultimate point is, rather, that these supposed theories are completely empty. This reading of the *Tractatus* has tensions of its own. For if the propositions of the *Tractatus* are nonsensical in exactly the same way as a string of nonsense words like 'piggly wiggle tiggle', how does the therapeutic process work? How does the *Tractatus* even give the appearance of advancing a positive philosophical theory; and how does it succeed in revealing the emptiness of that theory? And what on this view explains why the propositions of the *Tractatus* are nonsensical? On the conventional view, the nonsensicality of the *Tractatus*'s own propositions follows directly from the positive theory of language that Wittgenstein is advancing. But if we insist that the *Tractatus* embodies no positive theory of language at all, there seems nothing to say about why Wittgenstein judges his own propositions to be nonsensical.

On any account, then, there is a serious tension in Wittgenstein's position. On the conventional interpretation, the propositions of the *Tractatus* succeed in communicating a positive theory of language and logic. On the 'new' interpretation, they succeed in taking us through a therapeutic process in which we are first apparently presented with a philosophical view and then shown that it is unintelligible. But if Wittgenstein's propositions are nonsensical, as he says they are, it is hard to see how they can do either of those things. So whichever reading we favour, it is hard to see exactly how Wittgenstein's position is supposed to work. My own view, though, is that the difficulties for the 'new' reading of the *Tractatus* are more acute. In the first place, on the evidence of the *Tractatus* itself it is hard to believe that Wittgenstein is not advancing a specific and detailed theory of language and logic: a theory which he takes to be correct, though he also thinks that it cannot intelligibly be stated. Second, Wittgenstein seems in the *Tractatus* to take entirely seriously the idea that there are things that are shown by language but that cannot be said. Third, the 'new' reading is hard to reconcile with many comments about the *Tractatus* that Wittgenstein made soon after completing the book, and also in later years. Such comments include, for example, the passages from his 1919 letters to Ficker and Russell that were quoted at the beginning of section 2 above – which make it clear both that Wittgenstein took himself to have propounded definite theses about language and logic, and that he was absolutely serious in distinguishing between what can be expressed by propositions and what can only be shown.

Suppose that, for the reasons just given, we accept that the *Tracta-tus* does contain a substantive theory of language and logic – albeit a theory that, by its own lights, cannot coherently be stated. That does not resolve the question we left unanswered at the end of section 1 above, about the status of the *Tractatus*'s metaphysical remarks and the nature of the metaphysical vision it embodies. Even if it is wrong to think that the book advances no positive philosophical doctrines at all, it might be right to maintain that the positive vision of the *Tractatus* is concerned only with language and logic, and that Wittgenstein takes a wholly deflationary view of metaphysics. On that view, attempts to state realism or idealism are not on a par with pseudo-propositions such as 'There are 2 objects' or 'The name "*a*" refers to an object'. For when we come out with pseudo-propositions like those, there really is something that we want to say: something that is shown by our use of ordinary, meaningful propositions. But (on the current view) what we want to say when we come out with the pseudo-propositions of realism or idealism is not shown by anything at all: for there is no such thing to show. On this view, it is right to interpret the *Tractatus* as taking a deflationary approach towards the grand metaphysical debate between realists and idealists; in that respect, the 'new' reading of the *Tractatus* is correct. But it is wrong to think that the *Tractatus*'s deflation-ism extends to language and logic.

SUMMARY

The opening sections of the *Tractatus* set out a view of reality. The world is the totality of facts; a fact is the existence or non-existence of states of affairs; a state of affairs is a combination of objects; objects are sim-ple and are common to all imaginable worlds. Wittgenstein does not know what these simple elements of reality will turn out to be; that is something that will be revealed by logical analysis. But, he argues, there must be such simple elements; otherwise, language would be impossible. The content and purpose of the *Tractatus*'s remarks about metaphysics are controversial. On one view, the *Tractatus* advances a form of realism: reality has an intrinsic structure, and that structure determines the structure of any possible language; it is because reality is made up of simple objects in the way it is that any language ade-quate to describe reality must be made up of names that are correlated with those objects. On a second interpretation, the *Tractatus* proposes a form of idealism: the general structure of language is basic; the general structure of reality is a reflection of the language we use to describe it. So Tractarian objects are not absolute, metaphysical simples; they are simply the worldly correlates of whatever happen to be the simple elements in our system of representation. On a third interpretation, the *Tractatus* takes a deflationary view of metaphysics, which rejects both realism and idealism as unintelligible.

The *Tractatus* concludes with the remark: 'What we cannot speak about we must pass over in silence' (TLP: 7). That remark, Wittgenstein says, 'sums up the whole sense of the book' (TLP: Preface p. 3). The *Tractatus* aims to chart the limits of thought by charting the limits of language – by distinguishing meaningful propositions from nonsensical pseudo-propositions. The only meaningful propositions, it holds, are those that state matters of contingent fact: what Wittgenstein calls the propositions of natural science. So the *Tractatus* rules out as nonsensical many classes of propositions that we would ordinarily take to be perfectly intelligible. There are three areas that Wittgenstein regards as lying beyond the limits of intelligible language: the logical properties of language and the world; ethics, aesthetics, the meaning of life, and the mystical; and philosophy itself. Notoriously, Wittgenstein maintains that the propositions of the *Tractatus* are themselves nonsensical. That generates a serious tension: for he also says that the *Tractatus* communicates 'thoughts' whose truth is 'unassailable and definitive'. But how can true thoughts be communicated by a set of nonsensical pseudo-propositions? Different interpretations of the *Tractatus* attempt to resolve this tension in different ways.

FURTHER READING

The introductory books on the *Tractatus* listed in the Further Reading section of Chapter 2 are all helpful on the topics of the present chapter. See:

Anscombe, G. E. M. (1959) *An Introduction to Wittgenstein's* Tractatus, London: Hutchinson University Library.

Black, M. (1964) *A Companion to Wittgenstein's* Tractatus, Cambridge: Cambridge University Press.

Morris, M. (2008) *Wittgenstein and the* Tractatus Logico-Philosophicus, London: Routledge.

Mounce, H. (1981) *An Introduction to Wittgenstein's* Tractatus, Oxford: Blackwell.

White, R. (2006) *Wittgenstein's* Tractatus Logico-Philosophicus: *A Reader's Guide*, London: Continuum.

There is a much-discussed interpretation of the metaphysics of the Tractatus, and of Wittgenstein's treatment of solipsism (a topic I have had no space for here) in chapters 4, 5, and 7 of:

Pears, D. (1987) *The False Prison* vol. 1, Oxford: Oxford University Press.

Pears, along with Anscombe and Black, offers a realist reading of the metaphysics of
the Tractatus, on which the logical form of reality determines the form that must be
taken by any possible language. Opposition to that reading can be found in:

Ishiguro, H. (1969) 'Use and Reference of Names', in P. Winch (ed.) *Studies in the Phi-
losophy of Wittgenstein*, London: Routledge.
McGuinness, B. (1981) 'The So-Called Realism of the Tractatus', in I. Block (ed.) *Per-
spectives on the Philosophy of Wittgenstein*, Oxford: Blackwell; reprinted as 'The Supposed
Realism of the Tractatus', in B. McGuinness (2002) *Approaches to Wittgenstein*, London:
Routledge.

A different kind of opposition to realist readings of the Tractatus can be found in the
works of Cora Diamond and James Conant, the most prominent exponents of the
'new' or 'resolute' reading. For their interpretation, see:

Diamond, C. (1991a) 'Throwing Away the Ladder: How to Read the Tractatus', in Diamond, *The Realistic Spirit*, Cambridge, MA: MIT Press.
Diamond, C. (1991b) 'Ethics, Imagination and the Method of Wittgenstein's Tractatus',
in R. Heinrich and H. Vetter (eds) *Wiener Riehe: Themen der Philosophie*, Vienna: Oldenbourg; reprinted in A. Crary and R. Read (eds) (2000) *The New Wittgenstein*, London:
Routledge.
Conant, J. (1989) 'Must We Show What We Cannot Say?', in R. Fleming and M. Payne
(eds) *The Senses of Stanley Cavell*, Lewisberg, PA: Bucknell University Press.

For critiques of this 'new' reading of the Tractatus, see:

Hacker, P. M. S. (2000) 'Was He Trying to Whistle It?', in A. Crary and R. Read (eds)
(2000) *The New Wittgenstein*, London: Routledge.
Proops, I. (2001) 'The New Wittgenstein: A Critique', *European Journal of Philosophy*, 9:
375–404.

And for a helpful discussion of the issues, see:

Sullivan, P. (2004) 'What is the Tractatus about?', in M. Kölbel and B. Weiss (eds) *Wittgenstein's Lasting Significance*, London: Routledge.

Four

For 10 years after completing the *Tractatus*, Wittgenstein abandoned philosophy. When he returned to philosophical work in 1929, he began by explaining and developing the ideas of the *Tractatus*: amending them in various ways as he applied the abstract theories of the *Tractatus* to the actual analysis of parts of language. But the character of his work quickly changed: what began as a development of his own earlier views soon developed into a series of ideas that were fundamentally different from those of the *Tractatus*. In the words of Wittgenstein's preface to *Philosophical Investigations*, written in 1945, he was 'forced to recognize grave mistakes in what [he] wrote in [his] first book' (PI: p. viii). This chapter discusses some of those 'mistakes'. It focuses on three themes: (i) Wittgenstein's repudiation of the project of philosophical analysis that had informed the *Tractatus*, and his development of the idea that philosophy aims to achieve clarity by gaining a 'surveyable representation' of our use of words; (ii) his rejection of the *referentialism* of the *Tractatus* – its view that meaning is to be accounted for in terms of the reference of words and the truth or falsity of propositions – and his new emphasis on the diversity of kinds of word and sentence; (iii) the transition from the *Tractatus* doctrine that understanding a proposition involves knowing what is the case if it is true to Wittgenstein's later idea that understanding a proposition involves knowing its use.

1. FROM LOGICAL ANALYSIS TO SURVEYABLE REPRESENTATION

According to the *Tractatus*, ordinary language disguises the underlying form of the thoughts it expresses. As Wittgenstein puts it:

> Language disguises thought. So much so, that from the outward form
> of the clothing it is impossible to infer the form of the thought beneath

it, because the outward form of the clothing is not designed to reveal the form of the body.

(TLP 4.002)

One way in which ordinary language's outward form is misleading, Wittgenstein thought, is that it often uses a word with two or more different meanings. (For example, the word 'is' is used in at least three different ways: as a sign of identity ('Cicero is Tully'); as a way of linking a noun and an adjective ('Julia is tall'); and as a sign of existence ('There is a tavern in the town').) Or again, words that function in very different ways 'are employed in propositions in what is superficially the same way' (TLP: 3.323). (For example, the propositions 'Nothing works faster than Anadin' and 'Ibuprofen works faster than Anadin' have the same superficial structure. But the word 'Nothing' functions differently from the name 'Ibuprofen'; the underlying structure of the two propositions is quite different.) It is the task of philosophy, as the *Tractatus* conceives it, to display the real, underlying form of thought. And that task is to be carried out by analysing sentences of ordinary language into sentences in a sign-language that excludes the 'fundamental confusions [that] are easily produced' (TLP: 3.324) by ordinary language: a sign-language in which each word has only one meaning, and in which words that function differently are not used in ways that are superficially the same. 'It is obvious', writes Wittgenstein, 'that the analysis of propositions must bring us to elementary propositions which consist of names in immediate combination' (TLP: 4.221). And once we analyse ordinary propositions down to the deep level at which names are attached to simple objects, he thinks, we will get a completely clear account of their meanings. That account will, in turn, yield a solution to the traditional problems of philosophy. For 'most of the propositions and questions of philosophers', Wittgenstein thinks, 'arise from our failure to understand the logic of our language' (TLP: 4.003). With a correct understanding of ordinary language, we will see that the traditional problems of philosophy are empty pseudo-problems. 'We cannot give any answer to [traditional philosophical questions]', Wittgenstein writes, 'but can only point out that they are nonsensical' (TLP: 4.003).

When he returned to philosophy in 1929, Wittgenstein initially retained this conception of analysis. Our analysis of ordinary propositions, he wrote in 1929, 'must come to the point where it reaches propositional forms which are not themselves composed of simpler propositional forms' (RLF: 29). These elementary propositions, he says, 'are the kernels of every proposition'. And 'it is the task of the theory of knowledge to find them and to understand their construction out of the words or symbols'. The method for doing that, he continues, is 'to express in an appropriate symbolism what in ordinary language leads to endless misunderstandings'; so we must 'replace [ordinary language] by a symbolism which gives a clear picture of the logical structure, excludes pseudopropositions, and uses its terms unambiguously' (RLF: 29–30). That is essentially the view that he had advanced 10 years earlier in the *Tractatus*.

But in 1929, while retaining the Tractarian conception of analysis, Wittgenstein abandoned the Tractarian doctrine that elementary propositions are logically independent of one another. According to the *Tractatus*, 'it is a sign of a proposition's being elementary that there can be no elementary proposition contradicting it' (TLP: 4.211). For that reason, as we saw in Chapter 2 section 2.ii, Wittgenstein held that propositions ascribing colours to points in the visual field are not elementary propositions. A proposition that ascribes one colour to a point is logically incompatible with any proposition that ascribes a different colour to the same point; the truth of 'a is red', for example, entails the falsehood of 'a is blue', 'a is yellow', 'a is green', and so on. So these propositions do not meet the *Tractatus*'s condition for being elementary. Ascriptions of colour, Wittgenstein concluded, must be analysable as truth-functions of more basic propositions that *are* logically independent of one another. But in 1929 he abandoned that idea. For properties that admit of degree, he now thought, it is simply a basic feature that a thing's having a given degree of that property logically excludes its having any other degree of the same property. Any attempt to explain the incompatibility between the propositions 'a is red' and 'a is blue' by analysing them in terms of propositions at some lower level will simply reproduce the same basic incompatibility at the lower level; the lower-level propositions that figure in the analysis will not be logically independent of one another (see RLF: 32–3). And the same goes for any proposition that ascribes a given value of a property that admits of degrees: the proposition 'John is 2 metres tall' (which excludes 'John is 1 metre tall', 'John is 3 metres tall' etc.); the proposition 'The temperature outside is 22°' (which excludes 'The temperature is 12°', 'The temperature is 32°'), and so on. So, Wittgenstein concluded, ascriptions of colour, height, temperature, and so on are themselves elementary propositions. And that meant abandoning the idea that elementary propositions must be logically independent. So on Wittgenstein's new view, the rules that determine how elementary propositions may be combined into complex propositions are not exhausted by the rules for the logical constants 'and', 'not', 'or', and 'if'; they must also take account of the 'inner structure' of elementary propositions (WVC: 74), which rules out such combinations as '*a* is red and *a* is blue' or 'John is 2 metres tall and John is 3 metres tall'.

In 1929, then, Wittgenstein's initial position was to retain the *Tractatus* conception of analysis but to give up the *Tractatus*'s very demanding criterion for a proposition's being an elementary proposition: the idea that an elementary proposition must be logically independent of all other elementary propositions. But he soon made a much more radical move away from the *Tractatus*. By the end of 1929 he had abandoned the whole idea that the task of philosophy is to uncover the structure of thought by analysing the propositions of ordinary language into elementary propositions that are expressed in a quite different symbolism: a symbolism 'which gives a clear picture of . . . logical structure'. In a discussion in December 1929 he put it like this:

> I used to believe that there was the everyday language that we all usually spoke and a primary language that expressed what we really knew, namely phenomena. I also spoke of a first system and a second system. Now I wish to explain why I do not adhere to that conception any more.
>
> I think that essentially we have only one language, and that is our everyday language. We need not invent a new language or construct a new symbolism, but our everyday language already is *the* language, provided we rid it of the obscurities that lie hidden in it.
>
> (WVC: 45)

The 'primary language' that Wittgenstein says he no longer believes in is the symbolism envisaged in the *Tractatus*, in which the complete analysis of propositions of ordinary language was to be given. He now held that it was a mistake to think we can understand the features of propositions of our ordinary language by analysing them in terms of propositions in some other, as yet unknown, language. To achieve a philosophical understanding of ordinary propositions, he now thought, 'all that is possible and necessary is to separate what is essential from what is inessential in our language' (PR: 51). That is done by direct attention to the use of ordinary propositions so as to reveal what is essential in our language if it is to represent what it does and 'which parts of our language are wheels turning idly' (PR: 51): features that are inessential to its having the expressive capacity it does. And a method for getting clear about what is essential in our language is to compare our language with other languages, real or invented, that are different from ours but that also 'serve their purpose'. If we can replace our normal way of speaking with a different form of representation without loss, that will show that the features that are peculiar to our normal language are inessential: 'Each time I say that, instead of such a representation, you could also use this other one, we take a further step towards the goal of grasping the essence of what is represented' (PR: 51). (For an example of this method in action, see PR: 88–9 and WVC: 49.)

The idea that we can see what is essential in our language by seeing what it has in common with other languages with the same expressive power echoes something that Wittgenstein said in the *Tractatus*:

> A proposition possesses essential and accidental features.
>
> Accidental features are those that result from the particular way in which the propositional sign is produced. Essential features are those without which the proposition could not express its sense.
>
> So what is essential in a proposition is what all propositions that can express the same sense have in common.
>
> (TLP: 3.34–3.341)

But in 1929, this idea was understood in a new way. For what is essential in our language was now to be identified by attention to our use of ordinary propositions, not by analysing those ordinary propositions into elementary propositions at some lower level. 'I used to believe . . . that it is the task of logical analysis to discover the elementary propositions', Wittgenstein said in 1931; he had thought 'that the elementary propositions could be specified at a later date' (WVC: 182). But he now rejected the idea that, in philosophy:

> we can hit upon something that we today cannot yet see, that we can discover something wholly new . . . The truth of the matter is that we

have already got everything, and we have got it actually *present*; we need not wait for anything. We make our moves in the realm of the grammar of our ordinary language, and this grammar is already there. Thus we have already got everything and need not wait for the future.

(WVC: 183)

There were further developments in Wittgenstein's conception of philosophical method between 1929 and *Philosophical Investigations*. But the key themes we have highlighted here remained in place. First, that the features of our language must be understood by direct attention to our use of ordinary propositions, not by a process of Tractarian analysis. And second, that an important tool in achieving that understanding is the comparison of our ordinary form of representation with other possible forms of representation. As Wittgenstein puts it in *Philosophical Investigations*, the 'clear and simple language-games' he describes are put forward not as material for 'a future regimentation of language' but, rather, 'as *objects of comparison* which, through similarities and dissimilarities, are meant to throw light on features of our language' (PI §130).

A passage in *Philosophical Investigations* offers a simple illustration of Wittgenstein's objection to the *Tractatus* conception of analysis (see PI §§60–3). According to the *Tractatus*, propositions about complex objects are to be analysed in terms of propositions about the constituents that make up those complexes. For example, a broom is a complex object. Suppose its simple constituents are a broomstick and a brush. (Broomsticks and brushes, of course, are themselves complex objects with simpler parts. But for present purposes we can abstract from that point.) Then a proposition about the broom will be analysed as a conjunction of propositions about the broomstick and the brush. Thus, the proposition:

(1) The broom is in the corner.

will be analysed as the following conjunction:

(2) The broomstick is in the corner AND The brush is in the corner AND The broomstick is fixed in the brush.

But, Wittgenstein asks in *Philosophical Investigations*, in what sense is (2) a 'further analysed form' of (1)? It is not true, he thinks, that someone who says (1) 'really means' (2); she typically does not 'mean to speak either of the stick or of the brush in particular'. Nor is there any good sense in which (2) 'lies concealed' in (1). It is true that, if we were asked whether (2) has the same sense as (1), we would probably say that it does: or that 'they come to the same thing'. But that does not mean that (2) is *more fundamental* than (1), or that it *explains the meaning* of (1):

> To say that [2] is an 'analyzed' form of [1] readily seduces us into thinking that the former is the more fundamental form; that it alone shows what is meant by the other, and so on. We may think: Someone who has only the unanalyzed form lacks the analysis; but he who knows the analyzed form has got it all. – But can't I say that an aspect of the matter is lost to the latter no less than to the former?
>
> (PI §63)

The moral is a general one: the meaning of an ordinary proposition is not something that needs to be revealed by analysing that proposition into elementary propositions at some lower level.

That represents a huge shift away from the programme of analysis envisaged in the *Tractatus*. At the same time, however, there are significant continuities between the *Tractatus* and Wittgenstein's later work. In particular, the later work retains the idea that philosophical problems characteristically arise because we misunderstand the logic of our own language. 'In the use of words', Wittgenstein writes in *Philosophical Investigations*, 'one might distinguish "surface grammar" from "depth grammar"' (PI §664). Words that have the same 'surface grammar' may have very different 'depth grammars'. And philosophical problems arise when we are misled by 'certain analogies between the forms of expression in different regions of our language' (PI §90) into thinking that the phenomena we are talking about when we use those expressions are similarly analogous (we will shortly consider an example). So there is a significant parallel between Wittgenstein's early and later views about the source of philosophical problems. And there is a significant parallel in his view about the proper response to philosophical problems: we should not try to solve those problems by producing a philosophical theory; instead, we should dissolve them, by showing that they were not genuine problems at all. 'We cannot give any answer to [philosophical questions]', Wittgenstein writes in the *Tractatus*, 'but can only point out that they are nonsensical' (TLP: 4.003). Similarly, in *Philosophical Investigations*: 'The results of philosophy are the discovery of some piece of plain nonsense and the bumps that the understanding has got by running up against the limits of language' (PI §119). 'What I want to teach', he says, 'is: to pass from unobvious nonsense to obvious nonsense' (PI §464). 'The clarity that we are aiming at is indeed *complete* clarity. But this simply means that the philosophical problems should *completely* disappear' (PI §133).

But once Wittgenstein had rejected the *Tractatus* view of analysis, how did he think we should achieve the kind of clarity about words and propositions that would eliminate philosophical misunderstandings? He writes:

> A main source of our failure to understand is that we do not have an overview of the use of our words. – Our grammar is deficient in surveyability. A surveyable representation produces precisely that kind of understanding which consists in 'seeing connections'. Hence the importance of finding and inventing *intermediate links*.
>
> The concept of a surveyable representation is of fundamental significance for us. It characterizes the way we represent things, how we look at matters.
>
> (PI §122)

The idea, then, is to achieve 'an overview' of our use of words, a 'surveyable' or perspicuous representation of that use. But what does that involve?

'A philosophical problem', Wittgenstein says, 'has the form: "I don't know my way about"' (PI §123). Understanding a word involves mastering its use. But it is one thing to master the use of a word; it is another thing to have a reflective understanding of that use. And, Wittgenstein thinks, philosophical problems characteristically arise when we lack such reflective understanding. He illustrates the point with an example from Saint Augustine: 'What, then, is time? I know well enough what it is, provided that nobody asks me; but if I am asked what it is and try to explain, I am baffled' (Augustine 1961: Bk XI §14). Wittgenstein comments: 'Something that one knows when nobody asks one, but no longer knows when one is asked to explain it, is something that has to be called to mind. (And it is obviously something which, for some reason, it is difficult to call to mind)' (PI §89).

We have mastered the word 'time'; we understand it. But when we reflect on its meaning, we find it hard to explain. In particular, the fact that the word 'time' is a noun tempts us to think of time as a kind of thing. And then we wonder what kind of thing it can be; 'we are puzzled about the nature of time, [and] time seems to us a queer thing' (BB: 6). The cure for this puzzlement, Wittgenstein thinks, is to achieve a reflective understanding of our use of the word 'time' – to 'gain an overview', or command a clear view, of its use (PI §122). And the way to do that is to 'call to mind the kinds of statement that we make' when we use temporal language: 'Augustine calls to mind the different statements that are made about the duration of events, about their being past, present or future' (PI §90). By focusing on the actual use of temporal language we break the hold of the presumption that time is some kind of thing; and by breaking the hold of that presumption, we free ourselves of our sense of puzzlement about the nature of time.

Wittgenstein offers another illustration of the same process, also in connection with Augustine's reflections about time. Augustine wonders: 'How is it possible that one should measure time? For the past can't be measured, as it is gone by; and the future can't be measured because it has not yet come. And the present can't be measured for it has no extension' (BB: 26). It is tempting to conclude that time cannot really be measured at all. But we obviously do measure time. So there must be some mistake in the reasoning that suggests that we cannot. Wittgenstein's diagnosis is that the puzzle is generated by the surface similarity between different uses of the term 'measurement', which lead us to construe the measurement of time on the model of other kinds of measurement:

> Augustine, we might say, thinks of the process of measuring a length: say, the distance between two marks on a travelling band which passes us, and of which we can only see a tiny bit (the present) in front of us. Solving this puzzle will consist in comparing what we mean by 'measurement' (the grammar of the word 'measurement') when applied to distance on a travelling band with the grammar of the word when applied to time.
>
> (BB: 26)

As before, we solve (or rather, dissolve) the puzzle by achieving an 'overview', a 'surveyable representation', of our use of words; in this case, of our use of the term 'measurement'. And we achieve that overview not by finding 'something that lies *beneath* the surface', but by properly appreciating 'something that already lies open to view, and that becomes *surveyable* through a process of ordering' (PI §92): the pattern of analogies and disanalogies between our use of the word 'measurement' in different contexts. When we do that, our original problem – 'How is it so much as possible to measure time?' – is revealed for what it is: a mere artefact of a misleading analogy between different uses of the term 'measurement'. We see that the apparent problem was not a genuine problem at all.

Wittgenstein's repudiation of the *Tractatus* conception of analysis goes hand in hand with a repudiation of the *Tractatus's essentialism*. He set out in the *Tractatus* to give an account of the *essence* of language; the essential feature of any proposition whatever, he thought, is that it is a truth-function of elementary propositions (see TLP: 5.471, 6). When Wittgenstein gave up the *Tractatus* idea of analysis, he gave up the idea that there is anything that could be called the essence of a proposition or the essence of language:

> Instead of pointing out something common to all that we call
> language, I'm saying that these phenomena have no one thing in
> common in virtue of which we use the same word for all – but there
> are many different kinds of *affinity* between them. And on account of
> this affinity, or these affinities, we call them all 'languages'.
>
> (PI §65)

He illustrates the point by an analogy:

> Consider for example the activities that we call 'games'. I mean
> board-games, card-games, ball-games, athletic games, and so on.
> What is common to them all? – Don't say: 'They *must* have something
> in common, or they would not be called "games"' – but look and see
> whether there is anything common to all. – For if you look at them, you
> won't see something that is common to all, but similarities, affinities,
> and a whole series of them at that. To repeat: don't think, but look!
>
> (PI §66)

And, he thinks, what we find when we look is a whole host of similarities and differences between games of different kinds: in some games there is winning and losing, in others there is not; some games involve competition between players, others do not; there are games that are entertaining and games that are not; games that involve skill and games that do not; and so on.

> The upshot of these considerations is: we see a complicated network of similarities overlapping and criss-crossing: similarities in the large and in the small.
>   I can think of no better expression to characterize these similarities than 'family resemblances'; for the various resemblances between members of a family – build, features, colour of eyes, gait, temperament, and so on and so forth – overlap and criss-cross in the same way. – And I shall say: 'games' form a family.
>
> (PI §§66–7)

In Wittgenstein's view, then, there is no such thing as the essence of a game: no property or set of properties that is common to all and only the things that count as games. It follows that the meaning of the word 'game' cannot be analysed or explained by giving a set of conditions that are necessary and sufficient for something's being a game; for there are no such conditions. The word 'game', we might say, expresses a 'family-resemblance concept'. How, then, do we explain the meaning of the word? Simply by giving examples of games of different kinds and saying, 'This and similar things are called "games"' (see PI §69). The success of that explanation depends on the contingent fact that, given the explanation and the examples, people agree in going on to apply the word 'game' in new cases in more or less the same ways. But by and large, Wittgenstein thinks, we do all agree in going on from a set of examples to new cases in the same way. That fact, he thinks, is of fundamental importance in understanding our ability to use language and to follow rules.

Now Wittgenstein thinks that the points he makes about the word 'game' apply equally to the words 'language' and 'proposition'. There is, he thinks, no such thing as the essence of language, or the essence of a proposition: 'What we call "proposition", "language" has not the formal unity that I imagined, but is a family of structures more or less akin to one another' (PI §108). He imagines an objection: 'But haven't we got a concept of what a proposition is, of what we understand by "proposition"? Indeed we do', he replies, 'just as we also have a concept of what we understand by "game"' (PI §135). But, as the 'game' example shows, we can have the concept of a proposition without there being any set of necessary and sufficient conditions for something's being a proposition: 'Asked what a proposition is – whether it is another person or ourselves that we have to answer – we'll give examples . . . So, it is in this way that we have a concept of a proposition' (PI §135).

It is widely accepted in contemporary philosophy that, for many concepts, Wittgenstein's anti-essentialism is correct. Philosophers have traditionally aimed to analyse such fundamental concepts as knowledge, truth, goodness, causation, and so on. And they have traditionally taken the successful analysis of a concept to involve the identification of an informative set of necessary and sufficient conditions for something's falling under that concept. So, for instance, discussions of knowledge have traditionally focused on the question: What must be added to the conditions (i) that p is true, (ii) that S believes that p, and (iii) that S's belief that p is justified, in order to guarantee that S knows that p? But the consensus among contemporary philosophers is that it is impossible to analyse the concept of knowledge in that way; any proposed analysis will turn out either to be open to counter-examples or to employ concepts that presuppose the concept of knowledge. Instead of attempting to analyse knowledge in other terms, therefore, contemporary discussions tend to take knowledge as basic and unanalysable; they look for insight not by analysing knowledge but by exploring the relations between knowledge and other phenomena (belief, evidence, assertion, and so on), or by exploring the function or value of knowledge (see e.g. Craig 1990; Williamson 2000). The same goes for much contemporary discussion of truth, goodness, causation, and so on. That trend in contemporary philosophy is very much in agreement with Wittgenstein's repudiation of his own *Tractatus* conception of philosophical analysis. And it is in agreement with Wittgenstein's idea that philosophical understanding comes from achieving a 'surveyable representation' (PI §122), and from understanding the 'function' or 'structure' (PI §92) of the phenomena we are concerned with.

There is less widespread agreement in contemporary philosophy, however, when it comes to Wittgenstein's attempt to apply the same approach to the discussion of language, propositions, and meaning. Maybe Wittgenstein is right that there is no set of features that is common to *everything* that we are prepared to call 'a proposition': that the set of things we call 'propositions' displays the same kind of variety as the set of things we call 'games'. But what follows from that? Wittgenstein's own view is that philosophy must abandon the aim of saying anything general and systematic about language and propositions. Propositions, he thinks, form a family of different cases, related to one another in different ways; the best we can do is to chart the similarities and differences, and to say particular things about particular cases; but it is impossible to say anything about the nature of propositions as such – for there is nothing to say that applies to every case. But many philosophers take a different view. Even if there is nothing that is common to *everything* we are prepared to classify as a proposition, they think, we can nonetheless identify a set of central or paradigmatic cases of propositions. A philosophical account of language must start from these central, paradigmatic cases. And for propositions that belong to this central class, we *can* give a general, systematic account of what it is for something to be a proposition. On this view, Wittgenstein was right to point out the variety in the class of propositions as a whole. But he was wrong to think that meant that philosophy must abandon the attempt to give any general, systematic account of propositions and language. We will explore the issue between these two views in the following sections.

2. 'THE DIVERSITY OF KINDS OF WORD AND SENTENCE': WITTGENSTEIN'S REJECTION OF REFERENTIALISM

Early in *Philosophical Investigations*, Wittgenstein comments:

> It is interesting to compare the diversity of the tools of language and of the ways they are used, the diversity of kinds of word and sentence, with what logicians have said about the structure of language. (This includes the author of the *Tractatus Logico-Philosophicus*.)
>
> (PI §23)

The *Tractatus* offered a *referentialist* view of language. The fundamental notion in its account of meaning was the idea that a word stands for, or refers to, an object. As Wittgenstein put it, 'The possibility of propositions is based on the principle that objects have signs as their representatives' (TLP: 4.0312). And the essence of a proposition was to represent a state of affairs: to say that such-and-such is the case. A crucial failing of this Tractarian view, he came to think, was that it ignored the differences between different kinds of word and sentence, and between different uses of language. The importance of those differences is a central theme in the early sections of *Philosophical Investigations*.

Wittgenstein begins *Philosophical Investigations* with a quotation from Saint Augustine:

> When grown-ups named some object and at the same time turned towards it, I perceived this, and I grasped that the thing was signified by the sound they uttered, since they meant to point *it* out. This, however, I gathered from their gestures, the natural language of all peoples, the language that by means of facial expression and the play of eyes, of the movements of the limbs and the tone of voice, indicates the affections of the soul when it desires, or clings to, or rejects, or recoils from, something. In this way, little by little, I learnt to understand what things the words, which I heard uttered in their respective places in various sentences, signified. And once I got my tongue around these signs, I used them to express my wishes.
>
> (PI §1)

Augustine's words, according to Wittgenstein:

> give us a particular picture of the essence of human language. It is this: the words in language name objects – sentences are combinations of such names. – In this picture of language we find the roots of the following idea: Every word has a meaning. This meaning is correlated with the word. It is the object for which the word stands.
>
> (PI §1)

Wittgenstein's basic objection to this referentialist picture – 'Augustine's conception of language' (PI §4), as he calls it – is disarmingly simple. Some words do stand for objects, he thinks. Indeed, we can imagine a very primitive language that is made up entirely of words that stand for objects: 'a language for which the description given by Augustine is right' (PI §2). But it is obviously not true that all words in our actual language stand for objects. He illustrates the point with a simple example:

> Think of the following use of language: I send someone shopping. I give him a slip of paper marked 'five red apples'. He takes the slip to the

shopkeeper, who opens the drawer marked 'apples'; then he looks up
the word 'red' in a chart and finds a colour sample next to it; then he
says the series of elementary number-words – I assume that he knows
them by heart – up to the word 'five', and for each number-word he
takes an apple of the same colour as the sample out of the drawer. – It
is in this and similar ways that one operates with words.

(PI §1)

The words 'five', 'red', and 'apples' do not all function in the same
way; they do not all stand for objects. And understanding the words
does not in each case involve knowing what object the word stands
for. The shopkeeper understands the words 'five' and 'red'. But that
does not involve knowing objects that they stand for. Rather, Wittgenstein insists, it involves knowing how the words are used: in what circumstances they are appropriately uttered, what their use is meant to
achieve, how one should respond to their use, and so on. The lesson
is simple: we should not be misled by the surface similarity between
words of different kinds into ignoring the deeper differences between
them. Wittgenstein illustrates the point with an analogy:

Think of the tools in a toolbox: there is a hammer, pliers, a saw, a
screwdriver, a rule, a glue-pot, glue, nails and screws. – The functions
of words are as diverse as the functions of these objects. (And in both
cases there are similarities.)
   Of course, what confuses us is the uniform appearance of words
when we hear them in speech, or see them written or in print. For
their *use* is not that obvious. Especially when we are doing philosophy!

(PI §11)

We might put the moral of Wittgenstein's response to Augustine
like this. To say that a word signifies an object is a perfectly good way
of stating the function, or role, of some words: names. But not every
word is a name, and not every word signifies something. In a characteristic twist, however, Wittgenstein allows that the moral of his discussion might be expressed in a different way. Thus we *can*, if we want to,
say that every word signifies something: 'Napoleon' signifies a person;
'apple' signifies a kind of fruit; 'five' signifies a number; 'red' signifies
a colour; and so on (see PI §§10, 13–15). But if we do say that, he
insists, we will have to acknowledge that what signification is – what in

detail is involved in a word's signifying whatever it signifies – will be different for different kinds of words. We will have to give one account of what it takes for a proper name to signify a particular person; a different account of what it takes for a numeral to signify a particular number; a different account again of what it takes for a colour-word to signify a particular colour; and so on. (For example, it is very plausibly a necessary condition for the name 'Napoleon' to signify, or refer to, the man Napoleon that there is some kind of causal connection, however remote, between our use of the name and the man himself. But it cannot be a condition for the numeral '1' to refer to the number 1 that there should be a *causal* connection between our use of the numeral and the number 1; for numbers are not causally connected to anything. Similarly, though there may be a causal condition for the word 'red' to refer to the colour, red, that condition cannot be exactly the same as the causal condition that applies to the name 'Napoleon': for Napoleon is a particular, concrete object; redness is not.) If we do treat every word as signifying something, then, we will find that 'making the descriptions of the uses of these words similar in this way cannot make the uses themselves any more like one another! For, as we see, they are absolutely unlike' (PI §10). So we have a choice. We can think of signifying as a specific relation: the relation that holds between a proper name and the object it names. In that case, it is not true that every word signifies something; for it is not true that every word functions in the same way as a proper name. Alternatively, we can say that every word signifies something. But then the idea that a word signifies something will tell us nothing at all about the way that any word actually functions; in Wittgenstein's words, 'If we say "Every word in the language signifies something", we have so far said nothing *whatever*' (PI §13). The whole content of our account will be given by the particular accounts of signification that we go on to give, case by case; and those accounts will be different for each different kind of word.

A natural reaction to Wittgenstein's argument is to regard what he says as simply obvious. Of course different words function in different ways; and of course the relation between a proper name and its bearer is importantly different from the relation between a colour-word and a colour, say, or between a numeral and a number. But who is going to deny that? Maybe Wittgenstein's point counts against his own view in the *Tractatus*. (And even that is not obvious. The *Tractatus* said that elementary propositions are made up entirely of names, and that names stand for objects. But that is a claim about how language functions at the level of complete analysis, not a claim about ordinary language. So it is compatible with the idea that, in ordinary language, different words function in different ways: indeed, Wittgenstein positively insists that logical words such as 'and', 'not', and 'or', for example, do not function by naming objects (4.0312).) But even if Wittgenstein's point is fatal to his own earlier views, how radical a challenge is he posing to views that anyone else has actually wanted to hold? For whoever thought that every word *does* function in exactly the same way – by naming an object?

It might seem, then, that Wittgenstein is not, after all, posing a very radical challenge to other philosophers of language. It might seem that the point he makes in drawing attention to the diversity of kinds of word is a perfectly good one: but that it is readily accommodated within an orthodox, referentialist account of meaning of the kind promoted by Frege, Russell, and the *Tractatus*. On the orthodox view, meaning is explained in terms of the reference of words and the truth-conditions of propositions. The meaning of a sentence is a matter of what has to be the case for it to be true; and that is determined by the references of its component words. Take the sentence 'Julia is tall'. The name 'Julia' refers to a particular person: Julia. The expression 'is tall' refers to a particular property: the property of being tall. The whole sentence, 'Julia is tall', is true if and only if the person referred to by the name 'Julia' has the property referred to by the words 'is tall'. And in giving the sentence's truth-conditions in this way, we give its meaning. In saying all this, the referentialist can perfectly well acknowledge that an account of what it takes for the English word 'Julia' to refer to a particular individual will differ in various significant ways from an account of what it takes for the expression 'is tall' to refer to the property of being tall. But, on the orthodox view, that is no reason for giving up the idea that the notion of reference is central to an account of meaning. For without that idea, we have no idea at all how the meaning of a sentence is made up from the meanings of its parts. On this view, Wittgenstein's comments about the diversity of kinds of word remind us that we need a substantive account of what makes it the case that a given word refers to the object or property it does refer to. And they remind us that not every word functions by referring to a thing or a property: words such as 'Away!', 'Ow!', 'Help!', 'Splendid!', and 'No!', for example, do not (see PI §27). These are important points. But, on the orthodox view, they do not challenge the basic referentialist doctrine that the notion of reference is central to an account of meaning.

Wittgenstein, however, intends his critique of Augustine's conception of language to be much more radical than that. When he criticizes the idea that 'every word has a meaning; this meaning is correlated with the word; it is the object for which the word stands', he does not mean to be arguing for a more careful and subtle account of meaning of the same general kind that he had pursued in the *Tractatus* – a referentialist account on which the meaning of a word is a matter of what it refers to, and the meaning of a sentence is a matter of what has to be the case for it to be true. On the contrary, he is arguing that any such account gives an impoverished, one-sided, and inaccurate view of language. It is a mistake, he thinks, to treat reference as the fundamental feature in terms of which the meanings of all words are to be explained: some words refer, but not all do; and there is no reason to regard words that do refer as the paradigm case and others as merely secondary. Similarly, he thinks, it is a mistake to regard the condition under which a sentence is true as its fundamental feature, in terms of which its meaning is to be explained. The *Tractatus* held that 'the general form of a proposition is: This is how things stand' (TLP: 4.5); the essential property of a proposition is that it says that such-and-such is the case. In *Philosophical Investigations*, Wittgenstein totally repudiates that idea. We must, he says, 'make a radical break with the idea that language always functions in one way, always serves the same purpose: to convey thoughts – which may be about houses, pains, good and evil, or whatever' (PI §304). For there are 'countless different kinds of use' of language. Wittgenstein lists some examples:

Giving orders, and acting on them
Describing an object by its appearance, or by its measurements
Constructing an object from a description (a drawing)
Reporting an event
Speculating about the event
Forming and testing a hypothesis
Presenting the results of an experiment in tables and diagrams
Making up a story; and reading one
Acting in a play
Singing rounds
Guessing riddles

Cracking a joke; and telling one
Solving a problem in applied arithmetic
Translating from one language into another
Requesting, thanking, cursing, greeting, praying.

(PI §23)

Some of these uses of language involve uttering sentences that are true or false. But others, Wittgenstein insists – including giving orders, making up stories, guessing riddles, telling jokes, requesting, thanking, and so on – do not.

In itself, that observation is not an objection to orthodox, referentialist views in the tradition of Frege, Russell, and the *Tractatus*. The orthodox view acknowledges the existence of these different uses of language; and it acknowledges that a complete account of language must deal with them all. But, it holds, our account must start from the use of language to say things that are true or false. The words that make up the sentence 'The bird-box is nailed to the tree', for instance, can be used to do many things other than to say something that is true or false. They can be used to give an order ('Nail the bird-box to the tree!'), to ask a question ('Is the bird-box nailed to the tree?'), to tell a story ('Once upon a time, there was a bird-box nailed to a tree'), in jokes and riddles, in translations from one language to another, and so on. But, on the orthodox view, it is their use in saying something true or false that is fundamental in understanding their meaning. To explain what the words mean, we must say what a bird-box is, what a tree is, and what has to be the case for it to be true that a bird-box is nailed to a tree. That gives us an account of the meanings of the words that can be applied to other cases, where the same words are used to do something other than saying something true or false. But the use of words to say something true or false is basic. That is the referentialist view. And it is that view that Wittgenstein is challenging. When he draws attention to the diversity of uses of language, his point is that we should not treat the use of a sentence to say something true or false as fundamental and other uses as merely secondary or derivative: the different uses of sentences, he thinks, are on a par with one another; all of them will play an equal role in any account of language.

Wittgenstein is certainly right that there are many different kinds of word, and many different uses of language. He is right that an adequate account of language must accommodate all these phenomena. And it is true that philosophical discussions of language have often focused on a relatively small and restricted range of cases. But as we have seen, there are two attitudes we might take to this diversity of uses. On the orthodox view, recognizing the diversity of kinds of word and kinds of use of language is quite compatible with giving a general, systematic account of meaning: an account in which the basic feature of words is their reference, the basic use of words is their use in saying something true or false, and other features and uses of words are treated as being secondary to, or derivative from, these. On a different view, the diversity of kinds of word and kinds of use of language makes it impossible to give any systematic account of meaning at all: there is no one feature of words, and no one use of words, that can be taken as basic; and there is no systematic or uniform account to be given of what determines the meaning of a proposition. Wittgenstein favours this second view. But does he give us good reasons for agreeing with him?

The ultimate test for the orthodox approach to language is whether it can in the end successfully accommodate the diversity of words and uses of language within its framework of reference and truth-conditions. Contemporary researchers in philosophy and linguistics who work in the orthodox, referentialist tradition would certainly not claim to have given a complete account of all kinds of word or all kinds of use of language. But they would claim to be making steady progress; and they would certainly reject the contention that their project cannot succeed. For their part, those who are sceptical about the orthodox approach – including many who are influenced by Wittgenstein – continue to point to features or uses of language that, they think, resist any systematic treatment. But this dispute has the character of a live debate: and the debate has certainly not been resolved in favour of Wittgenstein's view that no orthodox account can in the end succeed.

In the light of that, our reaction to Wittgenstein's critique of referentialist accounts of meaning will partly depend on the attractiveness of the alternative, if any, that he offers. How *should* we think of the meanings of words, if not in a way that treats reference as fundamental? And how *should* we think of the meanings of propositions, if not in a way that treats their use to say something true or false as fundamental? In *Philosophical Investigations*, Wittgenstein suggests that 'the meaning of a word is its use in the language' (PI §43); and the sense of a proposition, he says, is its use. But what do those ideas amount to?

3. MEANING AND USE

Wittgenstein says in the *Tractatus* that the sense of a proposition is a matter of 'how things stand if it is true' (see TLP: 4.022). Accordingly, 'to understand a proposition means to know what is the case if it is true' (TLP: 4.024). In 1929 and 1930 he adopted a different slogan: 'The sense of a proposition is its method of verification' (WVC: 79). On this view, understanding a proposition involves knowing how it could be determined whether it is true. By 1932–33, he had formulated a third idea: 'The use of a proposition – that is its sense' (BT: 80). So to understand a proposition is to know how it is used. This last idea runs through Wittgenstein's later philosophy: 'Doesn't [the fact that two sentences have] the same sense consist in their having the same use?' he asks (PI §20). His question clearly expects the answer 'Yes'.

On the surface, then, there is a steady development in Wittgenstein's view of meaning: in the *Tractatus*, the meaning of a proposition is explained in terms of the conditions under which it is true; for a brief period in 1929–30, he holds the verificationist view that the meaning of a proposition is a matter of what would *show* that it is true; in his later philosophy, he holds that the meaning of a proposition is a matter of its use. That is the traditional view of the development of Wittgenstein's philosophy. And it is a reasonable first approximation. As we fill in the detail, we will see ways in which the sharp lines of the initial sketch need to be made more subtle. But before examining Wittgenstein's views, we need to see what it means to explain the meaning of a proposition in terms of its truth-conditions, or its method of verification, or its use. (The account that follows is indebted to the writings of Michael Dummett: for a summary of the relevant ideas, see Dummett 1994: 274–8.)

We can distinguish three features of a proposition. There is its truth-condition: what has to be the case for it to be true. There are the conditions that would justify believing or asserting the proposition; the conditions that count as *evidence* for its truth. And there are the *consequences* of believing or asserting the proposition: the effect that is produced by that belief or assertion. We can illustrate these three features by considering the proposition, 'Animals feel pain'. There is a state of affairs that has to obtain for the proposition 'Animals feel pain' to be true: the state of affairs of animals experiencing the sensation of pain. There are conditions that justify asserting the proposition: for example, the fact that, when animals are injured, their behaviour exhibits the same signs

of distress that we exhibit when we feel pain. And there are consequences of asserting or accepting the proposition. It is a consequence
of our accepting the proposition 'Animals feel pain', for example, that
we treat animals with care and consideration; if we did not believe that
animals felt pain, we would not behave towards them in the way that
we do. But what is the relation between these three features of a proposition? And how are they related to the proposition's meaning?

On the orthodox, truth-conditional view of meaning, the meaning
of a proposition is explained in terms of its truth-conditions. Thus,
what the proposition 'Animals feel pain' means is a matter of what has
to be the case for the proposition to be true; namely, that animals experience sensations of pain. Correspondingly, to understand the proposition is to know that it is that state of affairs – the state of affairs of
animals experiencing pain – that must obtain for the proposition to
be true. On this view, what counts as a justification for asserting the
proposition, and what the consequences are of accepting it, follow
from what the proposition means. It is *because* the proposition 'Animals
feel pain' means what it does that its assertion can be justified by the
relevant kinds of behavioural evidence. And it is *because* the proposition
means what it does that believing the proposition has the kinds of consequence it does.

But it is possible to take a different view of the relations between
meaning, truth-conditions, evidence, and consequences. The *verificationist* takes the evidence that we treat as justifying a proposition as its
basic feature, and explains the meaning of the proposition in terms of
that. The evidence that we treat as justifying the proposition 'Animals
feel pain' is that animals are disposed to behave in certain ways when
they are injured. And, for the verificationist, the fact that its assertion
is justified on the basis of that evidence is all there is to the proposition's meaning what it does. On this view, understanding a proposition
involves knowing what would justify us in asserting it. So if someone
has no idea what would verify a proposition – no idea how it could
be established whether it is true – she does not understand it at all. As
Wittgenstein put it in 1929: 'In order to determine the sense of a proposition, I should have to know a very specific procedure for when to
count the proposition as verified' (WVC: 47). On the orthodox view,
by contrast, it is perfectly possible to understand a proposition without
having any idea how it could be verified. For on that view, understanding a proposition is a matter of knowing what *has to be the case* for the

proposition to be true; and someone could know that without knowing how it could be established whether or not it is true.

Similarly, there are pragmatist views of meaning, which take the effects
of asserting or believing a proposition as basic and explain its meaning in terms of those. One consequence of accepting the proposition
'Animals feel pain', we saw, is that we are kind to animals (or at least,
kinder than we would otherwise be). So a pragmatist might regard the
proposition as a tool for producing that effect, and explain its meaning in terms of that function; the proposition's meaning what it does
consists in its having the function or effect of inducing people to treat
animals kindly. That reverses the orthodox way of seeing things, on
which the proposition has the consequences it does because it means
what it does. For the pragmatist, understanding a proposition will
involve grasping its consequences or function: using it to bring about
those consequences; and reacting in the right way to others' use of the
proposition.

The verificationist and the pragmatist each explain the meaning of a
proposition in terms of its use. But they differ in focusing on different
aspects of the use of a proposition: the verificationist focuses on what
justifies asserting the proposition; the pragmatist focuses on the effects or
consequences of asserting it. The idea that the meaning of a proposition
is a matter of its use may be developed in either of these ways. Or it
may be developed in a way that appeals to both features of use – with a
proposition's meaning being a matter of its whole use: the circumstances
that would justify us in asserting it, the point or purpose of asserting
it, the effects or consequences of asserting it, and so on.

With that background in place, we can return to the question of
how Wittgenstein's own view of meaning developed. The conventional
wisdom, I said, is that in the *Tractatus* Wittgenstein explained meaning
in terms of truth-conditions; that in 1929–30 he briefly held a verificationist view of meaning; and that in *Philosophical Investigations* he conceived of the meaning of a proposition in terms of its use. How does
the conventional wisdom look on closer examination?

According to the *Tractatus*, as we have seen, the sense of a proposition is 'how things stand if it is true' (TLP: 4.022). And 'to understand
a proposition means to know what is the case if it is true' (4.024). To
conceive of meaning in those terms just is to conceive of meaning in
terms of truth-conditions. But the *Tractatus* also associates meaning with
use. To know a sign's meaning, Wittgenstein says, 'we must observe

how it is used with a sense' (3.326); 'If a sign is *useless* it is meaningless' (3.328). And again: 'In philosophy the question, "What do we actually use this word or this proposition for?" repeatedly leads to valuable insights' (6.21). That stress on the relation between meaning and use might make it look as if Wittgenstein cannot, after all, be thinking of meaning in terms of truth-conditions – as if the *Tractatus* must be proposing some form of verificationism or pragmatism. But that would be a mistake: there is really no tension between these remarks, which link meaning and use, and the idea that the *Tractatus* offers a truth-conditional account of meaning.

In the *Tractatus*, Wittgenstein does hold that a proposition has the meaning it does because of the way that we use it. But what he means by that is that a proposition means what it does because we use it to represent the particular state of affairs we do: because we give it the particular truth-condition we do. To know what a sentence means, we have to 'observe how it is used with a sense' (3.326): that is to say, we have to see what state of affairs it is used to represent. But that has nothing to do with evidence or verification. The *Tractatus* expresses no interest in epistemology and includes virtually no discussion of questions of evidence or justification. And it contains no suggestion of the verificationist idea that the sense of a proposition is to be explained by reference to the grounds that would justify us in asserting it.

Similarly, the idea that we can derive 'valuable insights' by pressing the question, 'What do we actually use this word or this proposition for?' (6.21), is part of a fundamentally truth-conditional account of meaning, not a challenge to it. Wittgenstein makes that remark in the context of a discussion of mathematical propositions. We can get an insight into the nature of mathematical propositions, he thinks, by considering what we use them for. And, when we do consider how we use them, we find that 'we make use of mathematical propositions only in inferences from propositions that do not belong to mathematics to others that likewise do not belong to mathematics' (6.211). For example, we might use the mathematical proposition '7 + 5 = 12' to reason from 'There are 7 walnuts and 5 cashews in the bowl' to 'There are 12 nuts in the bowl'; that is an inference from one non-mathematical proposition to another. And, according to Wittgenstein, that is all we use mathematical propositions for. In particular, they are not used as pictures of states of affairs; they are not used to represent the world. So 'a proposition of mathematics does not express a thought'

(6.21). When Wittgenstein presses the question, 'What do we actually use this proposition for?', he is arguing that, if an apparent proposition is not used to say something true or false about reality, it has no sense. And that does not challenge the idea that the sense of a proposition is a matter of its truth-condition; it presupposes it. So the *Tractatus* does connect the meanings of words and propositions with their use. But it presents that connection in the context of an account that explains meaning in terms of truth-conditions.

If it is clear that the *Tractatus* conceives of meaning in terms of truth-conditions, it is equally clear that, for a period after Wittgenstein's return to philosophy in 1929, he thought that the sense of a proposition was to be explained in terms of the evidence that would establish its truth. 'How a proposition is verified is what it says', he wrote (PR: 200). And: 'In order to know the sense of a proposition, I should have to know a very specific procedure for when to count the proposition as verified' (WVC: 47). In keeping with that idea he proposed, for example, that the meaning of a proposition about someone else's toothache is to be explained in terms of the behavioural grounds on which we assert that she has toothache – rather than in terms of anything lying behind her behaviour, whose existence we could have no means of verifying (see PR: 88–9 and WVC: 49–50; the proposal is discussed in Chapter 6 section 1.i below). But verificationism in that form was a short-lived phase. G. E. Moore reports that in lectures in 1930 Wittgenstein 'made the famous statement, "The sense of a proposition is the way in which it is verified"' (Moore 1954–55: 59). But by 1932–33, Moore records, he had given up that idea in favour of the weaker thesis that 'You can determine the meaning of a proposition by asking how it is verified'. And even this weaker thesis, Wittgenstein now said, was 'a mere rule of thumb'. For one thing, 'in some cases the question "How is that verified?" makes no sense' (Moore 1954–55: 59). (For example, it makes no sense, according to Wittgenstein, to ask how one verifies the proposition 'I have toothache'. Nonetheless, the proposition is perfectly meaningful.) For another thing, the fact that we can verify a certain proposition in a particular way might tell us very little about its meaning. For instance, Wittgenstein said, 'statements in the newspapers could verify the "hypothesis" that Cambridge won the boat race, . . . yet these statements "only go a very little way towards explaining the meaning of 'boat-race'"' (Moore 1954–55: 60).

So Wittgenstein had abandoned his earlier verificationism long before he wrote *Philosophical Investigations*. But, though he gave up that form of verificationism, he did not give up the idea that there is a significant relation between the meaning of a proposition and the ways in which we can tell whether it is true or false. In *Philosophical Investigations* he writes: 'Asking whether and how a proposition can be verified is only a special form of the question "How do you mean?" The answer is a contribution to the grammar of the proposition' (PI §353). An account of how a proposition can be verified is a contribution to its 'grammar': to the kind of meaning it has. That is to say, it is one feature of its meaning: not the sole determinant. That is a much more restrained view than the out-and-out verificationism of 1929–30. But it still suggests that there is a close relation between the meaning of a proposition and the grounds on which it could be asserted: a much closer relation than Wittgenstein would have contemplated in the *Tractatus*. For example, Wittgenstein says in *Philosophy of Psychology – A Fragment* that 'the meaning of the word "length" is learned by learning, amongst other things, what it is to determine length' (PPF §338 [PI II xi p. 225]). His point is not that teaching people methods of measuring lengths is in fact an effective way to teach them the meaning of the word 'length'. It is that what 'the length of *x*' *means* is in part defined by how we measure the length of *x*; the meaning of the proposition 'The garden is 20 metres long', say, is in part a matter of how we determine whether it is true. When Wittgenstein associates the meaning of a proposition with its use, then, part of what he means by 'use' is the evidence on the basis of which we assert the proposition.

But *Philosophical Investigations* also suggest that the meaning of a proposition is in part a matter of what we use it for, or what we *do* with it. Consider the sentence 'I believe it's raining'. In many contexts, Wittgenstein points out, 'The utterance "I believe that this is the case" is used in a similar way to the assertion "This is the case"' (PPF §87 [PI II x p. 190]). So, for example, the purpose of saying 'I believe it's raining' is often to inform someone about the weather, rather than to inform them about one's beliefs. And in Wittgenstein's view, it seems, that is reflected in what the sentence means on these occasions: 'the statement "I believe it's going to rain"', he says, 'has a similar sense, that is to say, a similar use, to "It's going to rain"' (PPF §89 [PI II x p. 190]). Wittgenstein's view ties the sense of a sentence on an occasion to the point or purpose of uttering it. That contrasts with the traditional, and more orthodox, view that there is a sharp distinction between a sentence's *semantic* features (features having to do with its meaning) and its *pragmatic* features (features of its use that are not part of its literal meaning). On the traditional view, the sentence 'I believe it's going to rain' always means that the speaker believes that it is going to rain; it never means the same as 'It is going to rain'. And someone who utters the sentence is always saying something about herself; she is never saying something about the weather. Her *purpose* in saying 'I believe it's going to rain' may be to inform someone about the weather, rather than to inform them about herself. But that does not affect the meaning of the sentence she utters, or the content of what she says in uttering it. On this way of seeing things, there is a sharp distinction between the literal meaning of a sentence and the point or purpose of uttering it. But Wittgenstein rejects that distinction. In his view, as we shall see, there is no single standard of what a proposition means; and there is no clear, non-arbitrary division between a sentence's meaning and other aspects of its use. The very idea that a sentence has a 'strict and literal meaning', he thinks, is a philosopher's myth.

In *Philosophical Investigations*, then, Wittgenstein rejects the Tractarian idea that meaning is to be explained in terms of truth-conditions. He suggests that both the grounds on which we assert a proposition and the purposes for which we use it have a role in determining the proposition's meaning. He glosses 'the meaning of a proposition' as 'the use of the proposition'. And, as we saw, he suggests that for two propositions to have the same sense is for them to have the same use. It seems fair to say, then, that he does conceive the meaning of a proposition in terms of its use. But is there anything more definite to say about what he means by 'the use of a proposition' or about how he understands the idea that meaning is a matter of use?

When Wittgenstein says that the meaning of a proposition is its use, he is not advancing a general, systematic theory of meaning. Unlike the verificationist or the pragmatist, he does not think there is a single, uniform feature of the use of a proposition in terms of which we can give a systematic explanation of the meaning of every proposition. Nor is he offering a reductive account of meaning: an account that explains what it is for a proposition to mean what it does in terms that do not themselves presuppose the concept of meaning. That distinguishes Wittgenstein from some other philosophers who have also held that meaning is determined by use but who, unlike Wittgenstein, have had reductive ambitions. Such philosophers have wanted to show how the semantic properties of words, which they take to be prima facie puzzling or in need of explanation, can be accounted for within a scientific, or physicalist, picture of the world. For example, the twentieth-century American philosopher W. V. Quine construes the use of a sentence in terms of the pattern of sensory stimulations that would cause speakers to assent to, or dissent from, that sentence. Understood in that way, use is an entirely non-semantic matter; we can give a complete description of a sentence's use, in this sense, without referring either to its meaning or to the beliefs and intentions of those who use it. Quine's aim is to employ that notion of use to construct a well-defined and scientifically respectable notion of meaning; what he calls *stimulus meaning* (Quine 1960: ch. 2). Wittgenstein's version of the idea that meaning is use, is quite different. Unlike Quine, he does not start with a non-semantic conception of use and aim to construct meaning from that. But how exactly *does* he conceive of the use of a proposition?

For Wittgenstein, the 'use' of a proposition encompasses whatever would make us translate 'an otherwise unfamiliar kind of expression' into a given proposition in our familiar language (PPF §7 [PI II ii p. 175]). But, we might ask, what *does* make us translate one word or sentence by another? Wittgenstein writes:

> What characterizes an order as such, or a description as such, or a question as such, etc., is . . . the role which the utterance of these signs plays in the whole practice of the language. That is to say, whether a word of the language of [a] tribe is rightly translated into a word of the English language depends upon the role this word plays in the whole life of the tribe; the occasions on which it is used, the expressions of emotion by which it is generally accompanied, the ideas which it generally awakens or which prompt its saying, etc., etc. As an exercise ask yourself: in which cases would you say that a certain word uttered by the people of the tribe was a greeting? In which cases should we say it corresponded to our 'Goodbye', in which to our 'Hello'? In which cases would you say that a word of the foreign language corresponded to our 'perhaps'? – to our expressions of doubt, trust, certainty? You will find that the justifications for calling something an expression of doubt, conviction, etc., largely, though of course not wholly, consist in descriptions of gestures, the play of facial expressions, and even the tone of voice.

(BB 102–3)

Whether a given word is rightly translated by our word 'Goodbye', Wittgenstein thinks, is a matter of its use. And the use of the word is a matter of the role it plays 'in the whole life of the tribe', 'in the whole practice of the language'. But, we might ask, exactly *what* role must a word play in 'the whole practice of the language' for it to be right to translate it as 'Goodbye'? There are two things to highlight about the way that Wittgenstein would be likely to respond to that question.

First, Wittgenstein would say that there is no account to be given of *exactly* how a word must be used in order to be translated as 'Goodbye'. In actual cases, we can identify a given word in an unfamiliar language as corresponding to our word 'Goodbye'. We do so by seeing how it is used; given everything we know about these people and their use of their words, it makes best overall sense to translate this word as 'Goodbye'. But there is no prospect of systematizing or codifying the considerations that go into determining the correctness of that translation. Second, there is, for Wittgenstein, no single standard of whether or not two words or sentences have the same meaning. So there will be cases where it is right by one standard to translate a word or sentence in a particular way, but wrong by a different standard. And there is no question of one of those standards being correct and the other incorrect; of just one of the standards capturing the relation of genuine sameness of meaning. For there is no such relation. In Wittgenstein's view, the questions 'Do these two expressions have the same meaning?' and 'Is it correct to translate this expression in this way?' can be answered in different ways depending on the standards of sameness of meaning we are applying (for an example, see BB: 103–4; for related points, see PI §§531–2). That is a further reason why Wittgenstein holds that there can be no account of exactly what features of use are necessary for an expression to have a given meaning.

Wittgenstein's conception of the relation between use and meaning can seem elusive and difficult to state. But that is not because he has no positive view of meaning. It is, rather, because of the nature of his view. In particular, his account is anti-essentialist: there is, he thinks, no one feature or set of features that is essential for something to be a meaningful proposition – no one feature in terms of which its meaning is to be understood. It is anti-reductionist: he is not aiming to explain meaning by appeal to a notion of use that does not presuppose it. And it is anti-systematic: there is, he thinks, nothing general and systematic to say about exactly how an expression must be used in order to be rightly translated in a given way. As we shall see in succeeding chapters, these features – anti-essentialism, anti-reductionism, and anti-systematicity – run throughout Wittgenstein's later work.

SUMMARY

In the *Tractatus*, Wittgenstein offered a general account of the nature of all language. The meaning of a proposition, he thought, is a matter of what has to be the case for the proposition to be true. Propositions of ordinary language are analysable as truth-functions of elementary propositions. And elementary propositions are made up entirely of names, which function by standing for objects. In the years after his return to philosophy in 1929, Wittgenstein came to reject each of these features of his earlier view.

He abandoned the idea that philosophy must analyse ordinary propositions into truth-functions of more basic propositions. He still held that the aim of philosophy is to achieve clarity about the meanings of ordinary propositions, and that doing so would reveal traditional philosophical questions to be confused or nonsensical. But clarity was now to be achieved by attaining a 'surveyable representation' of our use of words, not by finding something hidden beneath the surface of ordinary use.

In opposition to the *Tractatus*'s essentialist and referentialist account of language, Wittgenstein stressed the diversity of kinds of word and sentence, and the diversity of uses of language. Some words, he thought, function by standing for objects. But many do not. And there are many different uses of language, only some of which involve saying something that is true or false. Accordingly, he abandoned the *Tractatus*'s referentialist doctrine that the reference of words, and the truth or falsity of sentences, are the fundamental notions in an account of language. It remains a topic of philosophical debate whether Wittgenstein was right to give up the Tractarian framework – or whether a broadly Tractarian, referentialist account can in fact be developed to accommodate the diversity of kinds of word and sentence to which he rightly drew attention.

Wittgenstein moved from a truth-conditional account of meaning in the *Tractatus*, through verificationism in 1929–30, to conceiving of meaning in terms of use. In saying that meaning is use, he is not offering a reductive account, which explains meaning in other terms. His conception of the use of a proposition is very catholic; it encompasses whatever features of use could be relevant to our translating a sentence one way or another. And it is flexible; two propositions may have the same use – and, therefore, the same meaning – by one standard, but a different use – and a different meaning – by another.

FURTHER READING

The developments in Wittgenstein's thinking immediately after his return to philosophy in 1929 can be traced through his writings and through records of his conversations. See:

'Some Remarks on Logical Form', *Proceedings of the Aristotelian Society Supplementary Volume*, 9: 162–71, 1929; reprinted in Wittgenstein, *Philosophical Occasions*.

Philosophical Remarks, ed. R. Rhees, trans. R. Hargreaves and R. White, Oxford: Blackwell, 1975.

Ludwig Wittgenstein and the Vienna Circle: Conversations recorded by Friedrich Waismann, ed. B. McGuinness , trans. J. Schulte and B. McGuinness, Oxford: Blackwell, 1979.

Notes taken by those who attended his lectures in Cambridge in the period 1930–35 continue the story of the evolution of his views:

Lee, D. (ed.) (1980) *Wittgenstein's Lectures: Cambridge, 1930–32*, Oxford: Blackwell.

Moore, G. E. 'Wittgenstein's Lectures in 1930–33', *Mind*, 63, 1954: 1–15, 289–315, and *Mind*, 64, 1955: 1–27, 264; reprinted in Wittgenstein, *Philosophical Occasions*.

Ambrose, A. (ed.) (1979) *Wittgenstein's Lectures: Cambridge, 1932–35*, Oxford: Blackwell.

Wittgenstein's discussions of Augustine's conception of language can be found in:

Philosophical Investigations §§1–136.

The Blue and Brown Books 1–20, 77–85.

For scholarly discussions of aspects of the transition from the *Tractatus* to *Philosophical Investigations*, see:

Hacker, P. M. S. (1986) *Insight and Illusion: Themes in the Philosophy of Wittgenstein*, Revised Edition, Oxford: Oxford University Press, chs. 5, 6.

Pears, D. (1988) *The False Prison: A Study of the Development of Wittgenstein's Philosophy*, vol. 2, Oxford: Oxford University Press, ch. 9.

Stern, D. (2004) *Wittgenstein's Philosophical Investigations: An Introduction*, Cambridge: Cambridge University Press, ch. 2.

Some of the themes of Wittgenstein's critique of Augustine's conception of language are discussed in:

Dummett, M. (1977) 'Can Analytical Philosophy be Systematic, and Ought it to Be?' in M. Dummett (1978) *Truth and Other Enigmas*, London: Duckworth.

Fogelin, R. (1996) 'Wittgenstein's Critique of Philosophy', in H. Sluga and D. Stern (eds) *The Cambridge Companion to Wittgenstein*, Cambridge: Cambridge University Press.

McGinn, M. (1997) *Wittgenstein and the Philosophical Investigations*, London: Routledge, chs. 1, 2.

Stern, D. (2004) *Wittgenstein's Philosophical Investigations: An Introduction*, Cambridge: Cambridge University Press, ch. 4.

Five

The later philosophy: intentionality and rule-following

In the *Tractatus*, Wittgenstein offered a general theory of representation: a theory that was intended to explain the representational character of both language and thought. As we have seen in the previous chapter, Wittgenstein came to reject that theory. It was committed to a programme of philosophical analysis that he came to reject. It ignored the diversity of kinds of word and sentence. And it was too abstract and programmatic to be philosophically illuminating. The connection between a thought and the state of affairs it represents, for example, was supposed to involve correlations between simple psychic elements and simple objects; but nothing was said about what exactly these correlations were, or how they were effected and maintained. The relation between thought and reality – the *representational* character of thought or, in philosophical jargon, the *intentionality* of thought – was one of the first topics that Wittgenstein explored when he returned to philosophy in 1929. And it remained a major theme throughout his later work.

As we shall see, Wittgenstein's treatment of thought and intentionality is closely related to his treatment of rules and rule-following. There are parallels between the philosophical questions that arise in each case. There are parallels between the negative phases of Wittgenstein's discussions: his criticisms of bad or mistaken accounts of intentionality and of rule-following. And there are parallels in the positive phases of his discussions: both at the level of detail; and at the level of overall strategy. In each case, Wittgenstein resists the demand for a reductive explanation: an explanation of intentionality or rule-following in other terms. And his view about the status of philosophical concerns about intentionality, and about the status of concerns about rule-following, is the same. Philosophical doubts about the very possibility of thought, or the very possibility of rule-following, he thinks, depend on misunderstandings: so those doubts are not to be addressed by producing a positive philosophical theory; they should, instead, be dispelled by removing the misunderstandings that generate them.

1. INTENTIONALITY

Suppose I wish for an apple. What makes it the case that it is *an apple* I am wishing for? Or suppose I am thinking that India is the world's largest democracy. What makes it the case that I am thinking *about India*; and that what I am thinking is that India *is the world's largest democracy*? 'A great many philosophical difficulties', Wittgenstein says in the *Blue Book*, 'are connected with . . . the expressions "to wish", "to think" etc. . . . .These can all be summed up in the question: "How can one think what is not the case?"' (BB: 30). (Notice the parallel with one of the questions that the *Tractatus* had aimed to answer: How is it possible for a proposition to be meaningful but false?) The question Wittgenstein is raising is how we should understand the *representational* or *intentional* character of thought.

One stimulus for the new thoughts about intentionality that Wittgenstein developed after 1929 was his dissatisfaction with the views he had advanced in the *Tractatus*. Another stimulus was the publication by some of his Cambridge acquaintances, in the early 1920s, of accounts of intentionality that he regarded as profoundly mistaken. He wrote scathingly to Russell about C. K. Ogden and I. A. Richards's book, *The Meaning of Meaning*, which he read while working as a schoolteacher in Austria:

> A short time ago I received 'The Meaning of Meaning'. Doubtless it has been sent to you too. Is it not a miserable book?! No, no, philosophy, after all, is not as easy as that! But it does show how easy it is to write a thick book.
>
> (7 April 1923, WIC: 137)

Wittgenstein was equally dismissive of the similar theory of intentionality advanced in Russell's own book, *The Analysis of Mind*, which was published in 1921. His objections to those views encouraged him to articulate his own thoughts.

i. Intentionality: Wittgenstein's negative arguments

Wittgenstein offers powerful arguments against two views of intentionality: the imagist view, which explains the intentionality of thought by appeal to mental imagery; and the causal views advanced by Russell and by Ogden and Richards, which explain intentionality by appeal to causal relations between thoughts and things.

According to the imagist, what makes my desire for an apple a desire *for an apple* is that it contains, or involves, a mental image of an apple; what makes my order to open the door an order *to open the door* is that it involves a mental image of the door's being opened; and so on. Such imagist views of representation have had a strong influence in philosophy: notably in the theory of ideas of Locke and Hume, for whom thought was made up of mental images copied from the experiences we enjoy in sense-perception and introspection. And the view is intuitively appealing, because the representational properties of mental images seem evident and unproblematic; so they seem to provide a straightforward explanation of the representative character of thought and language. 'It is clear that one can want to speak without speaking', writes Wittgenstein, 'just as one can want to dance without dancing. And when we think about this, we grasp at the *image* of dancing, speaking, etc.' (PI §338).

Wittgenstein's first argument against the imagist view is that having mental images is not necessary for thought. When I want an apple, I *might* form an image of an apple; and when I am looking for a red flower, I *might* form an image of a red flower. But, he points out, it is not necessary for me to form mental images. He often makes the point in connection with linguistic understanding. For the imagist, understanding an order involves forming an image of what one has been ordered to do.

> If I give someone the order 'fetch me a red flower from that meadow', how is he to know what sort of flower to bring, as I have only given him a *word*?
>
> Now the answer one might suggest first is that he went to look for a red flower carrying a red image in his mind, and comparing it with the flowers to see which of them had the colour of the image.
>
> (BB: 3)

That is the imagist view. But, Wittgenstein observes, 'this is not the only way of searching and it isn't the usual way'. Usually, 'we go, look about us, walk up to a flower and pick it, without comparing it to anything', and without forming mental images at all. In short, one can understand and obey an order without having a mental image of what one has been ordered to do. And Wittgenstein drives home the point with the following consideration:

> To see that the process of obeying the order can be of this kind, consider the order *'imagine* a red patch'. You are not tempted in this case to think that *before* obeying you must have imagined a red patch to serve you as a pattern for the red patch which you were ordered to imagine.
>
> (BB: 3; for other instances of the same argument, see BB: 12, and PI §451)

The observation that mental images are not necessary for thought was not original to Wittgenstein: related arguments were offered by William James (see James 1890), by Russell (see Russell 1921), and by early-twentieth-century behaviourists such as J. B. Watson. But the point is evidently a good one.

Wittgenstein's second argument against the imagist view begins with the observation that a mental image is not by itself sufficient to determine what a thought is about. A mental image of something, just like an actual picture on a piece of paper, can be taken or interpreted in numerous different ways. So the significance of a mental image is a matter of how it is understood or applied. As before, Wittgenstein often makes the point in connection with the idea that grasping the meaning of a word involves associating it with a mental image:

> Suppose that a picture does come before your mind when you hear the word 'cube', say the drawing of a cube. In what way can this picture fit or fail to fit a use of the word 'cube'? – Perhaps you say: 'It's quite simple; if that picture occurs to me and I point to a triangular prism for instance, and say it is a cube, then this use of the word doesn't fit the picture.' – But doesn't it fit? I have purposely so chosen the example that it is quite easy to imagine a *method of projection* according to which the picture does fit after all.
>
> (PI §139)

Any picture can be taken or applied in indefinitely many different ways. So a picture of a cube does not represent cubes in and of itself; it is only in virtue of being applied or understood in a certain way that the picture functions as a representation of cubes rather than prisms or anything else. And the same goes for mental images. Even if you do associate the word 'cube' with a mental image of a cube, the significance of that image is not determined by the image itself; it is a matter of the way you apply the image. You might associate the word 'cube' with a mental image of a cube, but misunderstand the word because you apply the image in the wrong way: to triangular prisms, say, rather than cubes. To understand the word 'cube', therefore, it is not enough to associate the word with a mental image of a cube; one must apply the image in the right way – to cubes, rather than prisms or anything else. But once we recognize that, we see that the appeal to mental imagery is redundant. What does the work in this account of understanding is not the mental image; it is the way the subject applies the image. And whatever account we give of how a subject must apply a mental image of a cube in order for it to function as a representation of cubes in general, that account could equally well be applied directly to the subject's use of the word 'cube'. The mental image plays no essential role. The same argument applies to wishing, expecting, and the rest. Even if an episode of wishing, say, involves a mental image of an apple, that will not be sufficient to make my wish a wish *for an apple*. For an image of an apple could be applied in numerous different ways, to represent different things. It will never be the mental image alone, therefore, that makes it the case that my wish has the object it does; it will be the way I apply the image. And then, as before, the image turns out to be inessential: we could do just as well without it.

At this point in the argument, Wittgenstein makes an interesting and characteristic move. Even when we are convinced by the arguments against the imagist view, he thinks, it remains extremely tempting to think that the representative character of thought *must* be explained by appeal to some kind of mental picture; the imagist model remains so deeply rooted in our way of thinking that we cannot shake it off. And, seeing that an ordinary mental picture will not do the job, we are then prone to think that thought must contain a special kind of image – a 'queer' or 'superlative' image – which, unlike an ordinary image, is not susceptible of being applied or interpreted in different ways:

'A mental image must be more like its object than any picture. For however similar I make the picture to what it is supposed to represent, it may still be the picture of something else. But it is an intrinsic feature

of a mental image that it is the image of *this* and of nothing else.' That is
how one might come to regard a mental image as a superlikeness.

(PI §389)

In a similar way, Wittgenstein thinks, we are prone to think that a
thought must contain a 'shadow' of the object or state of affairs it is
about: and 'we imagine the shadow to be a picture the intention of
which *cannot be questioned*' (BB: 36); we think of it as 'an unambiguous
shadow that admits of no further interpretation' (PG: 150). But, Wittgenstein objects, the idea that there is any kind of image or picture
that is not susceptible of being interpreted in different ways is a myth.
When we are doing philosophy, we can get into the frame of mind of
thinking that there must be such a thing. But, in reality, there is not.
Intentionality cannot be explained by ordinary mental images. And it
cannot be explained by 'queer' or 'superlative' images either. There are
no such things.

The second target of Wittgenstein's negative arguments is the kind
of causal theory advanced by Russell and by Ogden and Richards.
Those theories explained the intentionality of thought by appeal to
causal relations between thoughts, on the one hand, and external
objects, on the other. Their aim was to give a scientifically respectable
account of intentionality, which would avoid the traditional and, they
thought, scientifically objectionable idea that thought involves a special, *sui generis* relation between the mind and its objects. In that spirit,
Russell offers the following account of the relation between a desire
and the thing desired:

A hungry animal is restless until it finds food; then it becomes
quiescent. The thing which will bring a restless condition to an end
is said to be what is desired. But only experience can show what will
have this sedative effect, and it is easy to make mistakes. We feel
dissatisfaction, and think that such and such a thing would remove
it; but in thinking this, we are theorizing, not observing a patent fact.
Our theorizing is often mistaken, and when it is mistaken there is
a difference between what we think we desire and what in fact will
bring satisfaction.

(Russell 1921: 32)

So, for Russell, what makes it the case that it is food that the animal
wants is that getting food is what will bring an end to its restless

condition. And what makes it the case that I want *an apple* is that it is an apple that will remove my feeling of dissatisfaction. In a similar way, Russell appeals to the effects of words and images to explain their meanings (for a statement of that part of the theory, see, for example, Russell 1921: 209). Ogden and Richards appeal to slightly different causal facts to explain what determines the contents of our thoughts. But their theory belongs to the same general family as Russell's.

Wittgenstein's first objection to Russell is that it is neither necessary nor sufficient for something's being what one desires – for its being the object of one's desire – that it should remove one's feelings of dissatisfaction. On the one hand, something might be the object of one's desire even though it fails to remove one's feelings of dissatisfaction. (I wanted an apple. But eating an apple did not remove my feeling of dissatisfaction; I still felt dissatisfied, even though I got what I wanted.) On the other hand, something might remove one's desire without being the thing one desired. (On Russell's view, Wittgenstein argues, 'if I wanted to eat an apple, and someone punched me in the stomach, taking away my appetite, then it was this punch that I originally wanted' (PR: 64). But that is absurd; the fact that the punch removed my appetite does not make it the case that it was a punch that I wanted.) What makes something the object of one's desire, Wittgenstein concludes, is not that it removes a feeling of dissatisfaction. And similarly in other cases: what makes it the case that some event is the event one is expecting is not that it removes one's feeling of anticipation; what makes it the case that an action fulfils one's order is not that it produces a feeling of satisfaction; and so on.

A second objection to Russell's causal theory is that it radically misrepresents the character of our knowledge of our own minds. For Russell, a person's knowledge of what she wants involves a judgement about what would remove her feeling of dissatisfaction; her knowledge of what she expects involves a judgement about what would remove her feeling of anticipation; and so on. And these judgements are based on her past experience of herself. So her judgement that she wants an apple, or that she expects Jones to come, is, as Wittgenstein puts it, a hypothesis. But, Wittgenstein objects, we do not normally have to work out what we want or expect, by theorizing about what will remove our feeling of dissatisfaction or anticipation. In the normal case, we know what we want or expect immediately, and without inference: 'If I ask someone "whom do you expect?" and after receiving the answer ask again "Are you sure that you don't expect someone else?" then, in most cases, this question would be regarded as absurd' (BB: 21). On Russell's view, by contrast, it would not be at all absurd.

What should we make of Wittgenstein's case against causal theories of thought and meaning? That question is not of merely historical interest; for the idea that the contents of a person's thoughts, and the meanings of her words, are partly determined by causal relations with the things she thinks and talks about is widely accepted in contemporary philosophy of mind and language. Is that idea undermined by Wittgenstein's arguments?

Wittgenstein's discussion is decisive against his two most immediate targets: the idea, which was central to Russell's theory, that the object of a desire is, by definition, the thing that removes one's feeling of dissatisfaction (and similarly for the objects of expectation, hope, fear and so on); and the idea that one's knowledge of what one currently wants, expects, intends, and so on, involves a causal hypothesis about what would produce or remove certain feelings. Those ideas sometimes resurface in contemporary philosophy; and when they do, Wittgenstein's arguments remain effective against them. But his arguments do not (and are not intended to) refute the kinds of causal theory that are most common in current philosophy. Consider the following, which is typical of modern causal theories:

> In the simplest and most basic cases, words and sentences derive their meanings from the objects and circumstances in whose presence they were learned. A sentence which one has been conditioned by the learning process to be caused to hold true by the presence of fires will (usually) be true when there is a fire present; a word one has been conditioned to hold applicable by the presence of snakes will refer to snakes.
>
> (Davidson 1988: 44–5)

The basic idea expressed in that passage above is that the meaning of a particular utterance of the sentence 'That's a snake', say, is determined by the kind of thing that normally causes utterances of that sentence (more specifically, by the kind of thing that normally caused utterances of the sentence in 'the learning environment'). Similarly, Davidson thinks, the content of the thought one expresses in uttering the sentence is determined by the kind of thing that normally causes thoughts of that type. But this causal theory is quite different from Russell's; and Wittgenstein's objection to Russell's causal theory is not an objection to a theory of this form. Applied to the present example, Wittgenstein's fundamental point is that it is neither necessary nor sufficient for a particular thought's being a thought about snakes that that thought should be caused by the presence of a snake. A thought can be caused by a snake without being a thought about snakes. (That is what happens when one sees a snake and mistakes it for a stick: one's thought 'There's a stick' is caused by the presence of a snake; but it is a thought about sticks, not snakes.) And similarly, the thought 'There's a snake' can be caused by the presence of something that is not a snake (as when one sees a stick and mistakes it for a snake). But none of that is an objection to Davidson's causal theory. Davidson's theory claims that the content of a particular thought is determined by the *normal* cause of thoughts *of that kind*. And it is consistent with that that, as Wittgenstein insists, a thought about snakes might on occasion be caused by the presence of something other than a snake; and, on occasion, the presence of a snake might cause a thought about something other than snakes. Similarly, it is no part of a theory like Davidson's that one's knowledge of the contents of one's thoughts depends on a hypothesis about what caused those thoughts. Wittgenstein is quite right to object to the account of self-knowledge that is integral to Russell's account of intentionality. But it would be wrong to think that every kind of causal theory of intentionality faces the same objection.

Wittgenstein, then, gives decisive arguments against the causal theory of intentionality offered by Russell in the 1920s. But those arguments do not refute the kinds of causal theory most common in contemporary philosophy of mind and language.

ii. Intentionality: Wittgenstein's positive picture

Wittgenstein rejects imagist accounts of intentionality; and he rejects the causal theories of Russell and of Ogden and Richards. But what, if any, positive view of intentionality does he recommend? What in his view *does* make my wish a wish for an apple? And what *does* make it the case that I am expecting Jones to arrive at 3 p.m.? There are two recurrent themes in Wittgenstein's positive remarks. The first is the idea that 'it is in language that an expectation and its fulfilment make contact' (PI §445; PG: 140), that it is 'in language that wish and fulfilment meet' (PG: 151), and so on. The second is the suggestion that an attitude has the content it does in virtue of 'the *path* on which it lies' (PG: 147), or in virtue of 'certain transitions we made or would make' (LW i: 308). We can explore these ideas in turn.

In saying that a wish and its fulfilment make contact *in language* Wittgenstein is making two points. The first concerns the language *we* use to describe a subject's wish and its fulfilment. The second concerns the language *the subject* uses, or would use, to express her wish.

The first point is that the relation between a wish and its fulfilment is a conceptual relation (or, as Wittgenstein would say, an 'internal relation'). It is part of what it is for something to be a wish *for an apple* that it is fulfilled, or satisfied, by getting *an apple*; a wish that was fulfilled by something other than an apple would not be a wish *for an apple*. (By contrast, it is not part of what it is for something to be a wish for an apple that it is removed by getting an apple. A wish for an apple might be removed by a punch in the stomach. Even so, it was still a wish *for an apple*.) Wittgenstein puts the point like this:

> The statement that the wish for it to be the case that *p* is satisfied by the event *p*, merely enunciates a rule for signs:
>
> > (the wish for it to be the case that *p*) = (the wish that is satisfied by the event *p*)
>
> (PG: 161–2)

To make sense of that remark, we need to understand Wittgenstein's terminology. For Wittgenstein, an object or event 'satisfies' a wish if it fulfils the wish. So he distinguishes between satisfying *a wish* (i.e. fulfilling the wish) and satisfying *a person* (i.e. producing feelings of satisfaction). (Making use of that distinction, his objection to Russell's theory can be summarized thus: 'the fact that some event stops my wishing does not mean that it fulfils it. Perhaps I wouldn't have been satisfied if my wish had been satisfied' (PI §441).) The point Wittgenstein is making is this. If it is correct to describe someone as wishing *to be a millionaire*, say, then it is automatically correct to describe her wish as being satisfied by the event of *her becoming a millionaire*. Once we have established that someone can be described as wishing to be a millionaire, there is no further question, what it would take to fulfil her wish; to characterize her wish as a wish to be a millionaire *just is* to characterize it as a wish that will be fulfilled by her becoming a millionaire. That point is plainly correct. But it leads immediately to a further question:

under what circumstances is it correct to describe someone as wishing to be a millionaire? What makes it right to describe her as wishing just that? That question takes us to the second aspect of Wittgenstein's idea that a wish and its fulfilment make contact in language.

The simplest, most straightforward thing that can happen at the time of a wish to make it true that a person wishes *to be a millionaire*, Wittgenstein thinks, is that she *says* that she wishes to be a millionaire (see PG: 140). In such a case, it is the language the subject uses to express her wish that ties her wish to the particular event that will satisfy it. As Wittgenstein puts it, 'Where are we to find what makes the wish *this* wish . . .? Only in the expressed wish' (PG: 150): that is, in the words the subject uses to express her wish. But, as before, that is only the beginning of an account. In the first place, the fact that someone utters the words 'I want to be a millionaire' only makes it true that she does want to be a millionaire on two further conditions: first, that she is using words as we do – so her words 'I want to be a millionaire' mean *that she wants to be a millionaire*; and second, that she is sincere in uttering those words. But what makes it the case that those words *do* mean that the speaker wants to be a millionaire; and what makes it the case that she *is* speaking sincerely? In the second place, someone can want to become a millionaire without saying, or being disposed to say, that she wants to be a millionaire. In such a case, there is no linguistic expression to connect her wish to its fulfilment. What, then, *does* make it true that she wishes *to be a millionaire*? Furthermore, Wittgenstein recognizes that languageless creatures have beliefs, intentions, and emotions. A dog can believe that his master is at the door; it can be afraid his master will beat him, and so on (see PI §650; PPF §1 [PI II i p. 174]). But the dog has no language in which to express those attitudes. So what makes it true that he believes *that his master is at the door*, or that he is afraid *that his master will beat him* is not a linguistic expression. What, then, *does* give the dog's attitudes the contents they have?

Answering these further questions introduces Wittgenstein's second positive theme: the idea that what makes it the case that an attitude has the object it does is *the path on which it lies*. He illustrates the point of that idea in connection with the question, 'What makes my image of N into an image of N?'. Wittgenstein writes:

Suppose I say something like: 'What I see in my mind isn't just a picture which is like N (and perhaps like others too). No, I know that it

is him, that he is the person it portrays.' I might then ask: *when* do I
know that and what does knowing it amount to? There's no need
for anything to take place during the imagining that could be called
'knowing' in this way. Something of that sort may happen after the
imagining; I may go on from the picture to the name, or perhaps say
that I imagined N, even though at the time of the imagining there
wasn't anything, except perhaps a kind of similarity, to characterize
the image as N's. Or again there might be something preceding the
image that made the connection with N. And so the interpretation
isn't something that accompanies the image; what gives the image its
interpretation is the *path* on which it lies.

(PG: 147)

Or again:

What makes my image of him into an image of *him*? . . .
    Isn't my question like *this*: 'What makes this sentence a sentence
that has to do with *him*'?
    'The fact that we were speaking about him.' – 'And what makes our
conversation a conversation about *him*?' – Certain transitions we made
or would make.

(LW i: 308)

What Wittgenstein says about images in these passages can be applied
equally well to the other cases we have been considering. What makes
my wish the wish *to be a millionaire*, we might say, is 'the path on which it
lies'; what makes it the case that I was expecting *Jones to come at 3 p.m.* are
'certain transitions that I made or would make'; and so on. But what
does that mean?

Wittgenstein's idea is that what gives an attitude the content it has
is not something that was going on in the subject's mind at the time.
It is, rather, a matter of the circumstances of the case, and the context in which the attitude occurs. Those circumstances might include
what the subject said or did at the time; what she said or did earlier,
or later; what she would have said and done had she been asked what
her thought was about; her abilities (for example, the ability to speak
English); the environment in which she is situated; the institutions
and conventions of the community to which she belongs; and so on.
For instance:

> If I have two friends with the same name and am writing one of them
> a letter, what does the fact that I am not writing it to the other consist
> in? In the content? But that might fit either. (I haven't yet written the
> address.) Well, the connection might be in the antecedents. But in that
> case it may also be in what *follows* the writing.
>
> (Z: 7)

Thus, Wittgenstein thinks, the connection might lie in the fact that, if
someone asks me 'Which of the two are you writing to?', I reply by
identifying one friend rather than the other. What makes it true that
I am writing to this friend is that my activity 'lies on one path' rather
than another; it is the 'transitions I made, or would make', when I am
asked whom I am writing to. Or again:

> When I expect someone, – what happens? I perhaps look at my
> calendar and see his name against today's date and the note '5 p.m.'.
> I say to someone else 'I can't come to see you today, because I'm
> expecting N'. I make preparations to receive a guest. I wonder 'Does N
> smoke?', I remember having seen him smoke and put out cigarettes.
> Towards 5 p.m. I say to myself 'Now he'll come soon', and as I do so
> I imagine a man looking like N; then I imagine him coming into the
> room and my greeting him and calling him by his name. This and many
> other more or less *similar* trains of events are called 'expecting N to
> come'.
>
> (PG: 141–2)

We can highlight a number of features of Wittgenstein's view. In the
first place, his position is resolutely anti-reductionist. Wittgenstein is
not attempting to explain thought in other terms, or to reduce facts
about what people are thinking to facts that can be stated in non-
mental, non-intentional terms. For example, what makes it true that I
am expecting that N will come at 5 p.m., he thinks, are the circumstances
and context of the particular case. But some of the relevant circumstances and context are themselves characterized in mental or intentional terms: I make preparations to receive a guest; I wonder whether N
smokes, I remember him smoking, and so on. Wittgenstein's account is
not a reductive one.

Second, Wittgenstein's account is anti-systematic; he is not offering
a general, systematic account of how the facts about what someone

believes, or desires, or expects are related to facts about what she says and does, about what she would say and do, about the surrounding context, and so on. In any particular case, there will be something to say about why it is right to ascribe a person the attitudes that we do ascribe. So there is no mystery about the relation between what a person says and does, on the one hand, and her beliefs, desires, expectations, and so on. (We can see that by considering examples and reminding ourselves of how we actually do go about telling what people believe and desire in the light of what they say and do.) But the relation cannot be captured by any systematic theory.

Third, Wittgenstein's account stresses the crucial role of context in determining the content of a person's thoughts and attitudes. For example:

> Suppose I sit in my room and hope that NN will come and bring me some money, and suppose one minute of this state could be isolated, cut out of its context; would what happened in it then not be hope? – Think, for example, of the words which you perhaps utter in this space of time. They are no longer part of this language. And in different surroundings the institution of money doesn't exist either.
>
> (PI §584)

What would in one context be a case of hoping that someone will come and bring me some money, Wittgenstein thinks, would in another context be a case of hoping for something else. And, in a third context, it might not be a case of hoping at all.

It is sometimes said that Wittgenstein's positive remarks about intentionality are too sketchy: that he fails to give a sufficiently informative answer to questions of the form 'What makes it the case that Smith expects Jones to arrive at 3 p.m.?' All Wittgenstein tells us, it is objected, is that what makes it the case that Smith expects Jones to arrive at 3 p.m. is what she says and does, or would have said and done, and the overall context of the case. But that is not enough. We want to know exactly what it is about her and her context that makes it the case that she expects what she does. And it is the philosopher's business to tell us that; not simply to gesture in the general direction of an answer.

Wittgenstein's response to that objection would have two parts. In the first place, he would simply deny that there is anything more general and informative to say about the circumstances that make it true that someone wishes for such-and-such or expects that so-and-so. Facts about what people wish and expect are importantly related to facts about what they do and say, and to facts about the surrounding circumstances. But facts of the first sort cannot be reduced to facts of the second sort: everything is what it is and not another thing.

In the second place, Wittgenstein would argue that the feeling that it must be possible to give a more informative account is the product of a philosophical prejudice (this strand in Wittgenstein's treatment is very well articulated in McDowell 1992). When we adopt the detached standpoint of philosophy, he thinks, and reflect from that standpoint on the nature of thought, we are prone to think that there is something mysterious about the intentional character of thought – about the power of thought to represent something other than itself. This idea, Wittgenstein thinks – the idea that there is something inherently puzzling about thought: something that needs explaining – is partly the product of a tendency to think of all phenomena on the model of physical phenomena, and to take explanation in the physical sciences as the paradigm of what it is to understand something. That tendency leads to the demand for the intentional character of thought to be explained in scientific terms. (Exactly this line of thought, we saw, was explicit in the motivation for Russell's and Ogden and Richards's causal theories.) Wittgenstein's view, by contrast, is that there is nothing intrinsically mysterious about thought; the ability to represent objects and events in thought is a completely natural and familiar feature of the world. It is only made to *seem* mysterious when we reflect on it from certain philosophical perspectives: when, for example, we assume that the only genuine phenomena are those that can be described and explained in the terms of natural science; or when we suppose that, in order to represent a state of affairs, a thought must contain an 'unambiguous shadow' of that state of affairs 'that admits of no further interpretation' (PG: 150). But, Wittgenstein insists:

> One must remember that all the phenomena that now strike us as so remarkable are the very familiar phenomena that don't surprise us in the least when they happen. They don't strike us as remarkable until we put them in a strange light by philosophizing.
>
> (PG: 169)

Or again:

'A thought – what a strange thing!' – but it does not strike us as strange when we are thinking. A thought does not strike us as mysterious while we are thinking, but only when we say, as it were retrospectively, 'How was that possible?' How was it possible for a thought to deal with *this very* object?

(PI §428)

The lesson he draws is that we should not accept that there is an inherent mystery about thought, a mystery that must be resolved by explaining thought in other terms. Rather, we should reject the philosophical assumptions that created the sense of mystery in the first place. Once we do that, we will regain our ordinary sense of the familiarity and unmysteriousness of thought. And we will see that there is no need to say anything more general or informative about the relations between thought, words, actions, and context than Wittgenstein has offered us.

2. RULES AND RULE-FOLLOWING

Wittgenstein writes, in the preface to *Philosophical Investigations*, that 'The philosophical remarks in this book are, as it were, a number of sketches of landscapes which were made in the course of [the] long and meandering journeys' he took as he 'travel[led] criss-cross in every direction over a wide field of thought'. 'The same or almost the same points', he goes on, 'were always being approached afresh from new directions, and new sketches made' (PI p. 3). The discussion of rules and rule-following, which occupies a central place in *Philosophical Investigations*, is a good illustration of what he means. It picks up and develops a number of strands that have been explored in different contexts earlier in the book. One such strand comes from Wittgenstein's discussion of the imagist view of thought: any picture, he argues, can be interpreted in numerous different ways; so what a picture represents is a matter not of its intrinsic features but of how it is applied or understood; and the same goes for mental images. Another strand comes from the discussion of family resemblance, where Wittgenstein argues that our grasp of the concept *game* depends on the contingent fact that, having been introduced to the word in connection with a range of examples, we all find it natural to go on to apply it in new cases in the same way. As we shall see, versions of both those ideas play a central part in Wittgenstein's discussion of grasping and following rules.

Suppose we are teaching someone to count. We start by teaching him the series '0, 1, 2, 3, 4, . . .', and we reach the point where, judged by the usual criteria, the pupil has mastered that series (PI §§143ff.). Then we teach him other series of numbers: the series '2, 4, 6, 8 . . .', the series '3, 5, 7, 9 . . .', and so on. 'We have done exercises and tested his understanding up to 1000' (PI §185) and, judged by the usual criteria, he has mastered these series too.

> Then we get the pupil to continue one series (say '+ 2') beyond 1000
> – and he writes 1000, 1004, 1008, 1012.
>   We say to him, 'Look what you're doing!' – He doesn't understand.
> We say, 'You should have added *two*: look how you began the series!'
> – He answers, 'Yes, isn't it right? I thought that was how I *had* to do it.'
> – Or suppose he pointed to the series and said, 'But I did go on in the
> same way'. – It would now be no use to say, 'But can't you see . . .?' –
> and go over the old explanations and examples for him again. In such
> a case, we might perhaps say: this person finds it natural, once given
> our explanations, to understand our order as *we* would understand the
> order 'Add 2 up to 1000, 4 up to 2000, 6 up to 3000, and so on'.
>
> (PI §185)

Wittgenstein's example of the aberrant pupil raises two kinds of question. First, there are constitutive questions about rules and standards of correctness. What makes it the case that the correct continuation of the series '+ 2', the continuation that accords with the rule '+ 2', is '1000, 1002, 1004, 1006 . . .' and not '1000, 1004, 1008, 1012'? What makes it the case that someone who continues the series in the first way is going on in the same way as before, while someone who continues the series in the second way is not? Second, there are questions about our knowledge or grasp of rules. Most generally: what does it take to grasp the rule for adding 2; what makes it the case that I have grasped that rule? And more specifically, if I am following the rule '+ 2', how do I know what I have to do at each successive step in order to count as following the rule? 'How do I know that in working out the series + 2 I must write "20004, 20006" and not "20004, 20008"?' (RFM: 36).

Wittgenstein introduces these questions in connection with the case of a mathematical series. But the same questions arise in connection with ordinary descriptive words. Just as there is a distinction between a correct and an incorrect continuation of the series '+ 2', so there is a distinction between, say, a correct and an incorrect application of the word 'red'; there is a rule dictating what counts as a correct application of the word. And, as in the mathematical case, we can raise questions both about the constitution of the rule and about our knowledge of the rule. What *makes it correct* to apply the word 'red' to this colour (pointing to a ripe tomato) and incorrect to apply it to *that* colour (pointing to a spinach leaf)? And *how do I know* that this colour is called 'red' and that colour is not?

i. The constitutive question

What makes it the case that the correct continuation of the series '2, 4, 6, 8 . . .' is '1000, 1002, 1004, 1006 . . .' and not '1000, 1004, 1008, 1012 . . .'? What makes it the case that, having been given the usual training with the word 'red', the person who goes on to apply the word to a ripe tomato is using the word in the same way as before, while the person who applies it to a spinach leaf is using it differently?

Philosophers have traditionally answered such questions in either of two ways. On the one hand, there is *Platonism* about rules. On this view, there is an absolutely objective fact about which way of going on from the initial steps in a mathematical series is the *correct* continuation, and an absolutely objective standard of what it is to go on using a given descriptive word in the same way as before. Those standards, according to the Platonist, are dictated by the nature of reality. On the other hand, there is *constructivism* or *anti-realism* about rules. On the constructivist view, there is no absolutely objective standard of what counts as continuing a series correctly; for there are indefinitely many different possible ways of continuing a series, no one of which is absolutely better than any other. What counts as the correct way of continuing the series is determined by us; the standard for continuing the series correctly is constructed from the steps we actually take when we do continue it. And the same goes for applying a descriptive word; what counts as a correct application of a descriptive word is constructed from the applications we actually make when we apply the word.

Where does Wittgenstein stand in this debate? It is clear that Wittgenstein rejects the Platonist view of rules. It is less clear where his opposition to Platonism leaves him. Some commentators think he accepts some form of constructivism. Others think he takes a *quietist* or *deflationist* view of rules. On that interpretation, Wittgenstein regards the whole debate between Platonism and constructivism as fundamentally misguided. So his opposition to Platonism is not intended as an endorsement of constructivism. He rejects both sides in the traditional debate.

Platonism

According to the Platonist, it is an absolutely objective fact that the correct continuation of the series '2, 4, 6, . . . 996, 998, 1000' is '1002, 1004, 1006 . . .'. That continuation, she holds, is absolutely the *simplest* or *most natural*. Any other way of continuing the series – the aberrant pupil's '1004, 1008, 1012', for example – would be less simple, less natural. And it is not just that any such continuation would be less simple or natural *for us*; it would, says the Platonist, be *absolutely* less simple or natural than the usual continuation. So, for the Platonist, it is just a fact – an absolutely objective fact – that someone who continues the series by putting '1002, 1004, 1006 . . .' is going on in the same way as before, and that someone who puts '1004, 1008, 1012 . . .' is not going on in the same way as before. The same holds for the standards for applying a descriptive word. It is an absolutely objective fact that someone who is given the normal training with the word 'red', and who then goes on to apply the word to ripe tomatoes and British post-boxes, has gone on using the word in the same way as before – and that someone who goes on to apply the word to spinach leaves and Irish post-boxes is not using it in the same way as before.

Wittgenstein rejects this Platonist view. In the first place, he thinks, it is just evident that there are indefinitely many possible ways of continuing a series, no one of which has any better claim than any other to be absolutely the correct, or simplest, or most natural continuation. And the same goes for the use of a descriptive word. For example:

> If you have learned a technique of language, and I point to this coat and say to you, 'The tailors now call this colour "Boo"' then you will buy me a coat of this colour, fetch one, etc. The point is that one only has to point to something and say, 'This is so-and-so', and everyone who has been through a certain preliminary training will react in the same way. We could imagine this not to happen. If I just say, 'This is called "Boo"' you might not know what I mean; but in fact you would all of you automatically follow certain rules.

Ought we to say that you would follow the *right* rules? – that you
would know *the* meaning of 'boo'? No, clearly not. For which meaning?
Are there not 10,000 meanings which 'boo' might now have? – It sounds
as if your learning how to use it were different from your knowing its
meaning. *But the point is that we all make the SAME use of it.* To know its
meaning is to use it *in the same way* as other people do. 'In the right way'
means nothing.

(LFM: 182–3)

The word 'Boo' is defined by pointing at something and saying 'This
is called "Boo"'. Consistently with that definition, Wittgenstein says,
the word 'Boo' 'might have 10,000 meanings'. And Wittgenstein
thinks it is simply evident that no one of those possible meanings
is, absolutely, the right one: that no one way of going on to use the
word is absolutely correct, or absolutely simplest, or absolutely most
natural.

Second, Wittgenstein thinks it is impossible to justify the claim that
our way of continuing a series is absolutely the correct one, and that
other ways of continuing it are absolutely incorrect. We cannot, for
example, justify the claim that our way of continuing the series '2, 4,
6, 8 . . .' is the correct one by saying that the person who puts '1000,
1004, 1008, 1012 . . .' is not *going on in the same way*. Of course it is true
that, *by our standards*, he is not going on in the same way as before. But,
judged by his standards, he is. And there is nothing we can do to show that
our standards of correctness are themselves the right standards; that the
continuation that is correct by our standards is *absolutely*, or *objectively*,
the correct one.

That leads to Wittgenstein's third, and most fundamental point: that
the very idea that there is a way of continuing a mathematical series
that is absolutely correct, a continuation that is absolutely simplest or
most natural, makes no sense. The key point, then, is not that we cannot *tell* whether our way of continuing a series is absolutely correct:
whether it is absolutely simpler or more natural than any other. It is
that *there is no such thing* as one continuation's being absolutely correct,
or absolutely simpler or more natural than another. The idea that, lying
behind the facts about which continuation is correct, or simplest, or
most natural *by our standards* there is a further fact about which continuation is *absolutely* correct, or simplest, or most natural is, he thinks, an
illusion. And the same goes for the case of descriptive words.

Many readers of Wittgenstein find his arguments against the Platonist view of rules completely persuasive. But those arguments are not universally accepted. In response to Wittgenstein, the Platonist will accept that there are many different possible ways of going on from the initial steps in a series. But the fact that there are many possible ways of going on, she will say, does not show that they are all on a par. Some of them, the Platonist insists, are absolutely simpler or more natural than others; and there will often be one continuation that is absolutely the simplest. Second, the Platonist will agree that we cannot justify the claim that our way of continuing a series is absolutely correct by showing that it is correct by our standards. But, she will say, perhaps we can justify the claim in some other way. She might argue, for example, that the fact that our standards of simplicity and naturalness are integral to a system of thought that has evolved over the long history of successful human interaction with the world does give us reason to think that what strikes us as being simplest and most natural is, absolutely, simplest and most natural. Third, the Platonist will simply deny Wittgenstein's claim that we can make no sense of the idea of what is *absolutely* correct, or *absolutely* simplest or most natural: correct, or simplest, or most natural *by the standards of reality*. There is, she insists, no problem in making sense of the thought that our standards of correctness, simplicity, and naturalness may match, or fail to match, the standards that are built into reality.

I will not pursue this debate between Wittgenstein and the Platonist. But it is important to recognize that a significant number of contemporary philosophers accept a broadly Platonist view of rules and standards of correctness. And these philosophers have not merely ignored Wittgenstein's considerations. They know about Wittgenstein's arguments; they simply do not find them compelling (for an example, see Lewis 1983, 1984).

Wittgenstein himself, however, clearly rejects the Platonist's answer to the question, what makes it correct to continue the series '2, 4, 6, 8 . . .' by putting '1000, 1002, 1004, 1006 . . .'. But where, in his view, does the rejection of Platonism leave us?

Constructivism

Many commentators read Wittgenstein as advocating some form of constructivism or *anti-realism* about rules (see e.g. Dummett 1959, 1993; Wright 1980: chs 2, 12; Kripke 1982). For the constructivist, what counts as the correct application of a rule in any given case is determined by what we actually take to be correct when we consider that case and reach a verdict (or what we *would* take to be correct if we *were* to consider the case). So, for example, what counts as the correct continuation of the series '+ 2' at any particular point is determined by the way we actually continue the series when we reach that point. It is the fact that we all find it natural to continue the series by putting '1002, 1004, 1006 . . .' that makes that the correct continuation.

Some of what Wittgenstein says can certainly seem to suggest a constructivist view. He asks, for example: 'Is there a criterion for the continuation [of the series of cardinal numbers] – for a right and a wrong way except that we do in fact continue them that way, apart from a few cranks who can be neglected?' (LFM: 183). The answer, he thinks, is 'no': the right way of continuing the series '0, 1, 2, 3 . . .' is simply the way we all do in fact continue it. Or again:

> Russell said, 'It is possible that we have always made a mistake in saying 12 × 12 = 144.' But what would it be like to make a mistake? Would we not say, 'This is what we do when we perform the process which we call "multiplication". 144 is what we call "the right result" '?
>
> Russell goes on to say, 'So it is only probable that 12 × 12 = 144.' But this means nothing. If we had all of us always calculated 12 × 12 = 143, then that would be correct – *that* would be the technique
>
> (LFM: 97)

(We will see below that the interpretation of passages such as these is controversial: they can be read as suggesting a form of constructivism; but they can also be read in a non-constructivist way.)

The constructivist can allow that, in particular cases, it is possible for us all to make a mistake in applying our own rules. Suppose an evil demon contaminates our water supply with a drug that makes us find it natural to continue the series '2, 4, 6, 8 . . .' by putting '1000, 1004, 1008, 1012 . . .'. The constructivist need not conclude that that makes '1000, 1004, 1008, 1012 . . .' the correct continuation. For, she can say, when the effects of the drug wear off, we will judge that that continuation was wrong. But, she insists, it is not possible for the way we all continue the series in *normal circumstances* to be wrong. For all there is to a given continuation's being the correct continuation is that it is the continuation we all make, or would make, in normal circumstances.

It is natural to object that, when we follow a rule, it does not *feel* as though the way we apply the rule in a particular case plays any role in determining what counts as the correct application of the rule in that case; it *seems* as though our attempt to follow the rule is answerable to a standard of correctness that is entirely independent of any application we or anyone else actually makes. The constructivist agrees that that is how things *seem* when we are following a rule. But, she maintains, the *phenomenology* of rule-following is no guide to the actual *nature* of rules. And the truth is that what counts as the correct application of the rule at each step *is* constituted by the way we actually apply it at that step. Similarly, the constructivist acknowledges that the sentence 'Human beings agree in continuing the series "+ 2" by putting "1000, 1002, 1004 . . ."' does not *mean the same as* the sentence 'The correct continuation of the series "+ 2" is "1000, 1002, 1004 . . ."'. The first is an empirical claim about what people actually do when they continue the series; the second is a normative claim about what it is to continue the series correctly. But, she insists, the fact that the two claims differ in meaning is perfectly compatible with the constructivist view that the normative claim about what it is to continue the series correctly is true in virtue of the empirical claim about how people actually do continue the series. And there are passages where Wittgenstein seems to adopt exactly that view:

> The justification of the proposition 25 × 25 = 625 is, naturally, that if anyone has been trained in such-and-such a way, then under normal circumstances he gets 625 as the result of multiplying 25 by 25. But the arithmetical proposition does not assert *that*. It is so to speak an empirical proposition hardened into a rule.
>
> (RFM: 325)

There are two important consequences of this kind of constructivism about rules; consequences that sharply conflict with our ordinary way of thinking about rules, and that make the constructivist view deeply counter-intuitive. The first consequence is this. We ordinarily think that the series '+ 2' is an infinite series. The rule for adding 2, we think, dictates an answer to the question 'What is n + 2?' for any number whatever. Even if n is a number so unimaginably large that no human being could ever calculate the result of adding 2 to n, there is nonetheless a fact of the matter about what the correct result of that calculation would be. But the constructivist denies that. For her, the correct application of a rule in a given case is determined by the judgement we make, or would make, when we consider the case and reach a verdict. And there is no judgement we would make about how the rule applies in a case that is too large for us to compute; our calculative capacities do not reach that far. So, on the constructivist view, there is simply no fact of the matter about what counts as the correct application of the rule '+ 2' in such a case; there is nothing to determine what the correct application would be. And the same point applies quite generally: the standard for what counts as the correct application of any rule extends no further than our finite human capacity to apply that rule. That consequence of constructivism certainly conflicts with our ordinary view of rules.

A second counter-intuitive consequence of constructivism concerns the idea of objective truth (see McDowell 1984: 46). We ordinarily think that whether a sentence is true or false is independent of whether we judge it to be true or false. Take the sentence 'This table is square'. Whether or not that sentence is true, we think, depends on two things: what the words mean; and how the world is. We determine what the word 'square' means, by establishing a standard of correctness for the application of the word. But once we have done that, whether or not the word 'square' *does* apply to this table is determined by whether or not the table meets that standard. It is not determined by what, if anything, we say when we come to judge whether the table is square. But the constructivist must deny that. On her view, there is no standard of correctness for the application of the word 'square' to a particular object independent of the verdict we reach when we consider the question, whether or not the word applies to that object. But to say that is to give up the intuitive idea that whether a sentence is true or false is determined by how the world is, and not by anything we judge when we consider the matter and reach a verdict. Furthermore, we should note, Wittgenstein insists that we must not give up that idea:

'So you are saying that human agreement decides what is true and what is false?' – What is true or false is what human beings *say*; and it is in their *language* that human beings agree. That is agreement not in opinions, but in form of life.

(PI §241)

As I have said, many commentators read Wittgenstein as advancing some form of constructivism about rules, along the lines I have described. Others, however, think that the counter-intuitiveness of the constructivist view is a good reason not to ascribe it to Wittgenstein. Constructivism, they say, does not respect Wittgenstein's insistence that philosophy 'leaves everything as it is' (PI §124).

Deflationism

A different interpretation of Wittgenstein sees his view as a form of *deflationism* or *quietism* about rules (see e.g. McDowell 1984, 1992). The deflationist interpretation agrees with the constructivist interpretation that Wittgenstein rejects the Platonist view of rules; he rejects the central Platonist idea that there is just one way of continuing a series, and just one way of going on using a descriptive word, that is absolutely correct, or simplest, or most natural. But the deflationist disagrees with the constructivist interpretation about where Wittgenstein's opposition to Platonism leaves him. The constructivist reading represents Wittgenstein as constructing something normative (a standard of correctness for the continuation of the series '2, 4, 6, 8 . . .') from something non-normative (the fact that, having been trained in the usual way, human beings all by and large go on by putting '1002, 1004, 1006 . . .' after '1000'). On the deflationist reading, by contrast, Wittgenstein takes facts about rules and standards of correctness as basic and irreducible; he does not attempt to construct those facts from more basic non-normative facts. And, on this view, Wittgenstein takes it for granted that rules really do have the features we ordinarily think they have. When we grasp the rule for adding 2, we really do grasp a standard of correctness that extends to future cases independent of any judgement we make when we consider those cases; and the standard of correctness we grasp really is an infinite standard – a standard that is not limited by the finiteness of our actual capacity to apply the rule. On this view, Wittgenstein's discussion of rules does not offer a positive theory of rules; nor does it reject or revise anything we ordinarily think about rules. Wittgenstein's target is only the mythological, Platonic picture of rules.

We can bring out the disagreement between the constructivist and the deflationist readings in connection with Wittgenstein's idea that the correct way of continuing the series '2, 4, 6, 8 . . .' is simply the way we find it natural to continue the series. What does Wittgenstein mean by *the way we find it natural to continue the series*? For the constructivist, what we find it natural to do, having been given the usual training, is to go on by putting '1002, 1004, 1006 . . .' after '1000'. On this view, 'what we find it natural to do' is understood in a way that does not itself presuppose norms or standards of correctness. That is crucial, for on this view the appeal to what we find it natural to do is part of the project of constructing normative facts from non-normative facts. For the deflationist, by contrast, what we find natural when we are taught to count is not simply to go on from the steps '2, 4, 6, 8 . . .' by putting '1002, 1004, 1006 . . .' after '1000'; what we find natural is to take the steps '2, 4, 6, 8 . . .' as the initial stages of the mathematical series *add 2*. Similarly what we find natural when we learn to use the word 'red' is not simply to go on by uttering the word 'red' in response to *this*, *this*, and *this* particular thing; what we find natural is to take the word 'red', explained in this way, to mean *red*. On this reading of Wittgenstein, what we find natural (taking the steps '2, 4, 6, 8 . . .' as the initial stages of the mathematical series *add 2*; taking the word 'red' to mean *red*) is characterized in a way that presupposes norms, meanings, and standards of correctness (the rule for adding 2; the meaning of the word 'red'). So the purpose of Wittgenstein's appeal to what we find natural is not to construct something normative from something non-normative. It is, instead, to make a point against Platonism. The Platonist thinks there is a unique, absolutely correct way of continuing the series '2, 4, 6, 8 . . .': a continuation that is absolutely simplest or most natural. Wittgenstein rejects that notion of absolute correctness: there are indefinitely many possible ways of continuing the series, he thinks, no one of which is absolutely correct, or simplest, or most natural. So the correct continuation of the series is not the continuation that is absolutely the simplest or most natural; there is no such thing. The correct continuation is just the continuation that we find simplest or most natural. But, on the deflationist interpretation, Wittgenstein makes that anti-Platonist point without embracing constructivism. 'The continuation we find most natural' is the mathematical series *add 2*. And the way the series *add 2* proceeds is a basic, mathematical fact; the series cannot be reduced to, or constructed from, non-normative facts about how human beings do in fact go on.

At the start of section 2.i, we posed a constitutive question: What makes it correct to continue the series '+ 2' by putting '1002, 1004, 1006 . . .'? For the deflationist, what makes it correct is simply that the instruction '+ 2' means *add* 2, and that following the rule for adding 2 requires putting '1002, 1004, 1006 . . .' after '1000'. In saying that, the deflationist takes it for granted that the instruction '+ 2' means *add* 2. And she takes it for granted that following the rule for adding 2 requires putting '1002, 1004, 1006 . . .' after '1000'. But, she says, it is entirely legitimate to take those facts for granted; they are obvious truths – as clearly true as anything else. In real life, if someone doubts that '+ 2' does mean *add* 2 (rather than, say, *add* 2 *up to* 1000, 4 *up to* 2000, 6 *up to* 3000, *and so on*), we can respond to that doubt by explaining the meaning of the expression '+2' in the way we ordinarily explain it. Similarly, if anyone doubts that following the rule for adding 2 does require putting '1002, 1004, 1006 . . .' after '1000', we can respond to that doubt by explaining what adding 2 is; again, in the kinds of ways we explain it in everyday life. In giving those explanations we will, unavoidably, take it for granted that our words mean what we think they do, and that adding 2 after 1000 involves what we think it does. But as before, the deflationist insists, that is entirely legitimate. After all, any explanation must take *something* for granted. And no one could possibly explain what it is to follow a given rule correctly without taking the meanings of some words for granted.

It is helpful to see the relationship between deflationism, on the one hand, and Platonism and constructivism, on the other, in terms of two points of view. It is agreed on all sides that, from the point of view internal to our practice of adding 2 – the point of view we occupy when we are actually engaged in adding 2 – the correct continuation of the series '2, 4, 6, 8 . . .' is '1000, 1002, 1004, 1006 . . .' And it is agreed on all sides that, from this internal point of view, what makes that the correct continuation is simply that that is what adding 2 after 1000 involves. But the Platonist and the constructivist both think that philosophy can give a more informative answer to the question, what makes this the correct continuation. They both think that, as well as the point of view internal to our practice of adding 2, there is an external point of view: a point of view we can adopt when we reflect philosophically on the practice of adding 2 and consider the question, what makes it the case that the correct continuation of the series '2, 4, 6, 8 . . .' is '1000, 1002, 1004, 1006 . . .'. The Platonist and the constructivist give different answers to that question. The Platonist thinks that what makes the continuation '1000, 1002, 1004, 1006 . . .' correct is the *nature of numbers*: there is an absolute standard for continuing the series correctly; and that standard requires putting '1002, 1004, 1006 . . .' after '1000'. The constructivist thinks that what makes that continuation correct is *our nature*: it is the fact that, case by case, we all agree in developing the series that way. But the Platonist and the constructivist agree that it makes sense to adopt this external point of view and to seek an informative answer to the question, what makes '1000, 1002, 1004, 1006 . . .' the correct continuation of the series. The deflationist, by contrast, thinks the question makes no sense. The only point of view from which we can intelligibly consider our practice of adding 2, she thinks, is the point of view internal to that practice: the point of view that takes addition at face value, and does not attempt to reduce it to anything else. And once we have explained that the series we are writing down is the series *add 2*, there is no further explanation of why the correct continuation of the series is '1000, 1002, 1004, 1006 . . .'. All there is to say is that that is what adding 2 after 1000 is.

The deflationary interpretation of Wittgenstein's discussion of rules is extremely plausible. And it is in many ways more faithful to his philosophy than the constructivist reading. It takes his anti-reductionism seriously. On the deflationary reading, Wittgenstein takes rules and standards of correctness as basic features of our practice; he does not attempt to reduce normative facts about what a rule requires to non-normative facts about what people do when they apply the rule. That is in keeping with his pronouncement that 'Following according to the rule is FUNDAMENTAL to our language-game. It characterizes what we call description' (RFM: 330). And the deflationary interpretation respects Wittgenstein's opposition to positive philosophical theorizing, and his insistence that philosophy can neither justify nor criticize features of ordinary practice.

However, it is not clear that *everything* Wittgenstein says about rules is consistent with the deflationist view. In particular, some of his pronouncements about mathematical truth are decidedly constructivist in spirit. Consider, for example, what he says about Goldbach's conjecture: the proposition that every even number is the sum of two prime numbers. That conjecture has not been proved to be true; nor has it been proved to be false. But, we want to say, it *is* either true or false. And, we think, its truth or falsity is completely determined by the meanings of the words it contains; it does not depend on what, if anything, we would say if we were faced with a proof of its truth or falsity. That, at any rate, is the common-sense view. And it is the view that a deflationist about mathematical rules would take. But Wittgenstein takes a different view:

> Prof Hardy says: 'Goldbach's theorem is either true or false.' – We simply say the road hasn't been built yet. At present you have the right to say either; you have a right to *postulate* that it's true or that it's false.
>
> (LFM: 138)

In this passage (from lectures given in 1939), Wittgenstein apparently rejects the common-sense idea that the truth or falsity of Goldbach's conjecture follows directly from the meanings we have given to its component terms, regardless of whether or not we have any proof of its truth or falsity. Whether or not it is true or false, he suggests, is a matter of our 'building the road' one way or the other; of our producing something that people accept as a proof of its truth or falsity. And that involves a strikingly constructivist view of mathematical rules.

So the deflationary interpretation of Wittgenstein's discussion of rules is certainly more faithful to the main thrust of his remarks than the constructivist reading. But there are some passages in Wittgenstein that are hard to square with deflationism and strongly suggestive of constructivism. The truth, perhaps, is that there are genuinely conflicting strands in Wittgenstein's thinking about rules. The dominant trend is towards deflationism. But it is hard to deny that Wittgenstein sometimes says things that are strongly suggestive of a more constructivist view.

ii. Grasping a rule

When I am following a rule, how do I know what I have to do at each stage in order to follow that rule? How, for example, do I know what the rule '+ 2' requires me to put after 1000? It is plainly not enough to know only that the initial steps of the series are '2, 4, 6, 8, . . .'. Nor is it enough to know *every* step in the series up to 1000. For, as we have seen, there are indefinitely many different possible ways of continuing the series which agree on all the steps up to 1000 but diverge beyond that point; so I could know every step up to 1000 without knowing how I have to go on after 1000. In view of that, it is natural to think that what is needed is an instruction that explicitly specifies exactly which continuation of the series is the correct one: for example, the instruction 'You must always write the *same* sequence of numbers in the units: 2, 4, 6, 8, 0, 2, 4, etc.' (RFM: 36). That, it seems, will rule out the bizarre continuation '1000, 1004, 1008, 1012 etc.'; for someone who continues the series in that way is *not* 'writing the same sequence of numbers in the units column'. But of course, that depends on what counts as 'writing the same sequence of numbers in the units column'. And just as it was possible to take the initial steps in the series in different ways, so it is possible to take this further instruction in different ways. So, we are tempted to think, the further instruction ('You must always write the *same* sequence of numbers in the units') must itself be supplemented by an interpretation that specifies the correct way of taking that instruction. But *whatever* instructions we offer, and *whatever* interpretation of the instructions we supply, simply knowing those instructions and that interpretation will never by itself be sufficient for knowing what one has to do at each stage to count as following the rule. For any instructions, and any interpretation, can in turn be taken in indefinitely many different ways. As Wittgenstein says, 'interpretations by themselves do not determine meaning' (PI §198).

It is tempting, Wittgenstein thinks, to deny that. It is tempting to suppose that there must be *some* kind of interpretation that is not itself susceptible of being interpreted in different ways: a queer, or 'strange' (PI §195), or 'superlative' (PI §192) interpretation; an interpretation 'which makes the rule followable only in *this* way' (RFM: 341) by specifying what counts as the correct application of the rule at every future step in some absolutely unambiguous way. Unless understanding involved something like that, we are tempted to think, how could we ever know what we had to do in order to follow a given rule? But, Wittgenstein insists, there is no such thing as an interpretation that is not itself susceptible of being interpreted in different ways – just as (we saw him insisting earlier) there is no such thing as a picture or an image that is not itself susceptible of being taken in different ways. The idea of an interpretation that fixes its own interpretation is a philosophers' fiction.

The conclusion so far is negative: when I am continuing the series '+ 2', it is not by consulting any kind of interpretation that I know that I must put '1002, 1004, 1006' and not '1004, 1008, 1012'. How, then, do I know it? An exactly parallel question arises for our use of a descriptive word such as 'green': 'how do I know that the colour I am now seeing is called "green"?' (RFM: 336). Wittgenstein writes:

If I am drowning and I shout 'Help!', how do I know what the word Help means? Well, that's how I react in this situation. – Now that is how I know what 'green' means as well and also know how I have to follow the rule in the particular case.

(RFM: 337)

In the most basic cases of following a rule, Wittgenstein thinks, I do not consult anything that tells me how to apply the rule. I simply do what comes naturally, given my training: 'I obey the rule blindly' (PI §219), 'as a matter of course' (PI §238), 'without reasons' (PI §211). When I apply a familiar rule, Wittgenstein thinks, there is no intellectual procedure involved at the point of application; I simply act in the appropriate way. I know what the rule requires; but there is no *way in which* I know it.

Wittgenstein's anti-intellectualism about rule-following seems right. When I follow a familiar rule, I do act blindly and without reasons. But now we face a new question. For in such a case, what makes my action an instance of *following a rule*: why does something that I do blindly and without reasons count as a *correct* or *incorrect* application of a rule, rather than being a mere reaction – something I find it natural to do, but which cannot be assessed as correct or incorrect? Wittgenstein asks: 'When a thrush always repeats the same phrase several times in its song, do we say that perhaps it gives itself a rule each time, and then follows the rule?' (RFM: 345). There is a regularity in the thrush's behaviour: it sings a phrase and repeats it. But it is obviously not giving itself a rule and then following it. It is simply acting in a regular way. So what is the difference between what I do when I follow a rule and what the thrush does when it sings its song? What makes it the case that, when I write down the series of numbers '2, 4, 6, 8 . . .', acting blindly and as a matter of course, I am following the rule '+ 2', rather than, like the thrush, merely acting in a regular way?

Wittgenstein's answer to that question makes essential appeal to the *context* of my action. 'What, in a complicated surrounding, we call "following a rule"', he writes, 'we should certainly not call that if it stood in isolation' (RFM: 335). But what sort of 'complicated surrounding' is necessary in order for something to count as a case of following a rule? He considers an example:

Let us consider very simple rules. Let the expression be a figure, say this one:

|— —|

And one follows the rule by drawing a straight sequence of such figures (perhaps as an ornament).

|— —||— —||— —||— —||— —|

Under what circumstances should we say: someone gives a rule by writing down such a figure? Under what circumstances: someone is following this rule when he draws that sequence? It is difficult to describe this.

   If one of a pair of chimpanzees once scratched the figure |— —| in the earth and thereupon the other the series |— —||— —| etc., the first would not have given a rule nor would the other be following it, whatever else went on at the same time in the minds of the two of them.

   If however there were observed, e.g., the phenomenon of a kind of instruction, of showing how and of imitation, of lucky and misfiring attempts, of reward and punishment and the like; if at length the one who had been so trained put figures which he had never seen before one after another in sequence as in the first example, then we should probably say that the one chimpanzee was writing rules down, and the other following them.

(RFM: 345)

What Wittgenstein says about the chimpanzees is very plausible: we would not regard the case of one-off repetition as an instance of a rule being given and followed; and we probably would regard the more complex case as an instance of rule-following. But why would we describe these cases in that way? What is the crucial difference between them?

   '"Following a rule"', Wittgenstein says, 'is a practice' (PI §202). 'To follow a rule, to make a report, to give an order, to play a game of chess, are customs (usages, institutions)' (PI §199). And similarly: 'a person goes by a signpost only in so far as there is an established usage, a custom' (PI §198). In the case where one chimpanzee once scratches a figure and the other repeats it, he thinks, there is no practice or custom of giving and following rules; that is why we would not say that a rule had been given and followed. In the more complicated surroundings of the second case, however, there is a practice of following rules; that is what makes it reasonable to describe the first chimpanzee as giving a rule and the second as following it. But what does it take for there to be a practice, or custom, or institution of following rules, of going by signposts, and so on?

For Wittgenstein, the idea of a practice has at least two key elements. In the first place, a practice involves *regularity* and *repetition*: a regular or repeated pattern of activity. In the second place, it involves our *using* the rule, the signpost, or whatever in a particular way. We can expand on these points in turn.

Wittgenstein asks: 'Is what we call "following a rule" something that it would be possible for only *one* person, only *once* in a lifetime, to do? (PI §199). His answer is unequivocal:

> It is not possible that there should have been only one occasion on which only one person followed a rule. It is not possible that there should have been only one occasion on which a report was made, an order given or understood, and so on.
>
> (PI §199)

Something only counts as an instance of following a rule, making a report, or giving an order, he thinks, in a context in which there is regular following of rules, a repeated activity of making reports and giving orders. Similarly:

> It is possible for me to invent a card-game today, which however never gets played. But it means nothing to say: in the history of mankind just once was a game invented, and that game was never played by anyone. That means nothing. Not because it contradicts psychological laws. Only in a quite definite surrounding do the words 'invent a game' 'play a game' make sense.
>
> (RFM: 346; see also PI §204)

And that 'quite definite surrounding', Wittgenstein thinks, is a surrounding in which there is an actual activity of playing games, in which games are repeatedly played.

He anticipates an objection. Why must there be an actual activity of playing games if it is to make sense to say that someone once invented a game that no one ever played? Why couldn't everything that is required for something to count as a game – the whole background that, as things are, is supplied by the actual existence of the practice of playing games – be built into the intentions of the inventor, even if no one had ever played any game? Wittgenstein puts the objection like this:

> But that is just what is remarkable about *intention*, about the mental process, that the existence of a custom, of a technique, is not necessary to it. That, for example, it is imaginable that two people should play a game of chess, or even only the beginning of a game of chess, in a world in which otherwise no games existed – and then be interrupted.
>
> (PI §205)

But what makes it the case that someone *does* intend to play a game of chess? According to Wittgenstein, as we saw above in part 1 of this chapter, what makes an intention to Φ the intention to Φ is not something about the agent considered in isolation: it is not a mental image of Φ-ing, an 'unambiguous shadow' of Φ-ing, or anything else that is going through her mind at the time. That she intends to Φ is dependent on the whole context in which the intention occurs. In particular, he thinks, the possibility of intending to play a game of chess depends on the actual existence of a practice of playing chess: 'An intention is embedded in a setting, in human customs and institutions. If the technique of the game of chess did not exist, I could not intend to play a game of chess' (PI §337). The lesson, Wittgenstein thinks, is a general one: we cannot appeal to a subject's intention to follow a rule as a way of sidestepping the idea that following a rule requires a context in which there is an actual practice of following rules; for the possibility of intending to follow a rule itself depends on the existence of an actual practice of following rules.

The second crucial element in Wittgenstein's idea that following a rule is a practice is the claim that following a rule involves *using* or *relating to* the rule in a certain way. Consider the case of following a signpost. There is a difference between following a signpost and merely walking parallel with a board. Part of the difference is that following a signpost requires the existence of repetition and regularity, whereas walking parallel to a board does not: 'It cannot be said . . . that just once in the history of mankind did someone follow a signpost. Whereas it can be said that just once in the history of mankind did someone walk parallel with a board' (RFM: 346). But that is not the only difference. For people might regularly and repeatedly walk parallel to boards without thereby following signposts. In order to be following signposts, the people must also *use* the boards *as signposts*. But what does that require? How must people relate to something in order to be using it as a signpost? A practice of following signposts, Wittgenstein thinks, will involve such features as the following: that people treat a signpost as a *reason* for going a particular way; that they *explain* why they have gone that way by reference to a signpost; that they *correct* their own and other people's choice of route by reference to a signpost; and so on. It is the presence of features such as those that distinguishes the situation where there is a custom of following signposts from a situation in which people regularly walk parallel to boards without following signposts. And the same goes for following rules more generally: what distinguishes the case where people are following a rule from the case where they are merely acting in a regular way are such facts as that they *justify* or *explain* their actions by reference to the rule; that they *correct* their actions, or other people's, by reference to the rule; that they *teach* people to follow the rule, and so on.

This account of what is involved in following a rule has the same general character as Wittgenstein's account of intentionality and his account of the relation between meaning and use (discussed in Chapter 5 section 1.ii, and Chapter 4 section 3, respectively). In the first place, Wittgenstein's account is *anti-reductionist*. He is not attempting to explain what it is to follow a rule in more basic terms. The terms he uses in saying what it takes for there to be a practice of following rules – the notions of justifying, or explaining, or correcting an action by reference to a rule, and so forth – are no more basic than the notion of following a rule itself. That does not mean that we get no illumination from Wittgenstein's account. We do learn something about what it is to follow a rule by reflecting on the complex structure required for there to be such a thing. But the illumination is not reductive in character.

Second, and relatedly, Wittgenstein is not offering a general, systematic account of what it takes for someone to be following a rule, or to be following this rule rather than that. There is, he thinks, no set of non-circular necessary and sufficient conditions for someone's following a rule. But in any particular case, we can give reasons for saying that someone is following a particular rule. 'How are we to judge whether someone meant such-and-such?', asks Wittgenstein (PI §692). For example, how are we to judge that the teacher meant the pupil to continue the series by putting '1000, 1002, 1004, 1006 . . .'? In real life, he thinks, we have no difficulty in answering such questions: 'The fact that he has, for example, mastered a particular technique in arithmetic and algebra, and taught someone else the expansion of a series in the usual way, is such a criterion' (PI §692). Of course such ways of telling what someone meant, or what rule he is following, are not infallible. But they are just as reliable as our ordinary ways of telling anything else. In real life, Wittgenstein insists, there is no principled difficulty about knowing what rule someone is following.

Third, as we have already seen, Wittgenstein's account of following rules stresses the essential contribution of context: 'What, in a complicated surrounding, we call "following a rule" we should certainly not call that if it stood in isolation' (RFM: 335). Whether someone is following a rule, and what rule she is following, is not a matter only of what is true of her, considered in isolation. It depends essentially on the surrounding context.

As with Wittgenstein's account of intentionality, it might be objected that his account of following a rule is not sufficiently informative. He tells us that following a rule is a custom or a practice. And he makes some general comments about what it takes for there to be a practice of following rules. But he does not tell us *exactly* what it involves. So, it may be said, he leaves us unsatisfied. As before, Wittgenstein's response to that objection would have two elements. In the first place, he thinks, it is simply not possible to analyse the concept of following a rule in other terms; for the concept of following a rule is itself as basic as any other. So it is not a failing of his account that it offers no such analysis. In the second place, he would say, the demand for an informative analysis of this kind presupposes that the phenomenon of following a rule is in some way problematic or in need of explanation. But, Wittgenstein insists, there is nothing intrinsically mysterious about following a rule. It is only made to seem mysterious when we consider it in the light of particular philosophical assumptions. For example, suppose we start with the assumption that following a rule requires getting hold of an interpretation that dictates what the rule requires at every future step with no possibility of misinterpretation. Then the possibility of following a rule will indeed seem mysterious. For following a rule will seem to depend on an impossibility: an interpretation that is not itself susceptible of being interpreted in different ways.

> 'How can one follow a rule?' That is what I should like to ask.
>   But how does it come about that I want to ask that, when after all I find no kind of difficulty in following a rule?
>   Here we obviously misunderstand the facts that lie before our eyes.
>
> (RFM: 341)

What makes it seem as though there is a problem about how it is possible to follow a rule is a 'misunderstanding': a mistaken philosophical assumption about what it takes to follow a rule. Once we expose and remove that assumption, Wittgenstein thinks, we see that there is no real problem at all about the possibility of rule-following.

iii. Rules and communities

Wittgenstein says that following a rule is a 'practice', a 'custom', a 'usage', an 'institution'. But does he think it is an essentially *social* practice: that following rules necessarily involves a community of rule-followers? Or does he think the practice of *an individual* could be sufficient to sustain the existence of rule-following? There is sharp disagreement among commentators about Wittgenstein's answer to that question.

On one interpretation, Wittgenstein takes a social, or community, view of rule-following: he thinks there can be no rules without a community of rules. That is not to say that an individual cannot follow rules in isolation – even if, like Robinson Crusoe in Daniel Defoe's story, his isolation is prolonged. But, on this view, what makes it possible for an isolated individual like Crusoe to follow rules is that he is, or has been, a member of a community of rule-followers. In favour of this 'community interpretation' of Wittgenstein is the fact that the German words that are translated as 'customs', 'usages', and 'institutions' (*Gepflogenheiten, Gebräuche,* and *Institutionen*) are all strongly suggestive of something essentially social or communal: more strongly suggestive than their English translations (see Kusch 2006: 248–50). And consider this passage: 'Certainly I can give myself a rule and then follow it. But is it not a rule only for this reason, that it is analogous to what is called "rule" in human dealings?' (RFM: 344). That strongly suggests that there is something *essentially* social or communal about rules. For it implies that the existence of rules 'in human dealings' is the basic or paradigm case, and that something done by an individual counts as a rule only by analogy with the communal case.

But if Wittgenstein does think that rule-following is an essentially communal matter, what is his reason for thinking it? The most common suggestion is that he thinks that it is only a community's verdict about what a rule requires at each stage that can provide a standard of correctness for the efforts of an individual rule-follower (see e.g. Wright 1980: chs 2, 12; Kripke 1982; Malcolm 1986: ch. 9). In order for anyone to follow a rule, there must be a genuine difference between applying the rule correctly and applying it incorrectly. Now consider an individual developing the series '+ 2'. Suppose she continues the series in the usual way up to 1000, but then puts '1004, 1008, 1012 . . .'. What makes that the wrong continuation? If we consider the individual in isolation, the suggestion goes, there will be nothing to make one continuation right and the other wrong: *however* she continues the series, she will *seem to herself* to be continuing it correctly. And if there is no community of other people with whose continuation of the series her way of continuing it can be compared, there will be no independent standard at all by reference to which her continuation can count as being right or wrong. But in that case, there will be no content to the idea that she is continuing the series correctly or incorrectly: 'whatever is going to seem correct to [her] is correct. And that only means that here we can't talk about "correct"' (PI §258). If the individual belongs to a community of rule-followers, on the other hand, things are different. For the community's consensus in continuing the series one way rather than the other provides a standard of correctness by reference to which the individual's attempt to continue the series will count as right or wrong. That is the standard rationale for the claim that rule-following requires a community, and it represents Wittgenstein as taking a broadly constructivist view of rules: the standard of correctness for an individual's application of the rule is constructed from the applications made by other members of the community. (Other commentators have motivated the requirement for a community in different ways. For one suggestion, see McDowell 1984: 69–73. For another, see Bloor 1997: ch. 3.)

In stark contrast to this community interpretation of Wittgenstein, other commentators argue that, on Wittgenstein's view, there is nothing essentially communal about the activity of following a rule. They agree that, for Wittgenstein, the existence of a rule requires a custom or practice of following rules. But, on this interpretation, he does not require this practice to be a *communal* practice. On the contrary, it is said, the practice of an individual can provide the requisite regularity, it can provide the context that is needed for something to be used as a rule, and it can supply a genuine standard of correctness for the subject's attempts to apply the rule (see McGinn 1984: 77–92; Baker and Hacker 2009: 149–68). In favour of this interpretation is the fact that Wittgenstein does seem to have thought that an individual could follow linguistic rules without ever having belonged to a community of people following the same rules. He writes in *Philosophical Investigations* that: 'one could imagine human beings who spoke only in monologue, who accompanied their activities by talking to themselves. – An explorer who watched them and listened to their talk might succeed in translating their language into ours' (PI §243). This passage is not decisive; for the wording suggests that, though the monologuists use their language only to speak to themselves, they belong to a community with a shared language. But in an earlier version of the passage Wittgenstein says explicitly that there need be no shared language: 'Is it not imaginable, that each human being should think only for himself, speak only to himself? (In this case each person could even have his own language.)' (MS 124: 213; quoted in Baker and Hacker 2009: 163). So, at least when he wrote that passage, Wittgenstein does seem to have thought it conceptually possible for the rules that govern a person's language to be rules that are not, and never have been, shared with anyone else.

On the one hand, then, Wittgenstein describes following a rule in terms that strongly suggest the idea of a community: following a rule, he says, is a 'practice', a 'custom', a 'usage', an 'institution'. On the other hand, he allows that each individual might follow only her own linguistic rules, which are never followed by anyone else. What should we conclude? One suggestion is that Wittgenstein is genuinely agnostic about whether or not rule-following is an essentially social matter (see Pears 1988: 374–82). A different suggestion is that he does think that rule-following is essentially social – that it is, in its nature, a social phenomenon; but that, on his understanding of what it is for something to be 'essentially social', that is compatible with allowing, as a limiting case, the possibility of a life-long solitary rule-follower (see Canfield 1996).

When Wittgenstein talks about the 'essential features' of some phenomenon, he is not talking about a set of features that are possessed
by each and every instance of that phenomenon. For example, he
describes himself as trying to understand the nature, or essence, of
language – its function, its structure (see PI §92). But, he explains,
understanding the nature or essence of language in his sense does not
involve 'pointing out something common to all that we call language'.
Instead of that, he says:

> I'm saying that these phenomena have no one thing in common in
> virtue of which we use the same word for all – but there are many
> different kinds of *affinity* between them. And on account of this affinity,
> or these affinities, we call them all 'languages'.
>
> (PI §65)

The picture that suggests is one in which there are clear, central, paradigmatic cases of what we call 'language', and other cases that will
resemble the clear, central, or paradigmatic cases to a greater or lesser
extent; and there will be a gradual transition from cases that we are
prepared to call 'language' to cases that we are not. The same will go
for following a rule. There are cases that we certainly would describe
as rule-following, cases that we would certainly not describe as rule-
following, and a spectrum of cases in between. (We saw an example in
the passage about the two chimpanzees and the figure |– –|, quoted
above from RFM: 345. At one end of the spectrum was a case where we
would 'probably say that the one chimpanzee was writing rules down,
and the other following them'. At the other end was a case that we
would definitely not describe as one of rule-following. And there was
room for a range of intermediate cases.) In this framework, a feature
is 'essential' to rule-following if it is important to the 'function and
structure' of rule-following in the clearest, most central, cases: if it is
in some way involved in the *point* or *purpose* of the activity that we call
'following a rule' in those cases. And it seems plausible that Wittgenstein does think that rule-following is essentially social in that sense.
The clearest examples of rules – the central or paradigmatic cases – are
those whose point involves interactions between people: there are
rules laid down by one person or group to control or direct the behaviour of others; rules that are constitutive of social institutions such as
marriage; rules that allow people to coordinate their behaviour; rules

that facilitate interpersonal communication; and so on. The point of all these rules essentially involves their role in 'human dealings'. And, for Wittgenstein, these are the paradigmatic instances of rules. That does not mean that there cannot be rules that have nothing to do with interactions between different people: a person can give herself a rule to regulate her own behaviour. But such cases, Wittgenstein suggests, count as instances of rule-following only to the extent that they resemble the paradigm cases; and the paradigmatic cases of rule-following are ones that do involve interactions between people.

SUMMARY

The intentionality of thought – its power to represent objects and states of affairs – was one of the first topics that occupied Wittgenstein after his return to philosophy in 1929, and it remained a central theme in his later writings. Negatively, he offers a powerful critique of the imagist view (on which the representational features of thought are explained in terms of the representational qualities of mental images), and of Russell's causal theory of intentionality (on which intentionality is explained by appeal to causal relations between thoughts and feelings, on the one hand, and objects and states of affairs, on the other). Positively, two themes stand out in Wittgenstein's discussion: that it is in language that an expectation and its fulfilment make contact; and that a thought has the content it does in virtue of the 'path on which it lies' – the relations in which it stands to other thoughts, to what the subject says and does, to the context in which it occurs, and so on. Wittgenstein's account of intentionality, like his account of linguistic meaning, is non-reductionist and non-systematic. He sees intentionality not as something inherently mysterious, which needs to be explained in other terms, but as a natural feature of the world that we should accept at face value.

Wittgenstein's discussion of rules and rule-following raises questions of two kinds. There are constitutive questions. What makes this way of continuing a mathematical series, or this way of going on using a descriptive word, correct? What makes it the case that following the rule '+ 2' requires writing such-and-such at this point? And there are questions about our grasp of rules; for example, how do I know that the rule requires doing such-and-such at this point? The main thrust of Wittgenstein's discussion of the constitutive question is towards a deflationary view of rules, which takes rules for granted and resists the demand for an explanation of what makes a given way of following a rule correct. In response to the question about our grasp of rules, Wittgenstein offers an anti-intellectualist account of rule-following: when I follow a familiar rule, I act blindly and without reasons. And he holds that following a rule is a practice: one aspect of that idea is that rule-following involves regularity and repetition; another is that it involves a certain way of relating to rules.

FURTHER READING

Reflections on intentionality appear in many of Wittgenstein's writings. For some important early comments see:

Philosophical Remarks, 63–74.

There is a very accessible discussion, covering Wittgenstein's objections to the imagist view and to Russell's theory in:

The Blue and Brown Books, 1–43.

Some significant passages in Philosophical Investigations are:

Philosophical Investigations §§437–45, 572–86.

Russell's causal theory of intentionality, to which Wittgenstein was objecting, can be found in:

Russell, B. (1921) The Analysis of Mind, London: Allen and Unwin, chapter 3.

There is a very helpful account of Wittgenstein's discussion of intentionality in:

Budd, M. (1989) Wittgenstein's Philosophy of Psychology, London: Routledge, chapter 6.

An excellent discussion, which puts particular stress on Wittgenstein's opposition to positive philosophical theorising, and highlights the diagnostic and therapeutic element in his treatment of intentionality, is:

McDowell, J. (1992) 'Meaning and Intentionality in Wittgenstein's Later Philosophy', in P. French, T. Uehling, and H. Wettstein (eds) Midwest Studies in Philosophy XVII: The Wittgenstein Legacy, Notre Dame: University of Notre Dame Press; reprinted in McDowell, J. (1998) Mind, Value and Reality, Cambridge, MA: Harvard University Press.

On rules and rule-following, the most important texts are:

Philosophical Investigations §§139–242.
Remarks on the Foundations of Mathematics part VI.

Saul Kripke's discussion of Wittgenstein on rule-following has been hugely influential. It remains an excellent introduction, and is exceptionally clear and accessible. Kripke's reading is controversial. But it captures many strands in Wittgenstein's account very well. See:

Kripke, S. (1982) *Wittgenstein on Rules and Private Language*, Oxford: Blackwell.

For two introductory discussions of the rule-following passages in *Philosophical Investigations*, which both take a much more deflationary line than Kripke, see:

McGinn, M. (1997) *Wittgenstein and the* Philosophical Investigations, London: Routledge, chapter 3.
Stern, D. (2004) *Wittgenstein's* Philosophical Investigations: *An Introduction*, Cambridge: Cambridge University Press, chapter 6.

There is a helpful, book-length discussion of the rule-following passages, which is also critical of Kripke's reading, in:

McGinn, C. (1984) *Wittgenstein on Meaning: An Interpretation and Evaluation*, Oxford: Blackwell.

Other important contributions to the huge critical debate on the rule-following considerations include:

Baker, G. P. and Hacker, P. M. S. (2009) *Wittgenstein: Rules, Grammar and Necessity*, 2nd edition, extensively revised by P. M. S. Hacker, Oxford: Wiley-Blackwell.
McDowell, J. (1984) 'Wittgenstein on Following a Rule', *Synthese*, 58: 325–63; reprinted in McDowell, J. (1998) *Mind, Value, and Reality*, Cambridge, MA: Harvard University Press; and in A. Miller and C. Wright (eds) (2002) *Rule-Following and Meaning*, Chesham: Acumen.

For a recent and comprehensive survey of the literature on rule-following, with a defence of Kripke's reading of Wittgenstein, see:

Kusch, M. (2006) *A Sceptical Guide to Meaning and Rules*, Chesham: Acumen.

Six

The later philosophy: mind and psychology

1. SENSATIONS AND SENSATION LANGUAGE

How do we use language to talk about our own and other people's sensations? Take the word 'toothache', for example. It has a first-person use ('I have toothache') and a third-person use ('She has toothache'). But what is the relation between those two uses? Does the word 'toothache' have the same meaning in the first-person and third-person uses? Or does it mean something different? And either way, how exactly is its meaning to be understood?

Wittgenstein discussed these questions about sensation language, and about the relation between the first-person and third-person points of view, in some of the earliest work he did on his return to philosophy in 1929. They have a central place in his writings from the 1930s and in *Philosophical Investigations*. And they lead directly into the work on psychological concepts that occupied him in 1946–49, which was the basis for the work published under the title *Philosophy of Psychology – A Fragment* (or, in earlier editions, *Philosophical Investigations* part II).

i. Wittgenstein's 1929–30 account of sensation language

Wittgenstein's first discussion of sensation language can be found in writings and lectures from the period 1929–30, soon after his return to philosophy. That discussion aimed to do justice to two intuitions. First, that we can communicate successfully about our own and other people's sensations. Second, that our relation to our own sensations is fundamentally different from our relation to other people's sensations; and correspondingly, that there is a fundamental asymmetry between the first-person and third-person uses of sensation words. Wittgenstein thought that this asymmetry is obscured by our ordinary way of talking. On the surface, the difference between the propositions 'I have a toothache' and 'He has a toothache' is simply a difference in the identity of the person who is being said to have a toothache. In one case it is me who is said to have toothache. In the other case it is someone else. But, on the face of it, the rest of the proposition – the 'has a toothache' part – is exactly the same in each case. In Wittgenstein's view, however, there is a much deeper difference between the two propositions than that. To make that difference explicit, he says:

> We could adopt the following way of representing matters: if I, LW, have toothache, then that is expressed by means of the proposition 'There is toothache'. But if that is so, what we now express by the proposition 'A has toothache', is put as follows: 'A is behaving as LW does when there is toothache'. . . . It's evident that this way of speaking is equivalent to ours when it comes to questions of intelligibility and freedom from ambiguity. But it's equally clear that this language could have anyone at all as its centre.
>
> Now, among all the languages with different people as their centres, each of which I can understand, the one with me as its centre has a privileged status. This language is particularly adequate.
>
> (PR: 88–9)

He goes on to say, a page later, that there is a sense of the phrase 'sense-data' in which the word applies only to my own immediate experience; when the phrase is used in that sense, it is 'inconceivable' that someone else should have sense-data (PR: 90). But, he suggests, there is another sense of sensation words, such as 'toothache', in which 'the word "toothache" means the same in "I have toothache" and "He has toothache"' (PR 91).

Wittgenstein's idea was, in effect, that each person's sensation words have two meanings: a private, purely introspective meaning, in which her sensation words apply only to her own sensations and which only she understands; and a public meaning, which can be understood by other people as well as herself. When I use the word 'toothache' with its private meaning, the word refers to 'what is *primary*' (PR: 91) in my experience: to the immediate, subjective quality of my own toothache, which is known by me and no one else. Used in that way, the word gets its meaning by direct, introspective attachment to my own sensation. And that meaning cannot be understood by anyone else. But I can also use the word 'toothache' with a public meaning. Used in that way, the word gets its meaning by association with the distinctive pattern of behaviour that is characteristic of pain. So the sentence 'Jones has toothache', on my (William Child's) lips, means 'Jones is behaving as I (WC) behave when I have toothache'. Similarly, when Jones says 'WC has toothache', that means 'WC behaves as Jones does when I (Jones) have toothache'. No one can understand the private language that anyone else uses to describe her own sensations. But, Wittgenstein supposed, we can all understand the behavioural meanings of the sensation words we use to describe one another's sensations.

That account embodied two insights that Wittgenstein never abandoned: that a person's application of sensation words to herself is not based on the observation of her own behaviour; and that the meanings of the sensation terms we apply to others must be understood in a way that makes essential reference to their behaviour. However, he came to think that this early attempt to develop those insights was wrong. In the first place, the account of the first-person use of sensation words – their use by people for talking about what is 'primary' in their own experience – took it for granted that a word can be given a meaning by pure introspective attachment to a sensation, without relying on any links to external circumstances or behaviour. And that, he came to think, was impossible. In the second place, as we shall see below, the account of the public meanings of sensation words made the character of sensations irrelevant to communication. And that consequence, he later realized, is unacceptable.

We can trace the development of Wittgenstein's view from this point – his 1929–30 account of sensation language – to the account contained in Philosophical Investigations in three stages. First, we shall see why he came to think there could be no private, purely introspective sensation language. That is the burden of the 'private language argument' of Philosophical Investigations. Second, we shall examine his critique of the private linguist's attempt to explain how we make sense of the ascription of sensations to others, and his discussion of our knowledge of sensations. Third, we shall explore the positive view of sensation language that Wittgenstein explored in Philosophical Investigations and elsewhere.

ii. The private language argument

We can start by sketching the view of sensations and sensation language that Wittgenstein aims to undermine.

What individuates sensations? What makes a sensation the kind of sensation it is? When we reflect on that question, Wittgenstein thinks, we find it natural to think that sensations are individuated by their sub-jective, introspectible character. And we find it natural to think that its subjective character is a purely intrinsic feature of a sensation: a feature whose identity is entirely independent of anything to do with the sub-ject's behaviour or external circumstances. So, we think, it is perfectly possible for two people to be subject to all the same external stimuli, and to be exactly alike in every behavioural respect, but for the subjec-tive character of their sensations to be entirely different: it is possible, for example, 'that one section of mankind [has] one visual impression of red, and another section another' (PI §272). (To put the same point in contemporary philosophical jargon: it is possible for different peo-ple to have different colour qualia without there being any behavioural or environmental difference between them.) Such a view of sensations has been dominant in the history of philosophy; and it is popular in contemporary philosophy. And, Wittgenstein thinks, it exerts a natural appeal on anyone who reflects on the nature of sensations; though, as we shall see, he thinks the appeal of this view depends on misunder-standing the 'grammar' of our sensation language. Commentators often describe this as a *Cartesian view* of sensations ('Cartesian' after Descartes, who did much to promote it). And, though Wittgenstein himself did not use the term 'Cartesian' in this connection, it is a convenient label for the view of sensations that he criticized.

The Cartesian view of what individuates sensations goes hand in hand with particular views about knowledge of sensations and about the meanings of sensation words: views that have themselves been historically important and that have a natural appeal when we reflect on the epistemology and semantics of sensations. Thus, it is tempt-ing to think that the only person who can really know what sensation someone is having is the subject herself. 'Only I can know whether I am really in pain; another person can only surmise it' (PI §246), we think. Or, perhaps: 'I may know that he is in pain, but I never know the exact degree of his pain. So here is something that he knows and that his expression of pain does not tell me. Something purely private' (Z: 536). Similarly, if sensations are individuated in a way that has noth-ing to do with behaviour or external circumstances, it is tempting to think that words for kinds of sensations must get their meanings by direct, introspective attachment to the sensations themselves: I 'associ-ate the word with the feeling and use the word when the feeling reap-pears' (cf. Z: 545). But if sensation words get their meanings by direct attachment to sensations, and if no one can know the nature of anyone else's sensations, then, it seems, no one can know the meanings of anyone else's sensation words. So, it seems, each person's sensation language is a private language: a language that only she can understand.

That package of views about sensations and sensation language, Wittgenstein thinks, is extremely tempting. Indeed, his own 1929–30 account of sensation language had embodied elements of the package. But he argues in *Philosophical Investigations* §§243–315 that this picture of sensations is fundamentally mistaken; he aims to dislodge each part of the picture.

The discussion of sensations in *Philosophical Investigations* begins like this:

> Is it . . . conceivable that there be a language in which a person could write down or give voice to his inner experiences – his feelings, moods, and so on – for his own use? – Well, can't we do so in our ordinary language? – But that is not what I mean. The words of this language are to refer to what only the speaker can know – to his immediate private sensations. So another person cannot understand the language.
> (PI §243)

This passage builds in an important assumption: the assumption that the 'ordinary language' we use to talk about our 'inner experiences' – our pains, toothaches and so on – is not a private language. When I say 'I am in pain' or 'I have toothache', Wittgenstein thinks, my words 'pain' and 'toothache' do not refer to something that only I can know; and it is not true that my words can only be understood by me. On the contrary, it is perfectly evident that other people know exactly what I mean when I say that I have toothache. But, Wittgenstein is asking, *could* there be words that were used in the way he describes? Could it be that, as well as the ordinary word 'toothache', which everyone understands, each person had another word that meant, or referred to, only her *own* sensation of toothache, which was known only to her (see PI §273)? Wittgenstein argues that there could not.

The argument starts with the question, how the relation between a name and a private sensation could be set up. The private linguist's idea is that 'I simply *associate* names with sensations, and use these names in descriptions' (PI §256). But how, Wittgenstein asks, do I do that? He writes:

> Let's imagine the following case. I want to keep a diary about the recurrence of a certain sensation. To this end I associate it with the sign 'S' and write this sign in a calendar for every day on which I have the sensation. – I first want to observe that a definition of the sign cannot be formulated. – But all the same, I can give one to myself as a kind of ostensive definition! – How? Can I point to the sensation? – Not in the ordinary sense. But I speak, or write the sign down, and at the same time I concentrate my attention on the sensation – and so, as it were, point to it inwardly. – But what is this ceremony for? For that is all it seems to be! A definition serves to lay down the meaning of a sign, doesn't it? – Well, that is done precisely by concentrating my attention; for in this way I commit to memory the connection between the sign and the sensation. – But 'I commit it to memory' can only mean: this process brings it about that I remember the connection *correctly* in the future. But in the present case, I have no criterion of correctness. One would like to say: whatever is going to seem correct to me is correct. And that only means that here we can't talk about 'correct'.

> (PI §258)

In order to give a meaning to a word, I must establish a standard of correctness for the use of the word: a standard of what is to count as a correct application of the word. Now, Wittgenstein asks, how could that be achieved in the case of a word for a private sensation? The private linguist thinks that he can establish a standard of correctness for uses of the word 'S' by concentrating his attention on a particular sensation and undertaking to use the word 'S' for all sensations of the same type. Given that definition, he thinks, an application of the word 'S' to a sensation will be correct if the new sensation is the same kind of sensation as the one he originally called 'S'; it will be incorrect if the new sensation is of a different kind. But *what is it* for something to be the same kind of sensation as the one that was originally called 'S'? The lesson of the discussion of rule-following in Philosophical Investiga- tions §§143–242 is that we cannot just take for granted what it is for something to belong to the same kind as an ostended sample. When we are developing the series '2, 4, 6, 8', what counts as going on in the same way is not dictated by the world; it depends on a humanly created standard of similarity. And the same applies to the question, what counts as going on applying the word 'S' in the same way as before. What it takes for one private sensation to belong to the same kind as another is not determined by the nature of things; it must be understood by reference to a humanly created standard of similarity. And whatever the putative private linguist does with his word 'S', Wittgenstein thinks, he cannot establish a genuine standard of similarity: a standard by reference to which future applications of the word 'S' will count as correct or incorrect. But, we might ask, why not? What is it about the private linguist's situation that prevents him establishing a genuine standard of correctness for his uses of the word 'S'? Different interpreters have offered different views about Wittgenstein's answer to that question.

On one interpretation, Wittgenstein's argument against the possibility of a private sensation language essentially depends on taking a community view of rules. On the community view, the only standard by reference to which an individual's application of a word can count as correct or incorrect is the standard set by the community's application of the word. And that point applies across the board: to names of colours, shapes, numbers, animals, and so on, as well as to names of sensations. Now a central feature of a private sensation language is that its words are intelligible only to the private linguist himself. That means that there can be no communal consensus in the application of those words; for no one other than the private linguist himself can apply them at all. It follows, on the community view of rules, that there can be no standard of correctness for the private linguist's applications of his words. But if there is no standard of correctness for the application of his words, they are not meaningful words at all. On this reading, the impossibility of a private sensation language is just a special case of the impossibility of an individual following any rule at all without reference to a community.

That is a popular interpretation of Wittgenstein's argument. (For a prominent example, see Kripke 1982). But it is controversial. For, as we saw in Chapter 5, there are good reasons for doubting whether Wittgenstein *does* hold that the standard of correctness for an individual's applications of a word is constituted by the community's applications of the word. So is there an alternative reading of the argument: an alternative account of why, according to Wittgenstein, the practice of an individual could not establish a genuine standard of correctness for his applications of the private sensation word 'S'?

The private linguist thinks that he can give the word 'S' a meaning by an internal ostensive definition. And it might seem that it would be easy for him to do so. After all, Wittgenstein allows that ostensive definition is in general a perfectly good way of defining a word, provided that 'the role the word is supposed to play in the language is already clear' (PI §30). And he allows that one way to make the role of the ostensively defined word clear is by explicitly specifying the kind of thing we are naming: e.g. by saying 'This *colour* is called "sepia"' or 'This *number* is called "two"'' (PI §29). So why can't the private linguist simply specify the kind of thing he is naming: 'I shall call this kind of *sensation* "S"'? Isn't that enough to ensure that his internal ostensive definition does establish a standard of correctness for future applications of his word 'S', by identifying which of the many possible standards of correctness the word is intended to have? Wittgenstein's response to that natural suggestion is to press the question, what the private linguist means by 'sensation' when he says to himself, 'I shall call this kind of *sensation* "S"'? 'The word "sensation"', says Wittgenstein, 'is a word of our common language, which is not a language intelligible only to me' (PI §261). But if I am trying to set up a word with a private meaning, a meaning that is intelligible only to me, I cannot help myself to concepts or standards of correctness that are drawn from a public language. In particular, if I specify that the word 'S' is to be a word for a kind of 'sensation', and mean by the word 'sensation' what we ordinarily mean, then my word 'S' will not have a private meaning at all; it will be intelligible to other people too. (Wittgenstein's argument here depends on the assumption noted above: that the meanings of sensation words in our ordinary language are publicly intelligible. He takes that to be an obvious truth.) So, Wittgenstein argues, to succeed in giving the word 'S' a private meaning, I must find a way of specifying the kind of thing I am naming without relying on the resources of our ordinary, public language in any way at all. And that is a condition that it is impossible to meet. For example:

> it would not help [for the private linguist] to say that it need not be a *sensation*; that when he writes 'S', he has *Something* – and that is all that can be said. But 'has' and 'something' also belong to our common language.
>
> (PI §261)

So the private linguist cannot legitimately help himself to those words in defining his word 'S'. In fact, thinks Wittgenstein, he cannot use any of our ordinary words at all. For they all belong to a shared, public language. He must, then, conjure up absolutely everything he needs for defining his private words entirely from his own, introspective resources. And the idea that he can do such a thing, Wittgenstein thinks, is pure fantasy.

That line of thought is certainly suggestive. And it brings out the challenge that faces the private linguist. But can we say anything more definite or specific about exactly why, according to Wittgenstein, that challenge cannot be met? Consider, first, the case not of sensation words but of colour words ('red', 'green', 'blue', and so on). Could an isolated individual establish a standard of correctness for her own colour words without depending in any way on the resources of a shared, public language? If we take a community view of rules, our answer to that question will be 'no': on that view, there can be no standard of correctness for the application of any word unless there is a communal practice of applying that word. But suppose we reject the community view. Then we might think that it is in principle possible for the practice of a solitary individual to supply all that is needed for the existence of a genuine standard of correctness for a colour word. For, we might argue, the solitary individual could define her own colour word (call it 'wodj') in connection with a series of samples of that colour. When she goes on to apply the word 'wodj' to other things, there will be a genuine distinction between a correct and an incorrect application. For the original samples provide a standard of correctness for the judgement that this or that new thing is wodj: a standard that is independent of her impression that the thing is wodj. She might think that the word 'wodj' applies to a particular thing but discover, when she compares it with the original samples, that she was wrong. But, in Wittgenstein's view, things are different in the case of the private linguist's attempt to establish words for his private sensations. For in that case, there is nothing to play the role that is played by the colour samples in the solitary individual's use of the word 'wodj'. When the private linguist tries to apply his word 'S' today, and wonders whether that application is correct, he cannot compare today's sensation with yesterday's — as the solitary individual can compare the object she calls 'wodj' today with the set of samples in connection with which she defined the word. For, in the nature of the case, yesterday's sensation is no longer available for him to examine; sensations are simply too ephemeral. At most, Wittgenstein thinks, the private linguist can compare today's sensation with a memory image of the sensation he had yesterday, when he said to himself 'The word "S" refers to sensations of the same kind as this'. But that does not provide a genuine standard for the correctness of his application of the word 'S' to today's sensation, any more than a memory image of a set of colour samples would provide a genuine standard of correctness for the application of a colour word (see PI §265).

When Wittgenstein puts the argument this way – as he sometimes does –it can look as if his point is simply that the transience of sensations makes it impossible for the private linguist to tell whether he has applied his word 'S' correctly. That invites the objection that, even if he cannot know for sure whether his application of the word 'S' is correct, it does not follow that there is no fact of the matter as to whether or not it is correct. So Wittgenstein has not shown that there could not be a private sensation language; he has only shown that it would be hard for the private linguist to tell whether the statements he made when he used his private sensation language were true. But that objection misses the real point of the argument. Wittgenstein's fundamental idea is not that the private linguist succeeds in setting up a standard of correctness for his uses of the word 'S', but cannot tell when he has met the standard. Rather, he thinks that the private linguist does not succeed in establishing a standard of correctness for uses of the word 'S' at all. In the case of the solitary colour-word 'wodj', there are enduring physical objects that the solitary linguist can use in establishing a standard of correctness for applications of her new word. She can sort and resort those objects into those that are wodj and those that are not; she can compare new objects with those in the original set; she can arrange them by their degree of wodj-ness; and so on. All of that, in Wittgenstein's view, plays a crucial role in establishing a standard of correctness for uses of the word 'wodj'. In order to establish a standard of correctness, the solitary linguist must establish a practice of sorting and classifying things by their colours. And she can only do that because colour is a relatively enduring property, which sustains such a practice. But none of that is possible for the private linguist. He cannot sort and resort a set of private sensations into those that are S and those that are not: for a private sensation is available for inspection only as long as he can hold it in his attention; he cannot then retrieve the very same sensation and consider its qualities again. Nor can he compare the features of one private sensation with those of another that is enjoyed at a different time; or rank such sensations with respect to their degree of some feature they exhibit. So there is nothing to sustain the practices of sorting and classification that would be needed if the private linguist were to be able to establish standards of correctness for the use of his private sensation words. That is why the attempt to establish such standards of correctness cannot succeed.

Is Wittgenstein's argument successful? Does he succeed in showing that there could not be a language whose words 'refer to what only the speaker can know – to his immediate private sensations'? One way to challenge the argument would be to challenge Wittgenstein's rejection of Platonism. A crucial premise of the argument is the anti-Platonist principle that, when the private linguist tries to introduce his word 'S' in connection with a particular private sensation, the nature of the sensation does not itself determine what it is for something else to be the same kind of private sensation as the original sample. But an objector might reject that claim. If Platonism about private sensations is true, she might say, then the private linguist's internal ostensive definition *does* establish a genuine standard of correctness for future uses of her word 'S'. For if Platonism is true, it is straightforwardly true that *these* other private sensations belong to the same kind as the original sample and that *those* do not: and thus that it is correct to apply the word 'S' to *these* private sensations and incorrect to apply it to *those*. So someone who rejects Wittgenstein's case against Platonism may also reject the private language argument. A different kind of challenge to Wittgenstein's argument accepts his anti-Platonism: so it accepts that the private linguist cannot simply take for granted what it is for something to belong to the same kind of private sensation as the original sample; and it accepts that he must do something that *establishes* a standard of similarity for private sensations. But, on this view, Wittgenstein is wrong to think that it is impossible to establish a genuine standard of correctness in a way that uses only private, introspective, resources. The objector who takes this line argues that the private linguist can set up genuine standards of correctness for his words, by mimicking in his private inner world whatever we do in our shared public world to give meanings to our words for colours, numbers, and so on. (For an objection on those lines, see Blackburn 1984: 100–1.)

iii. Other minds

How do we make sense of the thought that other people have sensations and experiences? In Wittgenstein's words: 'What gives us *so much
as the idea* that beings, things, can feel?' (PI §283).

When philosophers discuss 'the problem of other minds', the problem in question is generally an epistemic one. They take it for granted
that we understand the claim that other people have thoughts, sensations, and so on. Their question is what reason we have for believing
that claim to be true. But when Wittgenstein asks 'what gives us so
much as the idea that living beings, things, can feel?', he is not asking
that epistemic question. He is raising a question about the concept of
other minds: how does anyone *make sense* of the thought that someone
other than themselves has sensations? That question poses a particular
challenge for the Cartesian view of sensations.

On the Cartesian view, 'it is only from my own case that I know
what the word "pain" means' (PI §293). I focus on my own sensation
of pain, and attach the word 'pain' to sensations with that intrinsic
character. That is how I know what the word means. As we have just
seen, Wittgenstein argues that it is impossible to give meaning to a
sensation word in that way. But, for the sake of argument, suppose that
it is possible. Suppose that, in the first instance, each of us understands
the word 'pain' in a purely introspective way. How could we then make
sense of ascriptions of pain to other people? The private linguist's idea
is that we can each use our purely introspective understanding of the
word 'pain', as it applies to ourselves, in coming to grasp what it is for
someone else to feel pain. But how exactly is this transition from the
first-person case to the third-person case supposed to work? Wittgenstein considers three proposals, and argues that each of them is unsuccessful. He concludes that even if the private linguist could give names
to his own private sensations, he could make no sense of the ascription
of sensations to others. And, since we evidently do understand ascriptions of sensations to other people, he thinks, that is a further reason
for rejecting the private linguist's Cartesian conception of sensations
and sensation language.

The private linguist's first proposal is that, having first understood by
introspection what it is for me to be in pain, I can understand what it is
for someone else to be in pain by *imaginative projection* from my own case.
I know by introspection what it is like for me to be in pain. That enables

me to form an image of pain, which I can use in imagining the state of affairs of someone other than me being in pain. And that gives me a way of understanding what it means to say, or think, that someone else is in pain. Wittgenstein's comment on that proposal is succinct:

> If one has to imagine someone else's pain on the model of one's own, this is none too easy a thing to do: for I have to imagine pain which I *don't feel* on the model of pain which I *do feel*. That is, what I have to do is not simply to make a transition in the imagination from pain in one place to pain in another. As from pain in the hand to pain in the arm. For it is not as if I had to imagine that I feel pain in some part of his body.
>
> (PI §302)

When I imagine a pain, he observes, what I am imagining is simply *being in pain*. But imagining being in pain cannot possibly give me the idea of someone other than me being in pain. As Wittgenstein puts it, I cannot derive the idea of pain that is felt by someone else – pain that I do not feel – by imagining pain that I do feel.

A second proposal is that, having first grasped the meaning of the word 'pain' in my own case, I come to understand its application to other people by way of the principle that for someone else to be in pain is for them to be in *the same kind of state* that I am in when I am in pain: 'if I suppose that someone has a pain, then I am simply supposing that he has just the same as I have so often had' (PI §350). But, Wittgenstein objects:

> That gets us no further. It is as if I were to say, 'You surely know what "It's 5 o'clock here" means; so you also know what "It's 5 o'clock on the sun" means. It means simply that it is just the same time there as it is here when it is 5 o'clock.' – The explanation by means of *sameness* does not work here. For I know well enough that one can call 5 o'clock here and 5 o'clock there 'the same time', but I do not know in what cases one is to speak of its being the same time here and there.
>
> In exactly the same way, it is no explanation to say: the supposition that he has a pain is simply the supposition that he has the same as I. For what's surely clear to me is *this* part of the grammar: that one will say that the stove has the same experience as I *if* one says: it's in pain and I'm in pain.
>
> (PI §350)

The principle, 'He is in pain when he is in the same state that I am in when I am in a pain', is true. But, Wittgenstein argues, if I did not already understand what it was for someone else to be in pain, I could not come to understand it by means of that principle. For if I do not understand what it is for someone else to be in pain then, by the same token, I will not understand what it is for someone else to be in the same state I am in when I am in pain. So the principle, though true, is no help to someone who is trying to acquire the idea of someone else being in pain.

A third proposal is that the transition from a purely introspective, first-personal conception of pain to a grasp of what it is for someone else to be in pain can be achieved by exploiting the relations between private sensations and behaviour. In the first instance, I use the word 'pain' to refer to my own private sensation of pain. I then correlate my private sensation of pain with my own pain behaviour. And I understand the claim that someone else is in pain by reference to their pain behaviour. So 'Jones is in pain' means 'Jones is behaving as I behave when I am in pain'. (As we have seen, that was the view that Wittgenstein himself proposed in 1929–30.) But Wittgenstein came to see that that account, too, was unacceptable; for it has the consequence that we never really communicate about the character of our sensations. Wittgenstein makes that point in a famous passage in *Philosophical Investigations*:

> Suppose everyone had a box with something in it which we call a 'beetle'. No one can ever look into anyone else's box, and everyone says he knows what a beetle is only by looking at *his* beetle. – Here it would be quite possible for everyone to have something different in his box. One might even imagine such a thing constantly changing. – But what if these people's word 'beetle' had a use nonetheless? – If so, it would not be used as the name of a thing. The thing in the box doesn't belong to the language-game at all; not even as a *Something*: for the box might even be empty. – No, one can 'divide through' by the thing in the box; it cancels out, whatever it is.
>
> That is to say, if we construe the grammar of the expression of sensation on the model of 'object and name' the object drops out of consideration as irrelevant.

(PI §293)

Wittgenstein does not think that the character of people's sensations *is* irrelevant to the meanings of sensation words in ordinary language. His point is, rather, that it *would be* irrelevant if we conceived of sensation language in the way he is considering: with each person using the word 'pain' in the first instance as a name for their own private, introspectively individuated sensation, and the communicative use of sensation words explained wholly in terms of behaviour. It is right, according to Wittgenstein, that an account of what it is for someone else to be in pain must make essential reference to the behavioural expression of pain. But when the appeal to behaviour in explaining the meaning of the word 'pain' in the third-person case is combined with a purely introspective explanation of the meaning of the word in the first-person case, we get the absurd result that the character of sensations themselves is irrelevant to the communicative use of sensation words.

The lesson Wittgenstein draws in *Philosophical Investigations* is that we must abandon the Cartesian idea that each person's conception of her own pain is a purely introspective conception. Even when we think about our own pains, he thinks, the concept of pain we employ already incorporates the relations to behaviour and bodily injury that we rely on when we ascribe pains to others. We will explore Wittgenstein's positive development of that idea in section 1.v below.

iv. Knowledge of sensations

What do we know about our own and other people's sensations? And how do we know it? The answer might seem obvious: each person has certain knowledge of her own sensations; no one really knows the character of anyone else's sensations. But Wittgenstein rejects both elements of that view. On the one hand, he claims, 'It can't be said of me at all (except perhaps as a joke) that I *know* I'm in pain. What is it supposed to mean – except perhaps that I *am* in pain?' (PI §246). On the other hand, 'If we are using the word "know" as it is normally used (and how else are we to use it?), then other people very often know if I'm in pain' (§246).

Many readers are puzzled by Wittgenstein's claim that it makes no sense to say that I know that I am in pain. But whether or not we agree with Wittgenstein, his claim is less puzzling once we see why he says what he does. His starting point is the idea that the concept of knowledge is part of a family of other epistemic concepts: it is essentially connected to the concepts of evidence, justification, observation, discovery, doubt, error, and so forth. So, he thinks, it is only possible for someone to know that p in the kinds of case where she can *learn* that p, where her belief that p can be *justified by evidence*, where she can coherently *doubt whether* p, and so on. But for the proposition 'I am in pain', he claims, none of those conditions is fulfilled. When I say 'I am in pain', I am not *inferring* that I am in pain on the basis of evidence; and my utterance is not the result of my having *learned*, or *found out*, that I am in pain; it is an immediate, non-inferential response to the pain. Similarly, Wittgenstein thinks, I cannot coherently *doubt whether* I am in pain: 'If someone said "I don't know if what I have is a pain or something else", we would think, perhaps, that he does not know what the English word "pain" means' (PI §288). And since the concepts of justification, evidence, doubt, and so on have no application to the proposition 'I am in pain', he thinks, neither does the concept of knowledge. In normal circumstances, at least, it makes no sense to say 'I know I am in pain'.

What should we make of that argument? Wittgenstein is absolutely right to say that we are not *observers* of our own mental lives, that we do not *find out* about our own sensations on the basis of evidence, and so on. But it does not follow from that that it is wrong, or even senseless, to say that a person knows that she is in pain. It seems better, and more in keeping with common sense, to say that a person who feels pain *does* normally know that she is in pain, while agreeing with Wittgenstein that one's knowledge that one is in pain, unlike one's knowledge of truths about the external world, is not normally based on evidence or observation. A plausible view of knowledge, which is widely accepted in contemporary philosophy, is this: one knows something if one believes it, one's belief is true, and it is no accident that one's belief is true. On that view of knowledge, a person who is in pain *does* normally know that she is in pain. After all, she believes she is in pain; her belief that she is in pain is true; and it is no accident that her belief is true. (Wittgenstein might respond that a person who is in pain cannot be said to *believe* that she is in pain – on the grounds that the concept of belief, like the concept of knowledge, is tied to the concepts of evidence, observation, and so on. But, as before, it seems better to say that she *does* believe that she is in pain, while acknowledging that she does not normally believe it on the basis of evidence.)

What of Wittgenstein's comments about our knowledge of other people's sensations? He acknowledges the temptation, when doing philosophy, to think that one person can never really know what sensation another person is having. But, he thinks, the temptation should be resisted. In real life, he points out, we do not for a moment think it is impossible to know the nature of someone else's sensation: 'Just try – in a real case – to doubt someone else's fear or pain!' (PI §303); or again, 'If I see someone writhing in pain with evident cause, I do not think: all the same, his feelings are hidden from me' (PPF §324 [PI II xi p. 223]). But Wittgenstein's rejection of the sceptical claim that we can never know what someone else is feeling does not depend merely on an appeal to ordinary language: to the fact that we do ordinarily say that we know about others' sensations. For he tries to show what is wrong with the reasoning that tempts us to make the sceptical claim. For example:

> 'I can only *believe* that someone else is in pain, but I *know* it if I am.'
> – Yes: one can resolve to say 'I believe he is in pain' instead of 'He is in pain'. But that's all. – What looks like an explanation here, or like a statement about a mental process, in truth just exchanges one way of talking for another which, while we are doing philosophy, seems to us the more apt.
>
> (PI §303; see also BB: 53–4)

If I say that I can never really know that someone else is in pain, Wittgenstein thinks, that is not because I think my evidence is never as a matter of fact strong enough for the belief that someone is in pain to qualify as knowledge. It is because I think that *no possible evidence* would be good enough for such a belief to qualify as knowledge. But in that case, I am simply stipulating that, however good my epistemic position vis-à-vis another's pain, it cannot amount to knowledge. We cannot stop someone deciding to talk that way. But even if someone does talk that way, there remains a genuine and important distinction between a case where I have no evidence about someone else's sensations and a case where I have extremely good evidence: for example, the case where 'I see someone writhing in pain with evident cause'. And, Wittgenstein thinks, it is merely quixotic to deny that, in these latter cases, I know that the other person is in pain. What more could be needed for knowing that someone else is in pain than what we all ordinarily acknowledge to be the best possible evidence?

v. Wittgenstein's positive view of sensations and sensation language

Wittgenstein rejects the private linguist's account of sensation language. But what is his own positive view? He writes:

> How do words *refer* to sensations? – There doesn't seem to be any problem here; don't we talk about sensations every day, and name them? This question is the same as: How does a human being learn the meaning of names of sensations? – For example, of the word 'pain'? Here is one possibility: words are connected with the primitive, natural, expressions of sensation and used in their place. A child has hurt himself and he cries; then adults talk to him and teach him exclamations and, later, sentences. They teach the child new pain-behaviour.
>
> 'So you are saying that the word "pain" really means crying?' – On the contrary: the verbal expression of pain replaces crying, it does not describe it.
>
> (PI §244)

The suggestion in this passage is that the expression 'I'm in pain' is a learned addition to our natural, pre-linguistic expressions of pain. And in later writings, Wittgenstein makes a parallel proposal about our application of the word 'pain' to other people. Our use of the expression 'He's in pain', he suggests, is a development of our natural, pre-linguistic reactions to others' pains:

> It is a primitive reaction to tend, to treat, the part that hurts when someone else is in pain; and not merely when oneself is – and so to pay attention to other people's pain behaviour, as one does *not* pay attention to one's own pain behaviour.
>
> But what is the word 'primitive' meant to say here? Presumably that this sort of behaviour is *pre-linguistic*: that a language-game is based *on it*, that it is the prototype of a way of thinking and not the result of thought.
>
> [. . .]
>
> Being sure that someone is in pain, doubting whether he is, and so on, are so many natural, instinctive, kinds of behaviour towards other human beings, and our language is merely an auxiliary to, and further extension of, this relation. Our language-game is an extension of primitive behaviour.
>
> (Z: 540–1, 545)

What picture of sensations and sensation language emerges from these passages?

In saying that the words 'I am in pain', or 'It hurts', are replacements for the natural, pre-linguistic expression of pain, Wittgenstein is making two main points. The first concerns our acquisition of the concept of pain. Before she learns the word 'pain', a child's pre-linguistic expressions of pain already distinguish cases where she is in pain from cases where she is not. When we teach her to use the words 'I'm in pain' in circumstances where she already expresses the pain non-linguistically, she learns to apply the word 'pain' to herself in circumstances where she feels pain. That effects a connection between her feelings of pain and her use of the word 'pain'. And crucially, Wittgenstein thinks, the connection is achieved in a way that does not depend on introspection or on any supposed inner ostensive definition. Of course, being trained to produce the word 'pain' in circumstances where one is in pain does not suffice for knowing what the word means. One needs to master the rest of the use of the word, too, including its application to other people. But, Wittgenstein thinks, learning to supplement or replace one's natural expressions of pain with linguistic expressions of pain is a crucial first step. Wittgenstein's second main point in stressing that the words 'I am in pain' are a taught addition to pre-linguistic expressions of pain concerns epistemology. A child's pre-linguistic expressions of pain are an immediate, unthinking reaction to her pain; they are not the result of any process of introspection or self-observation. As she learns to supplement her natural pre-linguistic expressions of pain with verbal expressions, the character of her reactions changes: the original inarticulate cry of pain is replaced by the sentence 'I'm in pain'. But, Wittgenstein thinks, the verbal expression has the same epistemic immediacy as the original pre-linguistic expression: saying 'I'm in pain', like crying out in pain, is typically not the result of any process of self-observation.

What about the use of the word 'pain' in the third-person case? We are prone to think that 'you attend to the man who groans because experience has taught you that you groan when you feel such-and-such' (Z: 537). But in Wittgenstein's view, that gets things the wrong way round. The truth is that the inclination to attend to a person who groans comes first; the belief that such a person is in pain is a development of that natural response. As before, there are two points here. The first concerns our acquisition of the concept of another's pain. A pre-linguistic child who reacts with sympathy and concern to another person's expressions of pain does not yet have the full-blown belief that the other person is in pain; she does not yet have a full-blown concept of pain. But, through her behaviour, she is already discriminating cases where another person is manifestly in pain from cases where he is not. When – by imitation and teaching – she learns to say 'He is in pain' in cases that she already singles out through her sympathetic behaviour, she is learning to apply the word 'pain' to another person in circumstances where he really is in pain. That is a crucial element in learning the meaning of the word 'pain'. And, Wittgenstein thinks, this account shows how the child can acquire the concept of another's pain in a way that does not depend on some kind of extrapolation to the third-person case of a purely introspective conception of pain that she derives from her own case. Wittgenstein's second point concerns the epistemology of other minds. The sympathetic response of a pre-linguistic child to another person's pain is an immediate, unthinking, animal reaction. It is not the result of any inference or reasoning. When an adult sees someone who is manifestly suffering and believes that he is in pain, the adult's response to the other person's pain is different from, and more sophisticated than, the child's pre-linguistic action. But, Wittgenstein thinks, there is an important respect in which the adult's response – of coming to believe that the other person is in pain – is similar to the child's pre-linguistic reaction: for the adult's response, like the child's, is an immediate, non-inferential reaction to the other's pain; it is not the result of any process of reasoning. That point, he thinks, is an important corrective to the tendency to think of our knowledge of other people's sensations in a way that over-intellectualizes our relation to other minds: just as the observation that the utterance 'I'm in pain' is an immediate, non-inferential response to one's own pain is an important corrective to the tendency to over-intellectualize our relation to our own minds.

Wittgenstein's remarks about the relation between our use of the word 'pain' and our natural, pre-linguistic reactions to our own and other people's pains are insightful. But they are only a first step towards a full account of sensation language; and Wittgenstein only intends them as a first step. We can consider three questions that arise when we try to develop Wittgenstein's suggestion beyond the immediate points he makes: What exactly is implied by Wittgenstein's idea that the utterance 'I'm in pain' is an *expression* of pain? How well does Wittgenstein's account accommodate the fact that the word 'pain' has the same meaning in the first-person utterance 'I'm in pain' and in the third-person ascription 'He's in pain'? And can Wittgenstein's account be extended to sensations other than pain, and to mental phenomena other than sensations?

Expression versus description. A person who lets out a non-verbal cry of pain – who exclaims 'Aargh!' or 'Ouch!', say – thereby expresses her pain. Other people can tell from her cry that she is in pain. But she has not *described* herself as being in pain, or *said that* she is in pain. Suppose, however, that what she cries is not 'Ouch!' but 'I'm in pain!' or 'That hurts!'. In this case, too, it seems right to regard her utterance as an expression of pain: especially in cases where, like a non-verbal cry of pain, the utterance is an immediate, involuntary reaction to the pain. But it is also natural to think that, in uttering the sentence 'I'm in pain', she is not only expressing her pain but also, and simultaneously, *describing herself* as being in pain. After all, when she utters the sentence 'I'm in pain!', she says something that is true or false, and whose truth or falsity depends on whether or not she is, indeed, in pain. And that seems enough for her to count as having described herself.

But Wittgenstein seems to disagree. In his view, someone can only be said to describe herself when she stands back and engages in a process of reflection or self-observation. That is something we sometimes do. And in such cases, he allows, a person can truly be said to describe her mental state. But in the normal case, he thinks, when someone simply comes out with the utterance 'It hurts' or 'I'm in pain' without needing to pause for reflection, her utterance is not a statement or a description at all. (That this is Wittgenstein's view is strongly suggested by what he says in PPF §§67–85 [PI II ix].) Wittgenstein is plainly right that someone who utters the sentence 'I'm in pain' might be doing different things with those words in different contexts. In one case, she might be letting out an involuntary cry of pain; in another, she might be making a carefully considered report to her doctor; and so on. But he writes as if there is just one dimension along which such utterances can be classified: so if a given utterance of 'I'm in pain' is an expression, it is not a description; and vice versa. We do better to allow that utterances can be classified along a number of different dimensions. It is one question whether someone who says 'I'm in pain' is engaged in any activity of reflection or self-observation; it is a different question whether the words she utters have the semantic function of describing the speaker. If we make that distinction, we can accept the natural view that a speaker who cries out 'I'm in pain' is both expressing her pain and describing herself as being in pain.

The unity of the concept of pain. It is sometimes claimed that Wittgenstein's account of the word 'pain' says too little about what unifies the first-person and third-person uses of the word: that it fails to explain how the word that we apply to ourselves without evidence can have the same meaning as the word that we apply to others on the basis of their behaviour. His account, it is said, makes it look as though the word 'pain' has different meanings in its first-person and third-person uses. He describes the two different uses of the word 'pain': its first-person and third-person uses. But, the objector complains, he does not say what unifies these two uses.

That objection seems unfair, for Wittgenstein goes to some lengths to stress the mutual interdependence of the first-person and third-person uses of the word 'pain'. In teaching the child to replace her natural, pre-linguistic expressions of pain with the linguistic expression 'I'm in pain', we teach her to make first-person uses of the word that are not grounded in observations of her behaviour. But, at the outset, we teach her to make such first-person uses only in circumstances where she already expresses her pain non-linguistically and, therefore, where we can apply the word 'pain' to her on the basis of her behaviour. And she only qualifies as having grasped the meaning of the word if her first-person applications are consistent with the way we apply the word to her on the basis of her circumstances and behaviour; if she regularly says 'I'm in pain' in circumstances where, on the basis of the third-person criteria, we know that she is not, she has not properly mastered the first-person use. Later on, when we are confident that she has mastered the first-person use, we accept her self-ascriptions of pain as decisive in cases where we have no independent basis for making a third-person ascription of pain. But even then, her overall use of the term must not come apart from the third-person criteria. If she regularly applied the word 'pain' to herself in circumstances where there was no independent evidence that she was in pain, we would start to doubt whether she really did understand the word after all. So the first-person use is not independent of the third-person use. Similarly, Wittgenstein thinks, the third-person use is intimately tied to the person's first-person uses of sensation words. A word that was applied to others on the basis of their behaviour, but which people could not apply to themselves without reference to their behaviour, he suggests, would not be a word for a mental phenomenon at all. He makes the point in connection with the concept of thought:

> One might distinguish between two chimpanzees with respect to the way in which they work, and say of the one that he is thinking and of the other that he is not.
>
>   But here of course we wouldn't have the complete employment of 'think'. The word would have reference to a mode of behaviour. Not until it finds its particular use in the first-person does it acquire the meaning of mental activity.
>
> (RPP ii: 229–30)

The same is true, he would say, of the word 'pain'.

Extending the account beyond the case of pain. Wittgenstein's description of the way in which the word 'pain' is 'tied up with' our pre-linguistic expressive and sympathetic behaviour is an account of a single mental concept. How would he go on from the case of pain to an account of other sensation words? And what about words for mental phenomena other than sensations?

Pain provides a particularly good case for Wittgenstein's approach. It is extremely plausible that there is a pattern of pre-linguistic expressive behaviour that distinguishes pain from other sensations; the behavioural expression of pain is distinctive, and different from the behavioural expressions of other sensations. And it is at least arguable that there is a distinctive way in which a pre-linguistic infant reacts to another person's pains: that the child's pre-linguistic response to another's expressions of pain is different from her responses to expressions of other sensations. But even in the case of pain, it is not plausible that each type of pain that we distinguish in language has its own distinctive pattern of pre-linguistic behaviour. We classify pains as shooting, pricking, stabbing, throbbing, gnawing, stinging, dull, and so on. But it is hard to believe that each of those types of pain is associated with a unique pattern of pre-linguistic expressive behaviour. And beyond the case of pain, there are very few kinds of sensation that are uniquely identified by a distinctive pre-linguistic behavioural expression. There are even fewer kinds of sensation for which there is a distinctive pattern of pre-linguistic reactions to other people's sensations. So there are few if any cases in which the idea that words for sensations are a taught addition to our natural, pre-linguistic reactions can be developed in exactly the way Wittgenstein develops it for the case of 'pain'. But Wittgenstein would not regard that as an objection to his account. His aim in discussing the use of the word 'pain', he would say, is not to formulate a general theory of sensation language that is appropriate for every sensation word. He is simply trying to give an accurate account of the functioning of the particular word 'pain'. Accounts of words for other sensations will need to respect the same fundamental principles: they must not represent the meanings of sensation words as dependent on internal ostensive definitions; they must recognize that the identity conditions of sensations are not purely introspective but are linked to behaviour and external circumstances; they must account for the different but interrelated uses of sensation words in the first-person and third-person cases; they must not represent our grasp of the concept of others' sensations as involving an extrapolation from a purely introspective grasp of the concept of our own sensations. But within that general framework, there is room for significant differences between the accounts we give of words for different kinds of sensation.

So, for example, Wittgenstein acknowledges that there are many kinds of experience for which there is no uniquely identifying pattern of pre-linguistic behaviour. In these cases, he thinks, the most basic expression of an experience will be a linguistic expression. Like pain, the experience will be individuated in a way that links it to external circumstances and to the subject's behaviour. But the relevant behaviour will, from the outset, include linguistic behaviour. For example, 'What does it mean to say that I *"see the sphere floating in the air"* in a picture?', Wittgenstein asks. He writes:

> What is an expression for my not merely understanding the picture in this way, for instance (knowing what it is *supposed* to represent), but *seeing* it in this way? – It is expressed by, say, 'The sphere seems to float', 'One sees it floating', or perhaps, in a special tone of voice, 'It floats!'
>
> (PPF §169 [PI II xi p. 201])

There need be no natural, pre-linguistic expression of the experience of seeing the sphere floating in the air in the picture. The most basic expression of that experience, Wittgenstein thinks, may be a linguistic expression. And in that case, he thinks, we can only have the experience if we have a language in which to express it. (That contrasts with the case of pain; for a person can evidently experience pain without having a language at all.) And the same goes in many other cases. There are many kinds of experience, he thinks, for which: 'Only of someone who *can do*, has learnt, is master of, such-and-such, does it make sense to say that he has had *this* experience' (PPF §224 [PI II xi p. 209]). When you look at a triangle, for example, you cannot have the experience of seeing 'now *this* as apex, *that* as base – now *this* as apex, *that* as base' if you have 'only just met the concepts of apex, base, and so on' (PPF §222 [PI II xi p. 208]). One consequence of Wittgenstein's view is that our acquisition of a language for describing and expressing our experiences extends the range of experiences we are capable of having. And that is a plausible idea. It is very plausible, for example, that the budding wine connoisseur's acquisition of a sophisticated vocabulary for describing the tastes of different wines goes hand in hand with her coming to experience wines in richer, more complex ways. It is not that she learns to describe more accurately the experiences that she already had; rather, she comes to have different experiences.

The main themes of Wittgenstein's account of experience are equally important in his account of mental phenomena other than experiences. That comes out clearly, for example, in his account of belief. He asks:

> How did people ever come to use such an expression as 'I believe . . .'?
> Did they at some time notice a phenomenon (of believing)?
> Did they observe themselves and others, and so discover believing?
> (PPF §86 [PI II x p. 190])

The concept of belief, Wittgenstein thinks, is plainly not acquired by observing ourselves and other people and discovering a phenomenon of believing. Rather, he thinks, the phrase 'I believe' is acquired as an addition to a pre-existing pattern of behaviour that is expressive of belief. In the first instance, a child learns to say things about the world: 'That's red', 'There's a robin', and so on. In making those judgements, she is talking about the world, not about her beliefs. But she is at the same time expressing her beliefs; when she judges 'There's a robin', say, she expresses the belief that there is a robin nearby. Once she has mastered the practice of making judgements about the world, we then teach her to use the phrase 'I believe p' in circumstances where she is already prepared to judge 'p'. That gives her a way of moving from judgements that *express* her beliefs to judgements *about* her beliefs. Wittgenstein's idea is that the expression 'I believe' is a taught addition to a more basic use of language that already expresses our beliefs – just as our use of the expression 'I'm in pain' is a taught addition to our natural, pre-linguistic expressions of pain. And, as in the case of pain, Wittgenstein is making two kinds of point: one about concept-acquisition, the other about epistemology. An important part of acquiring the concept of believing that p is learning to apply the concept to oneself in circumstances where one does believe that p, and Wittgenstein's proposal shows how we can do that without depending on introspection or internal ostensive definition. A further point concerns epistemology. We normally know what we believe immediately and unthinkingly; we ascribe beliefs to ourselves without needing to consult any introspective or behavioural evidence about what we believe. The idea that mastering the expression 'I believe' involves learning to prefix it to judgements about the world that we are already prepared to make helps to explain that immediacy of our self-ascriptions of belief.

The same general features appear in Wittgenstein's remarks about the concept of intention. There are, he thinks, natural, pre-linguistic expressions of intention. Our use of language to ascribe intentions to ourselves is grafted onto that pre-linguistic basis. 'What is the natural expression of an intention?', he asks. 'Look at a cat when it stalks a bird; or a beast when it wants to escape' (PI §647). In the same way, the pre-linguistic child exhibits natural expressions of intention: she tries to reach a toy, she prepares to throw a ball, and so on. And an important stage in acquiring the concept of intention, Wittgenstein thinks, is learning to supplement or replace these natural expressions of intention with verbal expressions: 'I'm going to Φ', 'I'm about to Φ', 'I intend to Φ'. As before, the idea is to show how we can acquire the concept of intention without depending on any supposed introspective identification of an inner state of intention; and to show how we can ascribe intentions to ourselves without depending on a process of self-observation, or on any inference from our own circumstances or behaviour.

Wittgenstein's comments about belief and intention show some of the ways in which he adapts and extends the central elements of his account of sensations in giving accounts of mental phenomena of other kinds. The same basic principles run throughout his extensive writings on philosophy of mind and psychology.

2. THEMES IN THE PHILOSOPHY OF PSYCHOLOGY

Wittgenstein's discussion of sensations and sensation language has received more attention than any other aspect of his exploration of mental phenomena. But in the period 1946–49 he wrote extensively about many topics other than sensation: thinking, intention, belief, imagination and mental images, perception and perceptual experience, memory, the emotions, bodily awareness, and more. Those writings, from which Wittgenstein made the selection that makes up *Philosophy of Psychology – A Fragment* (in earlier editions, *Philosophical Investigations* Part II), are published in *Remarks on the Philosophy of Psychology* volumes I and II and in *Last Writings on the Philosophy of Psychology* volume I. He dealt with the same topics in his final lectures in Cambridge, in 1946–67. It is impossible to summarize all that work here. But we can illustrate some important themes by exploring Wittgenstein's responses to the works of two writers who were influential in early-twentieth-century psychology and philosophy: William James and Wolfgang Köhler. Unusually for him, Wittgenstein's writings and lectures contain explicit as well as implicit references to both authors. As his student A. C. Jackson reported, 'Wittgenstein very frequently referred to James in his [1946–47] lectures, even making on one occasion – to everyone's astonishment – a precise reference to a page number!' (quoted in Passmore 1966: 434).

i. Wittgenstein and William James

In 'The Stream of Thought', chapter 9 of his *Principles of Psychology* (James 1890), James sets out to describe some basic features of our inner, conscious life. A principal aim is to correct the view of consciousness contained in the theory of ideas of Locke and Hume. On that view, according to James, we are only ever conscious of objects and sensations; and all mental content is made up from 'images . . . of perfectly definite things' (James 1890: 246). But that, he argues, radically misrepresents the actual character of our conscious lives. For one thing, we are consciously aware not only of objects and their perceptible qualities but also of the relations between objects; *feelings of relation*, he thinks, are a crucial ingredient in the stream of thought. For example:

> We ought to say a feeling of *and*, a feeling of *if*, a feeling of *but*, and a feeling of *by*, quite as readily as we say a feeling of *blue* or a feeling of *cold*. Yet we do not: so inveterate has our habit become of recognizing the existence of the substantive parts alone, that language almost refuses to lend itself to any other use.
>
> (James 1890: 238)

And as well as these feelings of relation, James thinks, there are feelings of tendency. For example, there is a distinctive conscious state of intending to say the particular thing one is about to say:

> has the reader never asked himself what kind of a mental fact is his *intention of saying a thing* before he has said it? It is an entirely definite intention, distinct from all other intentions, an absolutely distinct state of consciousness, therefore; and yet how much of it consists of definite sensorial images, either of words or of things? Hardly anything! . . . It has therefore a nature of its own of the most positive sort, and yet what can we say about it without using words that belong to the later mental facts that replace it? The intention *to-say-so-and-so* is the only name it can receive.
>
> (James 1890: 245)

James's idea is that there is a distinct conscious experience of intending to utter a particular sentence; the intention to utter any other sentence would involve a different experience. And he offers another example of such 'feelings of tendency': the feeling one has, when searching for a word, of the word's being on the tip of one's tongue.

> Suppose we try to recall a forgotten name. The state of our consciousness is peculiar. There is a gap therein: but no mere gap. It is a gap that is intensely active. A sort of wraith of the name is in it, beckoning us in a given direction, making us at moments tingle with the sense of our closeness, and then letting us sink back without the longed-for term. If wrong names are proposed to us, this singularly definite gap acts immediately so as to negate them. They do not fit into its mould. And the gap of one word does not feel like the gap of another, all empty of content as both might seem necessary to be when described as gaps. When I vainly try to recall the name of

Spalding, my consciousness is far removed from what it is when I
vainly try to recall the name of Bowles.

(James 1890: 243)

Wittgenstein agrees with James in rejecting the idea that consciousness is entirely composed of a succession of sensations and mental
images; the content of experience, he thinks, is much richer and more
varied than that. But, he thinks, James goes too far in the opposite
direction, by treating as features of conscious experience phenomena
that are not experiential at all. He makes that point in connection with
James's discussions of both the examples just mentioned: feelings of
relation and feelings of tendency.

Wittgenstein raises a number of objections to James's idea that we
have feelings of *and*, *if*, *but*, and so on. First, even if there are feelings
associated with the use of the word 'if', he thinks, it is implausible that
there is some one particular feeling that we have whenever we use the
word:

Are you sure that there is a single if-feeling, and not perhaps several?
Have you tried saying the word in a great variety of contexts? For
example, when it bears the principal stress of the sentence, and when
the following word does.

(PPF §39 [PI II vi pp. 181–2])

Second, whether someone understands the word 'if' is a matter of
the use he makes of it, not a matter of the way the word feels to him:

Suppose we found a man who, speaking of how words felt to him, told
us that 'if' and 'but' felt the *same*. – May we not believe him? We might
think it strange. 'He doesn't play our game at all', one would like to
say. Or even: 'This is a different kind of human being.'
   If he *used* the words 'if' and 'but' as we do, wouldn't we think he
understood them as we do?

(PPF §40 [PI II vi p. 182])

Third, insofar as we really do have feelings of a particular sort in
connection with the word 'if', they are not something that we experience *whenever* we use the word. Rather, they arise only when we deliber-
ately focus on the feelings we have in using words and 'play the game'

of 'feeling the meaning of a word'. But the fact that we have such feelings in that context does not show that we have the same feelings in our ordinary everyday use of words; in fact, Wittgenstein suggests, we do not:

> If careful attention shows me that when I am playing this game I experience the word now *this* way, now *that* way – doesn't it also show me that in the stream of speech I often don't experience the word *at all*?
>
> (PPF §272 [PI II xi pp. 215–16])

What should we make of these criticisms of James? Each of Wittgenstein's points is entirely persuasive against its intended target. It is not clear, however, that James himself actually holds all of the views that Wittgenstein is attacking. For example, James does not argue that the presence of an if-feeling is a necessary and/or sufficient condition for the meaningful use of the word 'if'. Nor would he object to the suggestion that there is no single if-feeling. He explicitly rejects the assumption that the same grass always gives us the same feeling of green, the same sky the same feeling of blue, and so on (James 1890: 225–7); one would expect him equally to reject the assumption that the same relation always gives us the same feeling of relation. But the third of Wittgenstein's objections – the claim that we experience if-feelings only in contexts where we are actively looking for them – certainly does contrast sharply with James's view. For James holds that such feelings of relation are a ubiquitous element in our conscious awareness. If Wittgenstein is right, as is very plausible, then James misrepresents the character of our conscious life by populating it with myriad experiences that we do not actually have.

Wittgenstein also argues that James misrepresents the nature of the phenomena that he discusses in connection with 'feelings of tendency'. James's treatment of the intention to say something, Wittgenstein thinks, wrongly 'treats the intention like an experience' (LW i: 843). According to James, 'even before we have opened our mouths to speak, the entire thought is present to our mind in the form of an intention to utter that sentence' (James 1890: 269). With that passage, perhaps, in mind, Wittgenstein reports James as holding that 'the thought is already complete at the beginning of the sentence' (RPP i: 173). He offers a diagnosis of the motivation for that view:

Interrupt a man in quite unpremeditated and fluent talk. Then ask
him what he was going to say; and in many cases he will be able to
continue the sentence he had begun. – 'For that, what he was going to
say must already have swum into view before his mind.' – Is not that
phenomenon perhaps the ground of our saying that the continuation
had swum into his mental view?

(Z: 38)

James's view is that what someone is going to say precisely does 'swim
into his mental view' before he says it. What motivates that view, Wittgenstein suggests, is the idea that it explains something that would
otherwise be hard to understand: the speaker's ability, when interrupted, to continue the sentence he had started. For (the idea goes)
if the sentence has already run through his mind before he starts to
speak, that explains why it is so easy for him to continue the sentence
after interruption. Wittgenstein has three objections to that view.

In the first place, it simply falsifies what actually happens in such
cases. When I remember what I was going to say, I do not normally do
so by recalling a conscious decision to say it, or a conscious rehearsal
of the words I was going to use; for in most cases, there was no such
decision or rehearsal. Nor do I recall any other conscious process that
went on in me at the time, and from which I can subsequently read off
what I was going to say. Nor do I work out what I was going to say by
interpreting the thoughts and actions I had at the time, or the situation
I was in. I simply remember what I was going to say, without recalling
any experiences and without inferring it from anything else (see PI
§§633–7). In Wittgenstein's view, then, there is no basis in experience
for James's claim that the whole sentence someone is going to utter
comes before her mind before she says it.

Wittgenstein's second objection is that James makes a fundamental
error in treating the intention to say something as a kind of *experience*.
James thinks that, even if my state of consciousness before speaking
does not *explicitly* contain the sentence I am about to utter, it somehow *implicitly* contains it; it is, in James's words, 'an absolutely distinct
state of consciousness', specific to the particular sentence I intend to
utter. Or, as Wittgenstein puts the view, 'everything [I go on to say]
was already there from the beginning and was contained in the initial experience' (LW i: 843). So when I go on to report what I had
intended to say, I am simply articulating what was already there in my

experience. Wittgenstein allows that there might be experiences that are characteristic of intending to say something. But, he thinks, it is a mistake to think that, even though the words I intended to utter were not explicitly represented in the experience I had at the time, they were somehow built into the nature of that experience from the outset. It is a mistake to represent the experience I had at the time as a kind of 'logical germ' (LW i: 843) of the intended words: something that 'cannot grow into anything but' the particular set of words I go on to utter. There is, he thinks, no such thing as an experience that can only grow into one particular set of words. The idea of such a thing – like the idea of a picture that can be a representation of only one thing, or the idea of an interpretation that can be taken in only one way – is a philosophers' illusion.

Third, Wittgenstein argues that James's theory is unnecessary; we do not need to appeal to any conscious anticipatory experience in order to understand a person's ability to report what she was about to say when she was interrupted. We often do know what we were going to say in such a case. But that knowledge is primitive; it is not grounded in something else that is consciously present to one's mind. That point is another instance of Wittgenstein's anti-intellectualism. And it echoes a fundamental point in his discussion of rule-following: his insistence that our knowledge of how to continue a mathematical series, or how to go on using a descriptive word, is basic or primitive – that it is not grounded in anything that comes before the mind of the rule-follower.

ii. Wittgenstein and Köhler: seeing an aspect

Philosophy of Psychology – A Fragment, section xi, contains an extensive discussion of the phenomenon that Wittgenstein calls *seeing an aspect*. He introduces the idea like this:

Two uses of the word 'see'.

The one: 'What do you see there?' – 'I see *this*' (and then a description, a drawing, a copy). The other: 'I see a likeness in these two faces' – let the man to whom I tell this be seeing the faces as clearly as I do myself.

What is important is the categorial difference between the two 'objects' of sight.

[. . .]

> I observe a face, and then suddenly notice its likeness to another. I *see* that it has not changed; and yet I see it differently. I call this experience 'noticing an aspect'.
>
> (PPF §§111, 113 [PI II xi p. 193])

Wittgenstein goes on to discuss a range of different cases of noticing, or seeing, an aspect. For example, there is the famous duck-rabbit figure (PPF §118 [PI II xi p. 194]) shown in Figure 6.1.

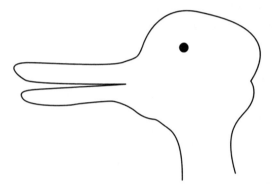

Figure 6.1

We can see the figure as a picture-duck or as a picture-rabbit; and we can experience a sudden shift from one aspect to the other. Another of Wittgenstein's examples is shown in Figure 6.2, which can be seen in numerous different ways: as a glass cube, as an upturned open box, as a wire frame of that shape, as three boards forming a solid angle, and so on (PPF §116 [PI II xi p. 193]). Wittgenstein discusses a wide variety of other cases.

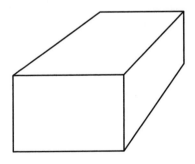

Figure 6.2

In the background of Wittgenstein's discussion are two opposing models of visual experience: models associated with competing traditions in philosophy and psychology. On the one hand, there is the Introspectionist view championed by Wilhelm Wundt and his followers. On the other hand, there is the Gestalt Psychology developed in opposition to Introspectionism by Max Wertheimer, Wolfgang Köhler, and others. For the Introspectionist, visual experience presents us with no more than a mosaic of shapes and colours. When I see a tree, for instance, it does not, strictly speaking, look to me as if there is a tree in front of me. What I really *experience* is just a pattern of shapes and colours. I then *judge*, on the basis of that experience, that there is a tree in front of me, because I know from past experience that visual experiences of this kind are normally caused by trees. Similarly, for the Introspectionist, the difference between 'seeing the duck-rabbit figure as a duck' and 'seeing it as a rabbit' is not strictly speaking an experiential difference. The experience I have is the same in each case; the difference between the two cases lies in the way I *take* or *interpret* the experience. So, though we ordinarily *say* that we see the duck-rabbit as a duck, and so on, that is just a *façon de parler* – a figure of speech. The phenomenon we call 'seeing an aspect' is not, properly speaking, an *experiential* phenomenon at all.

The Gestalt psychologists take the opposite view. The difference between seeing the duck-rabbit as a duck and seeing it as a rabbit, they think, involves a genuinely *sensory* difference. The visual field is intrinsically 'organized' or 'arranged'; we are presented in visual experience not with a mere mosaic of shapes and colours but with a field in which 'the contents of particular areas "belong together" as circumscribed units'. And 'this *organization* of the field', Köhler insists, 'is a sensory fact' (Köhler 1947: 137). Physical objects, for example, are *seen* as units, distinct from their surroundings. And collections of items are *seen* as grouped in particular ways. In Figure 6.3, for example, we *see* the patches as two groups of three patches, not as three groups of two patches (Köhler 1947: 142). And similarly, according to Köhler, the *change* in the organization of the visual field that occurs when we shift from seeing one aspect to seeing another is a genuine change in our experience: 'an actual transformation of given sensory facts into others' (Köhler 1947: 169).

Wittgenstein rejects both these theories of experience. In the first place, he thinks, there are clear objections to the specific claims that

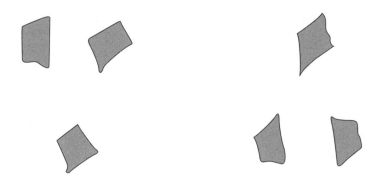

Figure 6.3

each theory makes about experience. In the second place, and more fundamentally, the two theories share a set of common assumptions about the nature of experience which, he argues, are mistaken.

Against the Introspectionist, Wittgenstein's argument is simple. There are some cases, he thinks, where we really do see a picture and *interpret* it in this or that way. And there are some cases where we really do know that something is a picture of such-and-such without being able to *see* it in that way. For example: 'When should I call it just knowing, not seeing? – Perhaps when someone treats the picture as a working drawing, *reads* it like a blueprint' (PPF §192 [PI II xi p. 204]; see also PPF §169, quoted above in section 1.v of this chapter). But it is evident that not every case is like that. 'To interpret', he says, 'is to think, to do something. [And] it is easy to recognize those cases in which we are *interpreting*. When we interpret we form hypotheses, which may prove false' (PPF §§248–9 [PI II xi p. 212]). But when I see the duck-rabbit figure as duck, say, I am plainly not engaged in any activity of interpreting. And it is plainly not a *hypothesis* that the figure is a representation of a duck; that it represents a duck is an immediately experienced feature of the figure. When we reflect on the cases in which someone really does see something and *take* it, or *interpret* it, as this or that, it is obvious that that is not what happens in every case. The Introspectionist, Wittgenstein thinks, makes the mistake of taking something that really does happen in some cases and treating it as a feature of every case.

Against the Gestalt theorist, Wittgenstein argues that organization and other aspect-properties are not, and could not be, built into the character of experience in the same way as shape and colour. He starts with an example:

> I suddenly see the solution of a puzzle-picture. Where there were
> previously branches, now there is a human figure. My visual
> impression has changed, and now I recognize that it has not only
> shape and colour, but also a quite particular 'organization'.
>
> (PPF §131 [PI II xi p. 196])

That is the Gestalt theorist's idea; when I suddenly see the human figure in the picture, I have a new visual experience; and the difference
consists in the fact that my visual impression is organized in a new way.
But Wittgenstein immediately questions that idea:

> My visual impression has changed – what was it like before; what is it
> like now? – If I represent it by means of an exact copy – and isn't that a
> good representation of it? – no change shows up.
>   And above all do not say 'Surely my visual impression isn't the
> *drawing*; it is *this* – which I can't show to anyone.' – Of course it is not
> the drawing, but neither is it something of the same category, which I
> carry within myself.
>   [. . .]
>   Someone who puts the 'organization' of a visual impression on a
> level with colours and shapes, would be taking it for granted that the
> visual impression is an inner object. Of course, this makes this object
> chimerical; a strangely vacillating entity. For the similarity to the
> picture is now impaired.
>
> (PPF §§131–4 [PI II xi p. 196])

According to the Gestalt theorist, seeing the solution to a puzzle-picture involves a change in sensory organization: a change in my visual
impression, as Wittgenstein puts it. But what is a visual impression;
and how does it change? If a visual impression really is like a picture,
then there will be no change in my visual impression when I see the
solution to the puzzle-picture. After all, the external picture does not
change when I see the picture differently; so if the visual impression is
simply an internal copy of the external picture, there will be no change
in the visual impression either. So the Gestalt theorist must think of the
visual impression as something that is radically different from an ordinary picture. An ordinary picture can be seen in different ways; it is
not intrinsically a picture of one thing rather than another. But, on the
Gestalt theorist's view, a visual impression is different; it is intrinsically

organized in one way rather than the other. That is why the fact that I have this visual impression rather than that one explains the picture's being seen in this way rather than that. But against that view, Wittgenstein objects that there is no such thing as a picture, or 'anything of the same category as a picture', that is intrinsically organized in one way rather than another. The idea of such a thing is a myth: an artefact of a bad way of thinking of experience. (Once more, Wittgenstein's point echoes his argument against the idea of an interpretation that is not susceptible of being interpreted in different ways.)

There is an obvious sense in which the Introspectionist theory of experience and the Gestalt theory are diametrically opposed to one another. But Wittgenstein thinks the two theories are importantly similar. For they share two crucial assumptions. The first assumption is that the phenomenon of seeing an aspect must fall into one or other of two categories: it must be either an experiential phenomenon or a cognitive phenomenon. The second, and related, assumption is that there is in every case a determinate fact of the matter as to which features of any given phenomenon are experiential features. Wittgenstein rejects both assumptions.

Consider the following case:

> I meet someone whom I have not seen for years; I see him clearly, but fail to recognize him. Suddenly I recognize him, I see his former face in the altered one. I believe that I would portray him differently now if I could paint.
>
> Now, when I recognize my acquaintance in a crowd, perhaps after looking in his direction for quite a while – is this a special sort of seeing? Is it a case of both seeing and thinking? Or a fusion of the two, as I would almost like to say?
>
> The question is: *why* does one want to say this?
>
> (PPF §§ 143–4 [PI II xi p. 197])

Suddenly recognizing someone, Wittgenstein thinks, is not 'a special sort of seeing'; for when I suddenly recognize my friend in the crowd, I do not see a new property of his face that I had not seen before. Nor is it a case of 'both seeing and thinking', for there are not two separate processes: first seeing him and then thinking that I know him; on the contrary, the recognition seems to permeate the experience. So, Wittgenstein thinks, it is tempting to conclude that suddenly recognizing someone is 'a fusion' of seeing and thinking. But he does not draw that tempting conclusion. Instead, he asks what makes the conclusion so tempting. What makes it tempting, he thinks, is the assumption that there are just two basic kinds of mental phenomena: experience and thought. All other mental phenomena, we think, must be accounted for in the framework of that dichotomy. Now the case of suddenly recognizing someone does not fit easily into this framework: it is not a case of seeing; nor is it a case of thinking; nor is it a case of both seeing and thinking. If we accept the initial assumption, that leaves us no option but to conceive of recognition as a 'fusion' in which the faculties of seeing and thinking are somehow fused into one. But, characteristically, Wittgenstein rejects that view; for he rejects the initial assumption that every mental phenomenon must be accounted for in terms of the dichotomy between experience and thought. Suddenly recognizing someone, he insists, is a phenomenon in its own right. It has interesting similarities to, and differences from, other phenomena, including the phenomenon of seeing and the phenomenon of thinking. But that does not mean that it must *really* be either a kind of seeing, or a kind of thinking, or else some kind of combination of the two. And the same goes for the other cases of seeing an aspect. 'There is', Wittgenstein says, 'an enormous number of interrelated phenomena and possible concepts' (PPF §155 [PI II xi p. 199]). To insist on describing everything in terms of a simple dichotomy between seeing and thinking is to oversimplify and distort the phenomena. That, in Wittgenstein's view, is a basic failing of both Introspectionism and the Gestalt theory.

The debate between the Introspectionist and the Gestalt theorist repeatedly comes back to the question: do we really *see* a thing differently when we notice a new aspect; is the *visual experience* different? Both sides take it for granted that, in every case, that question has a definite yes or no answer. But, as before, Wittgenstein rejects that shared assumption. There is, he thinks, no single, complete way of characterizing an experience, which captures what is really experienced on any occasion. He writes: 'What is the criterion of the visual experience? What should the criterion be? A representation of "what is seen" ' (PPF §146 [PI II xi p. 198]). That is to say, whether or not something is part of my experience is a matter of whether or not it figures in the way I represent what I see. And, he continues: 'The concept of a representation of what is seen, like that of a copy, is very elastic, and so *together* with it is the concept of what is seen' (PPF §147 [PI II xi p. 198]). In

Wittgenstein's view, we should reject the idea that there is some one, definite answer to the question, exactly what is and what is not part of someone's experience on any given occasion. Suppose I suddenly recognize a face. I describe the face differently: to that extent, Wittgenstein thinks, I experience it differently. But I can equally report that the face looks exactly the same as it did before: to that extent, my experience is unchanged. Both reports, Wittgenstein thinks, are true. They go hand in hand with different notions of what is seen or experienced. And it is a mistake to think that just one of those reports captures what is *really* seen or experienced; the two reports are equally accurate and equally legitimate.

SUMMARY

The topic of sensations and sensation language was one of the first that Wittgenstein discussed when he returned to philosophy in 1929. At that stage, he proposed a view on which each person, in effect, has two sensation languages: a purely private language, based on introspection, for talking about her own sensations; and a shared, public language, based on behaviour, for talking about other people's sensations. He soon abandoned that view.

The celebrated private language argument of *Philosophical Investigations* is one element in a sustained critique of the 'Cartesian' view of sensations. On the Cartesian view, the identity conditions of sensations are purely introspective: sensations are individuated in a way that is entirely independent of any links to external circumstances or behaviour. Sensation words get their meanings by introspective attachment to one's own sensations; so each person knows what 'pain' means only from her own case. And, while each of us knows the character of our own sensations, no one can know the character of anyone else's. Against the Cartesian view, Wittgenstein argues that it is impossible to give meaning to a sensation word by pure introspection without relying in any way on links to external circumstances or behaviour. For it is impossible, he thinks, for the putative private linguist to establish a genuine standard of correctness for applications of her words. Standards of correctness are not laid down by reality; they are dependent on human practices of classification. And the private linguist lacks the resources to establish a genuine practice of classifying her private sensations. Wittgenstein argues, too, against the Cartesian claim that our understanding of ascriptions of sensation to other people involves an extrapolation from a purely introspective, first-personal conception of sensation. He also rejects the Cartesian view that no one can know the nature of anyone else's sensations.

The starting point of Wittgenstein's positive account of sensation language is the idea that our use of sensation words is a development and extension of our natural, pre-linguistic behaviour. That explains the meanings of sensation words in a way that does not make them dependent on inner ostensive definitions, and that sees the third-person use of sensation words as being just as fundamental as their first-person use. The same general principles inform Wittgenstein's account of our concepts of belief, intention, and so on.

Wittgenstein's extensive late writings on philosophy of psychology, from the period 1946–49, include important discussions of James and Köhler. Wittgenstein criticizes James's view that there are 'feelings of relation' – feelings of 'and', 'if', 'but', and so on. He also argues against James's account of the intention to say a specific thing, which treats it as a 'feeling of tendency'. Wittgenstein's treatment of Köhler's Gestalt Psychology is part of a wider discussion of the phenomenon of seeing an aspect: seeing the likeness between two faces, for instance, or seeing an ambiguous figure in one way rather than another. He argues against both the Introspectionist and the Gestalt theorist's accounts of that phenomenon. Seeing an aspect, he thinks, is a *sui generis* mental phenomenon: it has important relations to experience and to thought; but we should resist the temptation to analyse aspect-perception in terms of those other concepts.

FURTHER READING

Wittgenstein's 1929–30 account of sensation language can be found in:

Philosophical Remarks, pp. 88–9.
Ludwig Wittgenstein and the Vienna Circle: Conversations recorded by Friedrich Waismann, pp. 49–50.

There is a complex but rewarding discussion of this material in:

Pears, D. (1988) *The False Prison: A Study of the Development of Wittgenstein's Philosophy*, vol. 2, Oxford: Oxford University Press, ch. 12.

For a different perspective, see:

Stern, D. (2010) 'Another Strand in the Private Language Argument', in A. Ahmed (ed.) *Wittgenstein's Philosophical Investigations: A Critical Guide*, Cambridge: Cambridge University Press.

For Wittgenstein's later discussion of sensations and sensation language, including his argument against the possibility of a purely introspective, private sensation language ('the private language argument'), see:

Philosophical Investigations §§243–315.

There are illuminating remarks about our grasp of the concept of others' pain in: *Zettel* §§532–65.

There is a vast secondary literature on the private language argument. The following are good places to start:

Budd, M. (1989) *Wittgenstein's Philosophy of Psychology*, London: Routledge, ch. 3.
McGinn, M. (1997) *Wittgenstein and the* Philosophical Investigations, London: Routledge, ch. 4.
Stern, D. (2004) *Wittgenstein's* Philosophical Investigations: *An Introduction*, Cambridge: Cambridge University Press, ch. 7.
Stroud, B. (2001) 'Private Objects, Physical Objects, and Ostension', in D. Charles and W. Child (eds) *Wittgensteinian Themes: Essays in Honour of David Pears*, Oxford: Oxford University Press; also available in Stroud, B. (2000) *Meaning, Understanding, and Practice*, Oxford: Oxford University Press.

Those discussions are all broadly sympathetic to Wittgenstein's position. For a more sceptical treatment, see:

Blackburn, S. (1984) *Spreading the Word: Groundings in the Philosophy of Language*, Oxford: Oxford University Press, ch. 3 sections 4–5.

A recent book-length discussion of the private language passages in *Philosophical Investigations*, which emphasizes the dialogic and therapeutic form of the text, is:

Mulhall, S. (2007) *Wittgenstein's Private Language: Grammar, Nonsense, and Imagination in* Philosophical Investigations §§243–315, Oxford: Oxford University Press.

For a clear and helpful interpretation of Wittgenstein's discussion of the conceptual problem of other minds, see:

Kripke, S. (1982) *Wittgenstein on Rules and Private Language*, Oxford: Blackwell, Postscript on 'Wittgenstein and Other Minds'.

And for a discussion of Wittgenstein's use of the notion of expression in philosophy of mind, see:

Finkelstein, D. (2003) *Expression and the Inner*, Cambridge, MA: Harvard University Press.

The works by William James and Wolfgang Köhler discussed in this chapter are:

James, W. (1890) *The Principles of Psychology*, Cambridge, MA: Harvard University Press, 1983; see especially ch. 9, 'The Stream of Thought'.
Köhler, W. (1947) *Gestalt Psychology*, New York: Liveright Publishing Company.

Wittgenstein's discussions of James are scattered throughout his later writings on philosophy of psychology. But there are remarks on the topics discussed in this chapter in:

Philosophical Investigations §§633–93.
Philosophy of Psychology – A Fragment §§35–51, 298–300 [PI II vi, II xi p. 219].

For Wittgenstein's discussion of aspect perception, Introspectionism and Gestalt psychology, see particularly:

Philosophy of Psychology – A Fragment, section xi [PI II xi].

There is a book-length study of Wittgenstein's discussion of James:

Goodman, R. (2002) *Wittgenstein and William James*, Cambridge: Cambridge University Press.

and there is a very helpful table of correspondences between passages in James's *Principles of Psychology* and passages in Wittgenstein in:

Coope, C. *et al.* (1971) *A Wittgenstein Workbook*, Oxford: Blackwell, p. 48.

Two good treatments of Wittgenstein's discussion of aspect perception are:

Budd, M. (1989) *Wittgenstein's Philosophy of Psychology*, London: Routledge, ch. 4.
Mulhall, S. (2001) 'Seeing Aspects', in H.-J. Glock (ed.) *Wittgenstein: A Critical Reader*, Oxford: Blackwell.

Seven

Knowledge and certainty

In the last 18 months of his life Wittgenstein lived with family and friends in Vienna, Oxford, and finally in Cambridge. He continued to write philosophical remarks in his notebooks, dealing mostly with three topics: knowledge and certainty; colour; and the philosophy of psychology. His writings on the first of these topics are published in the book *On Certainty*, more than half of which was composed in the six weeks before he died. As he wrote in a letter in April 1951:

> An extraordinary thing has happened to me. About a month ago I suddenly found myself in the right frame of mind for doing philosophy. I had been *absolutely* certain that I'd never again be able to do it. It's the first time after more than 2 years that the curtain in my brain has gone up.
>
> (Malcolm 1984: 134)

The remarks in *On Certainty* are taken unrevised from Wittgenstein's notebooks. So the book is even rougher and more programmatic than most of Wittgenstein's posthumously published work. But it is a rich source of observations and insights about knowledge, certainty, and justification.

On Certainty was stimulated by Wittgenstein's reflections on two papers by G. E. Moore, which Wittgenstein discussed extensively with his friend Norman Malcolm during a visit to the USA in 1949: 'Proof of an External World' (Moore 1939) and 'A Defence of Common Sense' (Moore 1925). But similar themes appear in earlier work, including Wittgenstein's 1937 notebooks (see CE) and *Philosophical Investigations* §§324–6 and §§466–86. So *On Certainty* is not a completely new turn in Wittgenstein's philosophy; it develops thoughts that are already visible in his previous writings.

1. MOORE'S 'PROOF OF AN EXTERNAL WORLD'

In his paper 'Proof of an External World', Moore offers the following proof of the existence of external objects (Moore 1939: 165–6):

1 Here is one hand (said as Moore holds up his hands and makes a gesture with the right hand).
2 Here is another hand (said as he makes a gesture with his left hand).

So:

3 Two human hands exist.

And since human hands are external objects, Moore says, it follows from the fact that two human hands exist that:

4 External objects exist.

Moore realizes that his proof will seem ineffective or question-begging. But, he contends, it is in fact 'a perfectly rigorous proof' (Moore 1939: 166). After all, Moore says, the premise of the proof ('Here is one hand and here is another hand') is different from the conclusion ('Two human hands exist' and hence 'External objects exist'). The premise is known to be true. And the conclusion follows from the premise. So the proof, he thinks, is perfectly adequate. To drive the point home, Moore reminds us that 'we all of us do constantly take proofs of this sort as absolutely conclusive proofs of certain conclusions' (Moore 1939: 167). For example, we accept that someone can prove that there are at least three misprints on a given page 'by taking the book, turning to the page, and pointing to three separate places on it, saying "There's one misprint here, another here, and another here"' (Moore 1939: 167).

Wittgenstein states a fundamental criticism of Moore's proof in the very first section of On Certainty:

> When one says that such and such a proposition can't be proved, of course that does not mean that it can't be derived from other propositions; any proposition can be derived from other ones. But they may be no more certain than it is itself.
>
> (OC: 1)

His point is this. It is true that Moore's conclusion – 'External objects exist' – can be derived from his premises – 'Here is one hand' and 'Here is another' (plus the further premise that human hands are external objects). The premises of Moore's argument do entail the conclusion. But for a proof that external objects exist to be philosophically satisfying, Wittgenstein objects, it is not enough that the premises of the argument entail its conclusion; the premises must also be more certain than the conclusion. And Moore's proof fails that further condition. For the proposition 'Here is one hand and here is another' is not more certain than the proposition that external objects exist. Indeed, it is if anything less certain that my two hands exist than that external objects exist in general; it would be much easier for the belief that I have two hands to be wrong than for the belief that there are external objects to be wrong. For Wittgenstein, a proof must be capable of giving one grounds for believing something that one does not already know; it must be capable of extending one's knowledge. Moore's proof cannot do that, for no one could be justified in believing the premise of the proof ('Here is one hand and here is another') without already knowing that the conclusion ('External objects exist') is true. If we were genuinely unsure whether there is an external world at all, we could not appeal to the existence of our own hands as a reason for thinking that there are external objects; for whatever reasons we had for doubting the existence of the external world would equally be reasons for doubting that we had two hands. So, Wittgenstein concludes, Moore's 'proof' of the existence of an external world is not a genuine proof at all.

Wittgenstein offers a second criticism of Moore's proof – that it is ineffective against the philosophical opponents Moore means to be arguing against: idealists, who deny that there is an external, mind-independent world at all; and sceptics, who hold that, even if there is an external world, we cannot know that there is. Moore starts from the claim that he has two hands: a claim which, he says, he knows to be true. But of course Moore's opponents will deny either that the premise is true or that Moore knows that it is. And we cannot argue against such opponents simply by restating the common-sense views that they reject. Even if Moore is right, and the idealist and the sceptic are wrong, an intellectually satisfying refutation of idealism and scepticism requires not just the *assertion* of something that Moore accepts and that his opponents reject, but a *diagnosis* of exactly where and how the idealist and the sceptic go wrong. Wittgenstein puts it like this:

If Moore is attacking those who say that one cannot really know such a thing, he can't do it by assuring them that *he* knows this and that. For one need not believe him . . . .

Moore's mistake lies in this – countering the assertion that one cannot know that, by saying 'I do know it'.

(OC: 520–1)

Similarly:

'I know' often means: I have the proper grounds for my statement. So if the other person is acquainted with the language-game, he would admit that I know . . . .

The statement 'I know that here is a hand' may then be continued: 'for it's *my* hand that I'm looking at'. Then a reasonable man will not doubt that I know. – Nor will the idealist; rather he will say that he was not dealing with the practical doubt which is being dismissed, but there is a further doubt *behind* that one. – That this is an *illusion* has to be shown in a different way.

(OC: 18–19)

Wittgenstein here contrasts two kinds of doubt that someone might have about the claim that I know that there is a hand here. There are 'practical' doubts: doubts that are internal to our ordinary talk about knowledge and justification; the kind of doubts we might have about such a claim in real life. And there are 'further' doubts: doubts that are external to our ordinary practice; the kind of doubts for which there is no provision in ordinary life. If someone rejects the claim 'I know that this is a hand' on *internal* grounds, she accepts the ordinary standards for knowing that there is a hand here; but she thinks I fail to meet those standards. (Perhaps I am surrounded by convincing waxworks and I cannot distinguish a waxwork hand from a real hand. Or perhaps it is too dark for me to tell whether the thing in front of me is a hand or not.) Someone who rejects the knowledge claim on *external* grounds, on the other hand, accepts that I meet the ordinary standards for knowledge; she allows that, judged by the ordinary standards, I do know that there is a hand here. But, she maintains, there are different, philosophical standards for knowledge; and, she insists, by these strict, philosophical standards I do not know that there is a hand here. Now Wittgenstein's point is that Moore's proof only ever addresses *internal* doubts about our knowledge of the external world. Moore reminds us that, when I say 'I know that there is a hand here', I have what we all ordinarily accept as proper grounds for my belief: I am looking at a hand in front of me; it is my hand; there is nothing unusual about the circumstances; and so on. So 'a reasonable man will not doubt' that, by the ordinary standards for knowledge, I do know that there is a hand here. But, Wittgenstein insists, Moore's point is completely ineffective against the philosopher who raises an *external* doubt about my claim to know. For such a philosopher allows that I meet the ordinary standards for knowledge – that I can rebut any 'practical' doubt about whether there is a hand here. He is raising a 'further' doubt about human knowledge – an external doubt. So our response to this sceptic must respond in some way to that external doubt.

The response Wittgenstein suggests in the passage quoted above (OC: 18–19) is that the sceptic's external doubt is 'an illusion'; we cannot make sense of the idea that, even when we have responded to all the ordinary reasons there might be for doubting whether there is a hand here, there remain further philosophical reasons for doubt. But even if that is right, it is just a first step. For, Wittgenstein thinks, if we are to deal satisfactorily with scepticism, we cannot just *assert* that the external philosophical doubt is illusory; we have to *show why* it is illusory. In this passage, Wittgenstein does not go on to that next step – of showing why the sceptic's external doubts about human knowledge make no sense. But the point he does make is certainly right. If someone raises an external doubt about the very possibility of having knowledge of the external world, it is not an effective response simply to show that, judged by our ordinary internal standards, we do know many things about the external world. We need in some way to engage with the external doubt, and to show why it need not trouble us.

2. MOOREAN PROPOSITIONS

In 'A Defence of Common Sense', Moore sets out to defend the common-sense view of the world against idealism and scepticism. At the start of the paper, he gives a 'list of truisms' which, he says, he 'know[s], with certainty, to be true' (Moore 1925: 107). He writes:

> There exists at present a living human body, which is *my* body. This body was born at a certain time in the past, and has existed continuously ever since . . . . Ever since it was born, it has been either in con-

tact with or not far from the surface of the earth; and, at every moment since it was born, there have also existed many other things, having shape and size in three dimensions . . . . Among the things which have . . . formed part of its environment . . . there have, at every moment since its birth, been large numbers of other human bodies . . .
[And] the earth had existed also for many years before my body was born . . . .

(Moore 1925: 107)

Wittgenstein agrees with Moore that the kinds of propositions Moore identifies have a special status. As Wittgenstein puts it, the propositions that the earth exists and has existed for many years, that I am a human being, that I have never been far from the surface of the earth, and so on, belong to the 'world-picture [which] is the substratum of all [our] enquiring and asserting' (OC: 162). And he lists a series of other propositions that have a similar status: 'For months I have lived at address A' (OC: 70), 'All human beings have parents' (OC: 240), 'Motor cars don't grow out of the earth' (OC: 279), 'My name is L.W.' (OC: 328), and more.

However, though Wittgenstein credits Moore with a real insight in drawing attention to this class of propositions, he thinks Moore has misidentified the significance of that class:

When Moore says he *knows* such and such, he is really enumerating a lot of empirical propositions which we affirm without special testing; propositions, that is, which have a peculiar logical role in the system of our empirical propositions.

The propositions, however, which Moore retails as examples of such known truths are indeed interesting. Not because anyone knows their truth, or believes he knows them, but because they all have a *similar* role in the system of our empirical propositions.

(OC: 136–7)

We can focus on two aspects of Wittgenstein's discussion of these 'Moorean propositions'. First, Wittgenstein suggests in On Certainty that Moore is wrong to think that we know the kinds of 'common-sense truisms' he lists. But why does he think that? And are his reasons good reasons? Second, Wittgenstein thinks that Moore in some way misunderstands the nature of the propositions he identifies. The Moorean propositions are important 'not because anyone knows their truth', but because they have 'a peculiar logical role in the system of our empirical propositions'. But what exactly is that 'peculiar logical role'?

Wittgenstein has at least two sorts of reason for thinking that it is wrong to say that I know that I have two hands, or that the earth existed for years before my birth, or that my name is William Child, and so on. In the first place, he thinks, if someone knows something there must be an answer to the question, 'How does she know?' (OC: 550, 484); it must be possible for her to give grounds for what she believes (OC: 243); she must be able to 'satisfy herself' (OC: 3) or 'make sure' (OC: 23) that her belief is true. But in the normal case, Wittgenstein thinks, we can give no grounds for believing the Moorean propositions. In his view, a ground for believing a proposition must be something that is more certain than the proposition itself (OC: 243), and in normal circumstances there is nothing we can cite as a reason for believing a Moorean proposition that is more certain than the proposition itself. For example:

> My having two hands is, in normal circumstances, as certain as anything that I could produce in evidence for it.
>   That is why I am not in a position to take the sight of my hand as evidence for it
>
> (OC: 250)

Or again:

> If a blind man were to ask me 'Have you got two hands?' I should not make sure by looking. For if I were to have any doubt of it, I don't know why I should trust my eyes.
>
> (OC: 125)

Similarly, my belief that I have never been on the moon, Wittgenstein thinks, is not based on evidence. For 'my not having been on the moon is as sure a thing for me as any grounds I could give for it' (OC: 111). Since, in Wittgenstein's view, knowing something essentially involves having grounds for believing it, it follows that we do not know such Moorean propositions as 'I have two hands' or 'I have never been to the moon'. And Wittgenstein's point is not that we fail to know them: that we are ignorant about whether we have two hands or have ever been to the moon. Rather, he thinks, our relation to the Moorean propositions should not be conceived in terms of knowledge or ignorance at all.

A second consideration is this. The proposition 'I know that p', Wittgenstein suggests, only makes sense in contexts where there is some point or purpose in asserting it. And there is only a point or purpose in saying 'I know that p' if, in the context of utterance, there is some doubt about whether p is true, or some doubt about one's warrant for believing that p. Consider the proposition 'I know that that's a tree'. There are, Wittgenstein thinks, some contexts in which that proposition makes perfectly good sense: there are, for instance, contexts where there is a genuine doubt about whether the thing in question is a tree. For example:

> I look at a plant that I take for a young beech and that someone else thinks is a blackcurrant. He says 'that's a shrub'; I say it is a tree. – We see something in the mist which one of us takes for a man, and the other says 'I know that that's a tree'.
>
> (OC: 349)

But suppose someone simply comes out with the proposition 'I know that that's a tree' in a context where it is perfectly obvious to everyone that the thing in question is a tree. In that case, Wittgenstein suggests, her utterance is not merely pointless; it is actually *meaningless* or *nonsensical*. Or again: imagine someone saying 'I know that a sick man is lying here' in a situation where she is sitting by his bed and looking attentively into his face (OC: 10). Moore would say that her utterance is true: she does know that a sick man is lying there. But Wittgenstein disagrees: in such a situation, he suggests, the utterance 'I know that there's a sick man lying here' is actually 'nonsense'.

So Wittgenstein gives two reasons for holding that, in normal circumstances, we do not *know* the Moorean propositions: we can give no grounds for believing them; and a claim to know them would be pointless or uninformative and hence, he thinks, nonsense. But he acknowledges that there are other circumstances in which we *can* truly be said to know such propositions. For example, suppose I have just come round from an operation in which my hands may have been amputated. In that context, there is a real doubt about whether I have two hands. Accordingly, I really can *find out* that I still have two hands; and I really can take the sight of my hands as *evidence* that I have two hands. In unusual circumstances like that, Wittgenstein thinks, it is right to say that I know I have two hands (OC: 23). Similarly, according to Wittgenstein, if I have been sitting at my desk all morning and circumstances are perfectly normal, it would be wrong or even meaningless to say that I know I am now sitting in a chair. But in other circumstances (when I am sitting in the ruins of my office just after an earthquake, for instance) I could truly be said to know that I am sitting in a chair (OC: 553): for in those circumstances, there would be such a thing as finding out that I was sitting in a chair. And the same is true, Wittgenstein suggests, for all of Moore's propositions. For each one of them, we can imagine circumstances in which it would be true to say that we knew them (OC: 622). But in normal circumstances, he insists, Moore's truisms are not 'known with certainty to be true'.

What should we make of that claim? The obvious response to Wittgenstein is to agree with the specific points he makes about the characteristics of Moorean propositions but to reject the conclusion that, in normal circumstances, we do not know them. Thus, we might think, Wittgenstein is right that in normal circumstances I do not have grounds for believing that I have two hands which are more certain than that belief itself. But that is no reason for saying that I do not know that I have two hands. It is plausible to think that I know that p if, roughly speaking, I believe that p, it is true that p, and it is no accident that my belief is true. And my belief that I have two hands certainly meets those conditions: I believe that I have two hands; my belief is true; and it is no accident that my belief is true. The same is true of my beliefs in the other Moorean propositions.

Similarly, we might think, Wittgenstein is right that in normal circumstances it would be pointless or uninformative for me to say that I know I have two hands. But he is wrong to think that that makes the proposition 'I know I have two hands' *senseless* in such a context. For whether there is any point in asserting a proposition is one thing; whether the proposition is meaningful is another. That objection depends on distinguishing a proposition's semantic features from the pragmatic features of asserting it. And, as we saw in Chapter 4 section 3, there is a strand in Wittgenstein's work that denies that distinction, by tying the meaning of a proposition in a context directly to the point or purpose of uttering it (that is one aspect of the idea that the meaning of a proposition is a matter of its use). So Wittgenstein's response to the objection might simply be to insist that the meaningfulness of an utterance of the proposition 'I know I have two hands' really does depend on its having a point or purpose. Interestingly, however, there are points at which he hints at a different view. For example:

> Do I know that I am now sitting in a chair? – Don't I know it?! In the present circumstances no one is going to say that I know this . . . But now, even if one doesn't say it, does that make it untrue??
>
> (OC: 552)

The suggestion in that passage is that I *do* know that I am now sitting in a chair, even if it would be pointless and uninformative for anyone to say that I know it. So perhaps Wittgenstein would in the end sympathize with the ordinary view that, in normal circumstances, I *do* know that I am sitting in a chair. And whatever Wittgenstein actually thought, it would certainly be open to him to accept the ordinary view while insisting, as he does, that we do not normally have grounds for believing the Moorean propositions, that we do not normally accept them on the basis of evidence, that it would normally be pointless to say that we know that they are true, and so on.

We can turn now to the second question we raised at the start of this section. Wittgenstein says that Moore's propositions 'play a peculiar logical role in our system of empirical propositions'. What exactly is that role? He uses a number of images to express it. For example, he compares Moore's propositions to hinges: 'The questions that we raise and our doubts depend on the fact that some propositions are exempt from doubt, as it were like hinges on which those turn' (OC: 341). He describes Moorean propositions as the *axis* on which our enquiries turn:

> Regarding [Moore's propositions] as absolutely solid is part of our *method* of doubt and enquiry.
>
> I do not explicitly learn the propositions that stand fast for me. I can *discover* them subsequently like the axis around which a body rotates. This axis is not fixed in the sense that anything holds it fast, but the movement around it determines its immobility.
>
> (OC: 151–2)

And he speaks of Moore's propositions as making up our world-picture:

I did not get my picture of the world by satisfying myself of its correctness; nor do I have it because I am satisfied of its correctness. No: it is the inherited background against which I distinguish between true and false.

(OC: 94)

Or again:

In general I take as true what is found in text-books, of geography for example. Why? I say: All these facts have been confirmed a hundred times over. But how do I know that? What is my evidence for it? I have a world-picture. Is it true or false? Above all it is the substratum of all my enquiring and asserting.

(OC: 162)

But how should we flesh out these suggestions? How exactly does Wittgenstein understand the place of Moorean propositions in our system of beliefs?

One theme that stands out from the passages just quoted is that it is a mistake to over-intellectualize or over-rationalize our relation to Moorean propositions: 'I do not explicitly learn the propositions that stand fast for me', Wittgenstein observes; 'I did not get my picture of the world by satisfying myself of its correctness'. Wittgenstein's point here is that I do not acquire beliefs such as that the earth has existed for many years before my birth by evaluating the evidence and satisfying myself that there is good reason to believe that they are true: 'I have not consciously arrived at [these] convictions by following a particular line of thought' (OC: 103). Rather, I simply pick them up in the course of my education and my interactions with others; I 'inherit' those beliefs, along with the rest of my world-picture. Similarly, it is not because I am 'satisfied of their correctness' that I continue to hold these beliefs; I simply retain them, without considering reasons for or against them at all. These observations about the acquisition and retention of our belief in the Moorean propositions seem exactly right. And they are an important corrective to philosophers' perennial tendency to over-intellectualize the process of forming and holding beliefs.

A further aspect of Wittgenstein's anti-intellectualism about Moorean beliefs is his stress on their relation to action. He writes:

Giving grounds, however, justifying the evidence, comes to an end;
– but the end is not certain propositions' striking us immediately as
true, i.e. it is not a kind of *seeing* on our part; it is our *acting*, which lies
at the bottom of the language-game.

(OC: 204)

That claim has a negative and positive element. Negatively, Wittgenstein is rejecting the traditional suggestion that justification terminates
in basic beliefs that are *self-evidently* true. Justification, he thinks, terminates at the point where we reach Moorean propositions that 'stand
fast for us'. But 'what stands fast', he writes, 'does so, *not because it is
intrinsically obvious or convincing*; it is rather held fast by what lies around
it' (OC: 144, emphasis added). The positive element in Wittgenstein's
claim is the idea that justification comes to an end in 'our *acting*'. The
end of giving grounds, he says, 'is not an ungrounded presupposition:
it is an ungrounded *way of acting*' (OC: 110, emphasis added). For example: 'Why do I not satisfy myself that I have two feet when I want to get
up from a chair? There is no why. I simply don't. This is how I act' (OC:
148). And, more generally, he suggests, our certainty about Moorean
propositions should be conceived 'as something that lies beyond being
justified or unjustified; as it were, as something *animal*' (OC: 359).

So far, then, Wittgenstein has told us that our acceptance of Moorean
propositions is not based on reasoning, and that it is rooted in our basic
ways of acting: 'At the foundation of well-founded belief lies belief
that is not founded. Any "reasonable" person behaves like this' (OC:
253–4). But at this stage we may wonder what bearing Wittgenstein's
reflections have on questions about the *epistemic status* of our beliefs. After
all, the philosophical sceptic agrees with Wittgenstein that our whole
system of beliefs rests ultimately on 'belief that is not founded'; he
agrees with Wittgenstein that we do not acquire our world-picture on
the basis of evidence; and he agrees that that world-picture is reflected
in the way we act. But, he insists, we are not ultimately *entitled* to hold
the beliefs we do; we have no epistemic *right* to think that our world-
picture is true. And that is something that Wittgenstein might seem to
concede, in insisting that we cannot *justify* our belief in the Moorean
propositions – that those beliefs are not *grounded in reasons*. But, where the
sceptic takes our lack of justification for our most fundamental beliefs
as a failing, Wittgenstein treats it as a perfectly acceptable feature of our
system of belief. What explains Wittgenstein's attitude?

Wittgenstein says elsewhere that 'to use a word without a justification does not mean to use it wrongfully' (PI §289; see also RFM: 406). That idea about our use of words has a parallel in Wittgenstein's view of Moorean propositions: to accept a Moorean proposition without a justification, we might say, does not mean to accept it wrongfully. But how should we understand this view? Why doesn't the fact that we cannot justify our belief in the Moorean propositions imply that we are not entitled to believe them at all? Commentators on *On Certainty* have detected in Wittgenstein's text a number of possible responses to that challenge. I shall focus here on one particularly prominent idea: that the status of Moorean propositions is akin to that of logical or mathematical *rules*. That, it seems, is what Wittgenstein means when he talks of the 'peculiar logical status' of Moorean propositions.

3. MOOREAN PROPOSITIONS AS RULES OF ENQUIRY

In a number of passages, Wittgenstein draws an analogy between the certainty of Moorean propositions and the certainty of basic logical or mathematical propositions. For example: 'I want to say: propositions of the form of empirical propositions, and not only propositions of logic, form the foundation of all operating with thoughts (with language)' (OC: 401). (The 'propositions of the form of empirical propositions' he has in mind are the Moorean propositions: 'The earth existed for many years before my birth', 'I have two hands', and so on.) Again, he writes: 'If the proposition $12 \times 12 = 144$ is exempt from doubt, then so too must non-mathematical propositions be' (OC: 653). Similarly: 'I want to say: If one doesn't marvel at the fact that the propositions of arithmetic (e.g. the multiplication tables) are "absolutely certain", then why should one be astonished that the proposition "This is my hand" is so equally?' (OC: 448). In passages like these, Wittgenstein seems tempted by the idea that Moorean propositions about material objects have a similar status to mathematical propositions like '$12 \times 12 = 144$'. But what, according to Wittgenstein, is that status?

Consider an extremely primitive stage in the development of mathematics. (The example that follows is adapted from one introduced by Dummett (Dummett 1959). My discussion is also indebted to Wright (2004).) At this primitive stage, we have a practice of counting collections of objects. But, so far, we have no concept of addition. So, we might count 5 walnuts in the bowl, and then count 7 cashew nuts. But, having counted the walnuts and the cashews, we have no procedure of determining the total number of nuts by adding the number of walnuts and the number of cashews; our only way of determining the total number is to start again and count the walnuts and the cashews together. Now it turns out that in every case (or virtually every case) when we count a group of 5 things and a group of 7 things, we find when we count the two groups together that there are 12 things. That gives us the idea of laying it down as a *rule* that $5 + 7 = 12$. The rule defines what it is to add 5 and 7 correctly. And in laying it down as a rule, we commit ourselves to not allowing anything to count against it. Suppose, for example, that having counted 5 walnuts and 7 cashews, someone proceeds to count the total number of nuts and gets the answer 13. We can explain what has happened in various ways: she might have made a mistake in counting the walnuts, or in counting the cashews, or in counting all the nuts together; or something might have been added between the initial counts and the final count. But the one thing we will not allow is that, on this occasion, $5 + 7$ did not equal 12. For it is a rule of correct counting that $5 + 7 = 12$: we have put the proposition '$5 + 7 = 12$' in the archives; we have decided not to treat anything as falsifying it. On this view of mathematical propositions, the question what justifies us in believing that $5 + 7 = 12$ is out of place. For the proposition '$5 + 7 = 12$' is not something that we accept on the basis of evidence. It is something we lay down as defining what it is to add 5 and 7. In that respect, Wittgenstein thinks, the proposition '$5 + 7 = 12$' is like a rule of a game. We cannot ask what justifies us in accepting the rule for moving a knight in chess. For the rule is not something that is correct or incorrect; it is not something that we accept on the basis of evidence. Rather, it is laid down as part of the definition of the game of chess. That, at any rate, is Wittgenstein's view.

Now Wittgenstein suggests that Moorean propositions have a similar status: they are propositions that we withdraw from testing and treat as 'norms of description' (OC: 167) – as partially definitive of correct description. For example: 'I could say: "That I have two hands is an irreversible belief." That would express the fact that I am not ready to let anything count as a disproof of this proposition' (OC: 245). We can flesh out Wittgenstein's suggestion as follows. Suppose that, in circumstances that are completely unremarkable, someone sincerely asserts that I do not have two hands. I might explain her assertion in various ways. I might, for instance, think that she is hallucinating; or that she has some bizarre delusion to the effect that many people she meets have no hands, but pretend to be two-handed; or that she has mistaken me for someone else whom she knows to have only one hand. But there is one thing that I will not treat as a genuine possibility: that her assertion is true, and I do not have two hands. For, in the current context, my having two hands is fundamental to my system of belief; whatever evidence I encounter, I am committed to maintaining the truth of that belief. And the same goes for other Moorean propositions. On this view, Moorean propositions are ones that we are committed to 'holding fast' come what may. We will not count anything as falsifying them. And that is not a merely *psychological* fact about us – just as it is not a merely psychological fact that we will not count anything as falsifying the mathematical proposition '5 + 7 = 12'. It is, rather, a *logical* feature of the role of the Moorean propositions in our system of empirical belief and enquiry. In the mathematical case, Wittgenstein thinks, it is partially definitive of our system of counting that nothing is allowed to falsify the proposition '5 + 7 = 12'. And similarly for the empirical case; it is partially definitive of our system of empirical belief and enquiry that nothing is allowed to falsify the Moorean certainties.

Wittgenstein presses this analogy between Moorean propositions and mathematical propositions. At the same time, though, he recognizes that there are important differences between them. In the first place, the incontrovertibility of mathematical propositions is absolute; there are no circumstances at all in which we would regard the proposition '5 + 7 = 12' as open to doubt. But there *are* circumstances where a Moorean proposition would be open to doubt – circumstances where we would not be committed to holding it true come what may. In normal circumstances the proposition 'I have two hands' is a basic certainty; I do not allow anything to falsify it. But, as we have seen, Wittgenstein acknowledges that there are circumstances in which that proposition *would* be subject to confirmation by experience. And in circumstances like that, it is plainly not a rule of enquiry that the world must be described in a way that maintains the truth of the proposition 'I have two hands'.

Second, and relatedly, the certainty of basic mathematical propositions is unchanging. The rule that 5 + 7 = 12 does not change over time. But in the case of Moorean propositions, Wittgenstein thinks, there can be changes over time in which propositions are accepted unquestioningly as the basis for empirical enquiry and which propositions are subject to doubt and confirmation. He expresses that point in a famous metaphor:

> It might be imagined that some propositions, of the form of empirical propositions, were hardened and functioned as channels for such empirical propositions as were not hardened but fluid; and that this relation altered with time, in that fluid propositions hardened, and hard ones became fluid.
>
> (OC: 96)

So, something that is at one point a solid element in our world-picture:

> may change back into a state of flux, the river-bed of thoughts may shift. But I distinguish between the movement of the waters on the river-bed and the shift of the bed itself; though there is not a sharp division of the one from the other.
>
> (OC: 97)

Wittgenstein's point is well illustrated by the changing status of such propositions as 'I have never been on the moon' and 'no one has ever been on the moon'. Writing nearly 20 years before the Apollo landings, Wittgenstein says that 'my not having been on the moon is as sure a thing for me as any grounds I could give for it' (OC: 111). That neither he nor anyone else had ever been on the moon was, for him, a basic certainty. But things would be different, he says, 'if a good many men had been on the moon' (OC: 111). And for us, 60 years on, it is plainly not a Moorean certainty that no one has been on the moon. So now, Wittgenstein would say, it is reasonable to ask for grounds for believing that a given person has never been to the moon – in a way that would not have been reasonable at the time he was writing.

According to Wittgenstein, then, there is a significant analogy between the role of Moorean propositions in our system of empirical beliefs and the role of basic mathematical propositions in our practice of counting and adding. There are significant differences, too. But despite the differences, he seems to suggest, the status of the Moorean propositions is fundamentally the same as the status of basic mathematical propositions. They are propositions that have, as it were, been hardened into rules governing the correct description of the empirical world. Their certainty lies in our commitment to count nothing as falsifying them. But is that a convincing view?

Wittgenstein is certainly right that any investigation must take some things for granted: we cannot simultaneously investigate everything. As he says, 'Whenever we test anything, we are already presupposing something that is not tested' (OC: 163); 'One cannot make experiments if there are not some things that one does not doubt' (OC: 337). Similarly, he is right that the Moorean propositions he discusses are fundamental to our system of thought and enquiry: we cannot produce any justification for believing them that is not directly or indirectly question-begging. He is right that self-evidence has little or no part to play in epistemology. And he is right that it is not by any process of conscious reasoning that we come to believe these Moorean propositions. But is he right that these very basic elements of our world-picture have a different *logical status* from ordinary empirical propositions: that, like mathematical propositions, they are *rules of description*? We will comment on Wittgenstein's analogy between Moorean propositions and rules in the next section. At this stage, we can simply note a natural alternative to Wittgenstein's position. On this alternative view, Moorean propositions really are the contingent empirical propositions they seem to be; and their foundational status in our enquiries stems simply from the fact that they are very well established and extremely unlikely to turn out to be false. It is indeed hard to imagine circumstances that would make us abandon our belief in the Moorean propositions. But the reason for that might not be that we have determined to allow nothing to count as falsifying such propositions. It might be, rather, that the Moorean propositions are so obviously true or so well established that, even though they could in principle be falsified, it is virtually impossible to imagine their actually turning out to be false. That alternative view of the logical status of Moorean propositions seems very plausible. But even if we accept this alternative view, we can, as I have said, agree with much of what Wittgenstein says about the structure of justification; and we can accept much of his anti-intellectualism about the acquisition and retention of belief.

4. THE THREAT OF RELATIVISM

My 'world-picture', says Wittgenstein, 'is the substratum of all my enquiring and asserting' (OC: 162); it is 'the inherited background against which I distinguish between true and false' (OC: 94).

All testing, all confirmation and disconfirmation of a hypothesis takes place already within a system. And this system is not a more or less arbitrary and doubtful point of departure for all our arguments; no, it belongs to the essence of what we call an argument.

(OC: 105)

A natural question immediately arises: What happens if different people, or groups of people, have different world-pictures – if the system of propositions that forms the substratum of our enquiring and asserting is different from the system that forms the substratum of their enquiring and asserting? If rational assessment of a claim is possible only within a system then, it seems, there can be no basis for the rational assessment of competing systems or world-pictures themselves. When we consider other people's world-picture from the standpoint of our own, we will judge our system to be superior to theirs. Similarly, when they consider our world-picture from the standpoint of theirs, they will judge their system to be better than ours. But, though each side has what it regards as compelling reasons for thinking that its system is better, neither side can point to anything that the other side will accept as a reason for thinking that the opposing system is better. For what each group counts as a good reason for believing something is itself a feature of that group's own world-picture. That is not to say that a person, or a group of people, can never be induced to give up their existing world-picture and adopt another one. They can. But, Wittgenstein insists, any such change of world-picture will ultimately depend on a process of persuasion or conversion rather than a process of giving reasons. Thus:

Suppose we met people who did not regard [a physicist's statement] as a telling reason. Now, how do we imagine this? Instead of the physicist, they consult an oracle . . . . If we call this 'wrong' aren't we using our language-game as a base from which to *combat* theirs?

[. . .]

I said I would 'combat' the other man, – but wouldn't I give him *reasons*? Certainly; but how far do they go? At the end of reasons comes *persuasion*. (Think what happens when missionaries convert natives.)

(OC: 609, 612; see also 262)

Suppose we accept, with Wittgenstein, that reasoning necessarily takes place within a system or world-picture. And suppose we accept that there is no neutral, external standpoint from which anyone could conduct a rational assessment of the relative merits of different world-pictures – no standpoint that does not itself involve acceptance of some particular world-picture. What follows from that? In particular, does it follow that there can be no objectively good reasons for thinking that one world-picture is superior to another – reasons that are not merely reasons 'within our system'? Does it follow that there is no fact of the matter about which world-picture is right or wrong, about which system of beliefs comes closer to characterizing the world as it really is? And does it follow that the truth or falsity of a belief is relative to the world-picture of the believer – so that a belief is true or false *in our system of beliefs* but can never be true or false *simpliciter*? That kind of relativism is deeply counter-intuitive. But it has seemed to many readers to be suggested by some of what Wittgenstein says in *On Certainty*. Is that really Wittgenstein's position?

There are passages in *On Certainty* that are easily read as suggesting some kind of relativism. For example:

> 'But is there then no objective truth? Isn't it true, or false, that someone has been on the moon?' If we are thinking within our system, then it is certain that no one has ever been on the moon. Not merely is nothing of that sort ever seriously reported to us by reasonable people, but our whole system of physics forbids us to believe it. For this demands answers to the questions 'How did he overcome the force of gravity?', 'How could he live without an atmosphere?' and a thousand others which could not be answered. But suppose that instead of all these answers we met the reply: 'We don't know *how* one gets to the moon, but those who get there know at once that they are there; and even you can't explain everything.' We should feel ourselves intellectually very distant from someone who said this.
>
> (OC: 108)

It is natural to agree with the thought underpinning the questions at the start of that passage: when Wittgenstein was writing in 1950, we want to say, it was objectively true that no one had been on the moon. And it is natural to think that Wittgenstein's comment at the end of the passage ('we should feel ourselves intellectually very distant from someone who said this') understates the appropriate reaction to someone who, in 1950, was convinced that people went to the moon but who had nothing at all to say about how they got to the moon, how they survived there, and so on. Of course Wittgenstein is right that we would 'feel ourselves intellectually very distant' from such a person. But, we want to insist, it is not just a matter of intellectual distance; the other person's beliefs would be false. And they would not just be false 'within our system'. They would be *absolutely* or *objectively* false.

And consider a second passage:

> One might simply say 'O, rubbish!' to someone who wanted to make objections to the propositions that are beyond doubt. That is, not reply to him but admonish him.
>   This is a similar case to that of showing that it has no meaning to say that a game has always been played wrong.
>
> (OC: 495–6)

But is the case of someone who objects to the Moorean propositions that are foundational for us really similar to the case of someone who says that a game has always been played wrong? Suppose someone claimed that everyone has always played chess wrong; that the rules we have always followed are the wrong rules. The right response to that claim, according to Wittgenstein, is that it 'has no meaning' to say that everyone has always played chess wrong. And the reason it has no meaning, he thinks, is that *all there is* to playing chess correctly is playing it in the way we all accept as correct. The correct rules of chess are simply the rules we all accept as correct. If we apply that analogy directly to the case of Moorean propositions such as 'the earth has existed for millions of years', we get the following position: 'It has no meaning to say that the Moorean propositions we accept are incorrect; that we ought to accept a different set of propositions as the unquestioned basis for all our beliefs. For Moorean propositions are like the rules of a game. The rules we accept define the game we are playing. And the Moorean propositions we accept define our world-picture. So, just as all there is to playing a game correctly is playing it by the rules that we all accept, all there is to having correct beliefs is having beliefs that accord with the Moorean propositions that define our world-picture.' But that position ignores a fundamental disanalogy between the rules of a game and the basic features of a world-picture. The rules of a game are answerable to nothing outside themselves. There really is nothing to the correctness of such a rule beyond the fact that we accept it as

correct. But Moorean propositions are different. Unlike the rules of
a game, Moorean propositions *are* answerable to something beyond
themselves; they are answerable to the way the world is. The correctness of the proposition 'the earth has existed for millions of years',
say, is not just a matter of its having a foundational role in our system
of belief; it is a matter of whether or not the earth really has existed
for millions of years. If Wittgenstein thinks that Moorean propositions
are like the rules of a game in *not* being answerable to any external
standard of correctness, his position seems radically and unacceptably
relativistic.

However, the evidence of this sort of relativism in *On Certainty* is
equivocal. The passages I have quoted can certainly be read as suggesting relativism. But there are other passages where Wittgenstein seems
happy to assert that our world-picture is right and some imagined
alternative is wrong. For instance:

> We all believe that it isn't possible to get to the moon; but there might be
> people who believe that that is possible and that it sometimes happens.
> We say: these people do not know a lot that we know. And, let them be
> never so sure of their belief – they are wrong and we know it.
>   If we compare our system of knowledge with theirs then theirs is
> evidently the poorer one by far.
>
> (OC: 286)

In that passage, Wittgenstein seems clear that, where there are fundamental differences between different systems of belief, it may be
straightforwardly true that one system is correct and the other incorrect. And that is surely the right view to take. We should agree with
Wittgenstein that the rational assessment of any claim necessarily
draws on a whole system of belief. And we should agree that there is
no completely neutral standpoint from which to carry out a rational
comparison between competing world-pictures or systems of belief;
a rational assessment of anything can only be made from within a
system of reasoning. But it does not follow that the most fundamental commitments of a world-picture are not straightforwardly true or
false. Nor does it follow that, if we encounter a world-picture completely different from our own, the process of comparing it with ours
and evaluating one or other as superior cannot be a process of reasoning. If Wittgenstein thought that those relativistic views did follow

from the insight that 'all testing, all confirmation and disconfirmation of a hypothesis takes place already within a system' (OC: 105), then he was wrong; but there is no clear-cut and unequivocal evidence that he did think that.

SUMMARY

On Certainty records Wittgenstein's last thoughts about knowledge, certainty, and justification. G. E. Moore had offered a proof that external objects exist: 'Here is one hand and here is another; so two human hands exist; so external objects exist'. Wittgenstein contends that this is not an effective proof of the existence of external objects. In the first place, the premise of Moore's proof is no more certain than the conclusion; so the proof cannot give anyone a reason for believing that there are external objects unless they already believe it. In the second place, Wittgenstein thinks, even if Moore is right that we know that there is an external world, his discussion of scepticism and idealism is philosophically unsatisfying because it fails to diagnose and explain how the sceptic and the idealist go wrong.

Moore's writings also draw attention to a class of propositions that are basic to our system of belief: propositions such as 'The earth has existed for millions of years' and 'I have two hands'. According to Moore, these are propositions that we know, with certainty, to be true. Wittgenstein agrees that these 'Moorean propositions' play a special role in our system of belief. But, he argues, it is wrong to say that we know them to be true. And, more generally, he argues against a tendency to over-intellectualize our relation to such propositions. We acquire our world-picture not by satisfying ourselves of its correctness but by picking it up, unreflectively, as part of the 'inherited background' of our enquiries. And our certainty in the Moorean propositions is grounded not in reasoning but in our ways of acting. Wittgenstein suggests that Moorean propositions have a status similar to that of basic logical or mathematical propositions: they are rules of enquiry, norms of description, which serve to define what it is to describe the world correctly. However, while Wittgenstein is right that the Moorean propositions are fundamental to our system of enquiry, and that we cannot justify them by appeal to anything more basic, it seems implausible that their logical status is really any different from that of any other empirical proposition.

Wittgenstein's suggestion that all testing and confirmation takes place within a system of reasoning creates a threat of relativism. For the idea that reasoning is only possible within a system or world-picture seems to imply that, where different world-pictures conflict, there can be no rational assessment of which is right and which is wrong. Many readers of On Certainty have detected a strand of relativism in Wittgenstein's remarks. But, though there are elements of relativism in some of what Wittgenstein says – for example, in his comparison of Moorean propositions to rules of a game – the evidence of relativism in On Certainty as a whole is equivocal.

FURTHER READING

The text discussed in this chapter is On Certainty. For earlier discussions involving similar themes, see:

'Cause and Effect: Intuitive Awareness', in Wittgenstein, *Philosophical Occasions*. *Philosophical Investigations* §§324–6, 466–86.

The works by G. E. Moore to which On Certainty responds are:

Moore, G. E. (1925) 'A Defence of Common Sense', in J. Muirhead (ed.) *Contemporary British Philosophy* (Second Series), London: George Allen & Unwin; reprinted in Moore, G.E. (1993) *Selected Writings*, ed. T. Baldwin, London: Routledge.
Moore, G. E. (1939) 'Proof of an External World', in *Proceedings of the British Academy* 25: 273–300; reprinted in Moore, *Selected Writings*.

For a very clear discussion of Moore's and Wittgenstein's views of knowledge and scepticism, which is broadly sympathetic to Wittgenstein, see:

McGinn, M. (1989) *Sense and Certainty*, Oxford: Blackwell.

More recent monographs on On Certainty include:

Moyal-Sharrock, D. (2004) *Understanding Wittgenstein's* On Certainty, Basingstoke: Palgrave Macmillan.

A helpful recent collection of papers sets out to offer a set of contrasting philosophical and interpretative approaches to On Certainty:

Moyal-Sharrock, D. and Brenner, W. (2005) *Readings of Wittgenstein's* On Certainty, Basingstoke: Palgrave Macmillan.

Two recent papers that discuss the main themes of On Certainty, and relate Wittgenstein's ideas to contemporary views in epistemology, are:

Williams, M. (2004) 'Wittgenstein's Refutation of Idealism', in D. McManus (ed.) *Wittgenstein and Scepticism*, London: Routledge.
Wright, C. (2004) 'Wittgensteinian Certainties', in D. McManus (ed.) *Wittgenstein and*

Scepticism, London: Routledge.

I have drawn on Wright's paper, in particular, in writing this chapter.

For a treatment with a different flavour, downplaying any concern with Moore or scepticism and arguing that Wittgenstein's primary interest was simply to provide 'a philosophically illuminating picture of the epistemic structure of language-games', see:

Kober, M. (1996) 'Certainties of a World-Picture: The Epistemological Investigations of *On Certainty*', in H. Sluga and D. Stern (eds) *The Cambridge Companion to Wittgenstein*, Cambridge: Cambridge University Press.

Eight

Religion and anthropology

1. RELIGION

Wittgenstein wrote very little about the philosophy of religion, almost none of which was intended for publication: the *Tractatus* contains two brief comments about God (TLP: 6.372, 6.432); there is a single parenthetical remark about theology in *Philosophical Investigations* (PI §373). But Wittgenstein's views about religion and the nature of religious belief have had a significant influence on theologians and philosophers of religion. The evidence for those views comes from a number of sources. There are students' notes of three lectures on religious belief given by Wittgenstein in 1938 (see LC: 53–72). There are various remarks on religion that Wittgenstein wrote in the philosophical notebooks he kept between 1929 and 1951, a selection of which appear in the volume *Culture and Value*. And there are reports of Wittgenstein's views from various friends and pupils.

In considering Wittgenstein's views about religion, we should distinguish two questions: what, if any, were Wittgenstein's own religious beliefs; and what was Wittgenstein's philosophical view about the nature of religious belief? This second question will be our primary concern. But we can start with some brief comments on the first.

i. Wittgenstein's 'religious point of view'

There is evidence that Wittgenstein regarded his own attitudes and way of thinking as being in some sense religious – or, perhaps, as having something importantly in common with religious belief. He is reported as saying, in a conversation in the late 1940s: 'I am not a religious man but I cannot help seeing every problem from a religious point of view.' And, in the same conversation: 'My type of thinking is not wanted in this present age, I have to swim so strongly against the tide' (Drury 1981: 94). Around the same time, he spoke of dedicating his work to the glory of God:

> I have had a letter from an old friend in Austria, a priest. In it he says he hopes my work will go well, if it should be God's will. Now that is all I want: if it should be God's will. Bach wrote on the title page of his Orgelbuchlein, 'To the glory of the most high God, and that my neighbour may be benefited thereby.' That is what I would have liked to say about my work.
>
> (Drury 1981: 182)

Those sentiments echo comments he wrote some 20 years earlier, in the preface to *Philosophical Remarks*:

> I would like to say 'This book is written to the glory of God', but nowadays that would be chicanery, that is, it would not be rightly understood. It means the book is written in good will, and in so far as it is not so written, but out of vanity, etc., the author would wish to see it condemned. He cannot free it of these impurities further than he himself is free of it.
>
> (PR: 7)

This earlier reference to God is again accompanied by the idea that the style or spirit of Wittgenstein's work runs counter to the dominant contemporary way of thinking:

> This book is written for such men as are in sympathy with its spirit. This spirit is different from the one which informs the vast stream of European and American civilization in which all of us stand. That spirit expresses itself in an onwards movement, in building ever larger and more complicated structures; the other in striving after clarity and perspicuity in no matter what structure. The first tries to grasp the world by way of its periphery – in its variety; the second at its centre – in its essence. And so the first adds one construction to another, moving on and up, as it were, from one stage to the next, while the other remains where it is and what it tries to grasp is always the same.
>
> (PR: 7)

An earlier draft identifies the way of thinking with which Wittgenstein contrasts his own as that of 'the scientists' (CV: 7 [revised edition: 9]).

Wittgenstein spoke of dedicating his book 'to the glory of God'. But that is not to say that he believed in God in the conventional sense. As an infant he was baptized into the Catholic Church. But, he told a friend, 'he lost his childish faith after conversations with his sister Gretl' (McGuinness 1988: 43). And Russell reported that, when Wittgenstein was first in Cambridge, he was a fierce critic of organized religion. But an incident around the same time, when Wittgenstein was in his early twenties, gave him a new sense of the possibility of religion. Norman Malcolm reports:

> He told me that in his youth he had been contemptuous of [religion], but that at about the age of twenty-one something had caused a change in him. In Vienna he saw a play that was mediocre drama, but in it one of the characters expressed the thought that no matter what happened in the world, nothing bad could happen to him – he was independent of fate and circumstances. Wittgenstein was struck by this stoic thought; for the first time he saw the possibility of religion. He said that during his service in the First War he came across Tolstoy's writings on the Gospels, which made a great impression on him.
>
> (Malcolm 1984: 58)

Wittgenstein was powerfully affected by Tolstoy's Christianity: he read Tolstoy's *Gospel in Brief* many times, and he carried it everywhere with him during the First World War. And he remained struck by the feeling he had seen expressed in the play in Vienna (the play was Ludwig Anzengruber's *Die Kreuzelschreiber* (The Cross-makers) (see McGuinness 1988: 94)). In a lecture given in Cambridge in 1929, he commented on 'the experience of feeling *absolutely* safe . . . the state of mind in which one is inclined to say "I am safe, nothing can injure me whatever happens"' (LE: 41). That feeling, he said, is sometimes given a religious expression: 'The experience of absolute safety has been described by saying that we feel safe in the hands of God' (LE: 42). And he spoke of having had that experience himself.

Wittgenstein was a deeply serious and spiritual person. He thought often of sin and guilt, and he had a powerful sense of his own unworthiness. Those qualities come across powerfully in the testimony of his friends. Paul Engelmann, a close friend of Wittgenstein's during the First World War, writes:

Was Wittgenstein religious? If we call him an agnostic, this must not
be understood in the sense of the familiar polemical agnosticism that
concentrates, and prides itself, on the argument that man could never
know about these matters.

  The idea of a God in the sense of the Bible, the image of God as the
creator of the world, hardly ever engaged Wittgenstein's attention
. . ., but the notion of a last judgement was of profound concern to him.
'When we meet again at the last judgement' was a recurrent phrase
with him, which he used in many a conversation at a particularly
momentous point. He would pronounce the words with an
indescribably inward-gazing look in his eyes, his head bowed, the
picture of a man stirred to his depths.

(Engelmann 1967: 77–8)

Perhaps it is not surprising that Wittgenstein should have been pre-
occupied with the idea of a last judgement at a time when he was
engaged in active combat. But Malcolm, who knew Wittgenstein
more than 20 years later, notes the same interest in the idea of a last
judgement:

If 'to be a religious person' means to lead 'a religious life', then I think
he was not a religious person. Yet he reflected often and deeply on
what it would mean to live such a life. He was dismayed by his own
character, perceiving himself as vain, cowardly, false. Sometimes he
suffered the anguish that has pushed others into a religious life.
Probably he had no real hope that his life would take a new direction,
that he would be 'turned around'. Probably he felt that he could not,
or would not, 'open his heart'. At times he felt a dread of the Last
Judgement – as when he wrote to me [in 1940] 'may I prove not too
much of a skunk when I shall be tried'.

(Malcolm 1984: 83)

Malcolm, like Engelmann, notes that Wittgenstein had no interest in
the idea of God as the creator of the world; his interest lay rather in the
ideas of guilt, redemption, and so on:

Wittgenstein [once said] that he thought that could understand the
conception of God, in so far as it is involved in one's awareness of
one's own sin and guilt. He added that he could not understand the

conception of a Creator. I think that the ideas of Divine judgement, forgiveness, and redemption had some intelligibility for him, as being related in his mind to feelings of disgust with himself, an intense desire for purity, and a sense of the helplessness of human beings to make themselves better. But the notion of a being making the world had no intelligibility for him at all.

(Malcolm 1984: 59)

Wittgenstein, then, was not a religious believer in the normal sense. But he was sympathetic to some aspects of religious thought, and he regarded his view of the world as having important similarities to the outlook that he associated with religious belief.

ii. Religion and the *Tractatus*

Wittgenstein says in the *Tractatus* that 'the meaning of life' and 'the sense of the world' do not consist in any fact or facts about how things are in the world. Accordingly, he thinks, it is impossible to say what the meaning of life is: that is something that cannot be put into words but that makes itself manifest. The *Tractatus* links those ideas about the meaning of life to a comment about God:

How things are in the world is a matter of complete indifference for what is higher. God does not reveal himself in the world.

[. . .]

It is not how things are in the world that is mystical, but that it exists.

(TLP: 6.432, 6.44)

God is not an item in the world. Nor does God reveal Himself in any empirical facts: in anything about how things are in the world. Rather, Wittgenstein suggests, He reveals himself in the existence of the world as such. Now suppose we treat the word 'God' not as the name of any kind of being, but as a term for the meaning of the world, or the meaning of life. Then the comment about God that we have just quoted (TLP: 6.432) will be a way of expressing the *Tractatus*'s view of the sense of the world and the meaning of life. And that is exactly how Wittgenstein puts things in his 1914–16 *Notebooks*:

What do I know about God and the purpose of life?
I know that this world exists. . . .

That something about it is problematic, which we call its meaning.
That this meaning does not lie in it but outside it . . .
The meaning of life, i.e. the meaning of the world, we can call God.
[. . .]
To pray is to think about the meaning of life.

(NB: 72–3, 4 July 1916)

And, four days later:

To believe in a God means to understand the question about the
meaning of life.
   To believe in a God means to see that the facts of the world are not
the end of the matter.
   To believe in God means to see that life has a meaning.

(NB 74: 8 July 1916)

On this view of God and religious belief, believing in God is not a matter of having any factual beliefs. It is, rather, a matter of seeing the facts
in a certain light: believing in God means seeing 'that the facts of the
world are not the end of the matter'; or seeing 'that life has a meaning'.
Similarly, the word 'God' does not function by referring to anything:
it does not refer to any item in the world; nor does it refer to an item
outside the world. Both these features of Wittgenstein's early conception of religion, as we shall see, carry through into his later view.

Is the *Tractatus* sympathetic to religious belief? It is, insofar as religious belief involves the idea that the world has meaning, or value,
that goes beyond any facts. For according to the *Tractatus*, fact-stating
propositions – the propositions of natural science – are silent on everything that really matters in life. To that extent, then, Wittgenstein agrees
with the religious believer: the facts of the world are not the end of
the matter. But traditional religion does not merely hold that there is a
meaning to life; it also appeals to God to explain why the world is as
it is, and why it exists at all. And Wittgenstein is unsympathetic to any
such appeal:

The whole modern conception of the world is founded on the illusion that the so-called laws of nature are the explanations of natural
phenomena.
   Thus people today stop at the laws of nature, treating them as
something inviolable, just as God and Fate were treated in past ages.

And in fact both are right and both wrong: though the view of the
ancients is clearer in so far as they have a clear and acknowledged
terminus, while the modern system tries to make it look as if *everything* were explained.

(TLP: 6.371–6.372)

The laws of nature, Wittgenstein thinks, are simply generalizations
about what always happens: about how the world works. But science
does not explain why the basic laws of nature are as they are. That is
why it is an illusion to think that the laws of nature explain natural
phenomena. Traditional religious belief, on the other hand, purports to
explain what science treats simply as a given; the laws of nature are as
they are, it says, because God has willed them to be that way. But that
explanation, Wittgenstein thinks, has no explanatory power. For the
nature and existence of God is itself a mystery; something that cannot
be explained. And if we can say nothing more about exactly what God
is, and why we should believe there is such a thing, the claim that God
created the world and established the laws of nature explains nothing.
In Wittgenstein's view, then, neither science nor religion really explains
why the world is as it is. But, he thinks, religion is preferable in that,
where the 'modern conception of the world' presents itself as giving
a complete explanation of natural phenomena, religion acknowledges
that its chain of explanations ends with something that is not itself
explained: the existence and creative power of God.

iii. Religion in Wittgenstein's later philosophy

Religious people are said to believe that the world was created by God;
or that there will be a Judgement Day; or that people's souls are rein-
carnated after death; and so on. But how are those beliefs to be understood? On the face of it, religious beliefs are factual beliefs: beliefs
that are true or false in exactly the same sense as any other. If someone
believes that there will be a Judgement Day, the truth or falsity of her
belief, it seems, depends on whether or not there will in fact be such a
day. In the same way, there is on the face of it a straightforward question about what justifies religious beliefs. We can ask what reason there
is to believe that there will be a Judgement Day. And if there is no good
reason for believing it, then the belief will be unjustified or irrational.
But Wittgenstein denies both these apparently common-sense points.
Religious beliefs, he thinks, are not beliefs about matters of empirical

fact. And they can neither be justified by appeal to evidence nor criticized on the grounds that they are not supported by evidence.

'In a religious discourse', Wittgenstein says, 'we use such expressions
as: "I believe that so and so will happen" '. But we 'use them differently
to the way in which we use them in science' (LC: 57). In particular, we
do not use those words to express the belief in the future occurrence of
an event of a particular kind. Rather, we use them to express our commitment to a certain way of seeing things and a certain way of living.
Thus: 'Suppose somebody made this guidance for this life: believing
in the Last Judgement. Whenever he does anything, this is before his
mind' (LC: 53). Such a person, Wittgenstein thinks, would be said to
believe in the Last Judgement. But the difference between the person
who believes in the Last Judgement and the person who does not is not
a disagreement about the occurrence of a future event. It is the difference between seeing the events of one's own and other people's lives
in terms of the concepts of divine judgement, reward, and punishment
and not seeing them that way.

> Suppose you had two people, and one of them, when he had to decide
> which course to take, thought of retribution, and the other did not. One
> person might, for instance, be inclined to take everything that
> happened to him as a reward or punishment, and another person
> doesn't think of this at all.
>
> If he is ill, he may think: 'What have I done to deserve this?' This is
> one way of thinking of retribution. Another way is, he thinks in a
> general way whenever he is ashamed of himself: 'This will be
> punished.'
>
> Take two people, one of whom talks of his behaviour and of what
> happens to him in terms of retribution, the other one does not. These
> people think entirely differently.
>
> (LC: 54–5)

But the difference, Wittgenstein thinks, is not – or not fundamentally
– a difference in their factual beliefs. Similarly, the difference between
someone who believes in God and someone who does not is not a
difference about the existence of an omnipotent and omniscient agent
who created the universe. To believe that God exists and is the creator
of the world is, rather, to accept a 'system of representation' in which,
in the words of a sympathetic commentator:

all aspects of nature and human nature are to be understood in terms
of their source in God and in terms of God's providential relation to his
creatures [and] all descriptions, decisions, etc., [are to be] formulated
or completed in terms of the notion of God's creative power, God's
judgements, God's grace, or God's love and anger.

(Arrington 2001: 176)

Wittgenstein sums up his view like this:

It strikes me that a religious belief could only be something like a
passionate commitment to a system of reference. Hence, although
it's belief, it's really a way of living, or a way of assessing life. It's
passionately seizing hold of this interpretation.

(CV: 64 [revised edition: 73])

A 'system of reference', for Wittgenstein, is a system of concepts: a
system for describing and assessing the world. The idea that religious
belief involves a *passionate commitment* to a system of reference reflects
the idea that the system of religious concepts has a peculiarly *central and
fundamental* place in the life of the religious believer. And it captures the
idea that religious belief involves not just a particular way of *thinking*
but a distinctive way of *leading one's life*.

According to Wittgenstein, then, religious beliefs are not factual
beliefs; they do not purport to represent how the world was, or is,
or will be. That is why he thinks it misconceived to try to justify
religious beliefs by showing that they are well supported by
evidence, or to criticize them on the grounds that there is insuffi-
cient evidence to show that they are true. Attempts to justify religious
beliefs in that way, he says, are 'ludicrous' (LC: 58), 'ridiculous'
(LC: 59), or even 'repellent' or 'repugnant' (CV: 29 [revised edition:
34]).

Wittgenstein's view of religious belief has attracted strong and committed support from some theologians and philosophers of religion.
But it has attracted equally strong rejection from others. Is it a convincing account? We can address that question in connection with
three objections that have been raised by Wittgenstein's critics: that his
account misrepresents the nature of religious belief; that it misstates
the role of justification in religious belief; and that it involves an unacceptable kind of relativism.

The nature of religious belief. Wittgenstein is plainly right that religious belief involves the things he says it does: the use of a set of distinctively religious concepts in describing and thinking about the world; a commitment to lead one's life in a certain way; and a certain pattern of evaluations of oneself and others. But is he right that that is *all there is* to religious belief? In particular, is he right to deny that religious belief essentially involves a host of factual beliefs: beliefs about the occurrence of particular historical events (the birth, crucifixion, and resurrection of Jesus, for example); beliefs about the existence of particular kinds of entity (God, immortal souls, etc.); beliefs about the nature of reality, and so on; all of which are true or false in the same way as any other belief?

We can start with the point that many religions, including Christianity, rest on a core of historical fact. Part of Wittgenstein's response to that point is that even if religious belief *requires* the acceptance of particular historical facts, such acceptance is not *sufficient* for religious belief. For one could believe in the historical core of Christianity, say, without having any religious belief; however indubitable the historical core might be, he says, 'the indubitability wouldn't be enough to make me change my whole life' (LC: 57). And it is an essential part of religious belief that it *does* change one's whole life. But Wittgenstein goes further than that; he suggests that the truth of the historical core of Christianity is not essential to Christian belief at all:

> Christianity is not based on a historical truth; rather, it offers us a (historical) narrative and says: now believe! But not, believe this narrative with the belief appropriate to a historical narrative, rather: believe, through thick and thin, which you can do only as the result of a life. Here you have a narrative, don't take the same attitude to it as you take to other historical narratives! Make a quite different place in your life for it . . . .
>
> Queer as it sounds: The historical accounts in the Gospels might, historically speaking, be demonstrably false and yet belief would lose nothing by this . . . because historical proof (the historical proof-game) is irrelevant to belief. This message (the Gospels) is seized on by men believingly (i.e. lovingly). That is the certainty characterizing this particular acceptance-as-true, not something else.
>
> (CV: 32 [revised edition: 37–8])

Now maybe, as Wittgenstein says, someone could continue to hold distinctively Christian beliefs while accepting that the account of Jesus's life in the Gospels is historically false – and false not just in minor details. That is probably the position of many contemporary believers who regard themselves as Christians. But what about the belief in a Judgement Day? Wittgenstein argues that it is not *sufficient* for believing in a Judgement Day that one has the empirical belief that there will be a day at some future time when some process of judging takes place; for that belief might not have the role or significance of the religious belief (see LC: 56). That is very plausible. But it would be wrong to conclude that the empirical belief is not even *necessary* for the religious belief. And it seems extremely plausible that religious beliefs of this sort do generally involve straightforwardly factual components. Whatever else the religious belief in a Judgement Day involves, it seems clear that it involves an empirical belief about the occurrence of a future event. If there will, in fact, never be any process of judgement in which a supernatural being holds people to account for what they have done, the religious belief is mistaken.

Wittgenstein would deny that. On his view, the belief in a Judgement Day, or the fundamental Christian beliefs articulated in the Nicene Creed, are not beliefs about the nature of reality and the occurrence of past and future events. They are, rather, expressions of a commitment to seeing the world in a particular way and to leading one's life in a certain way. It is plausible to respond that that is a reinterpretation of the nature of religious belief, rather than an account of religious belief as it has actually been held by most religious believers. For it entirely bleaches out the supernatural and metaphysical content of such belief. Wittgenstein's account might well be an accurate characterization of the beliefs of some sophisticated modern religious believers: people who have themselves revised or reinterpreted traditional religious belief – treating as metaphorical some of the core doctrines that have traditionally been taken as literal truths. And his account might be an accurate characterization of the most that could reasonably be involved in religious belief in the twentieth or twenty-first centuries; it might correctly characterize what religious belief *ought* to be. But, it seems plausible to think, his account does not accurately capture the character of the beliefs that most religious believers have actually held, either now or in previous generations.

Justification and religious belief. As we have seen, Wittgenstein holds that religious beliefs are not susceptible of justification or criticism by reference to evidence. Is he right about that? Theologians and religious believers do in fact offer proofs of the existence of God, and they do try to produce evidence for the truth of their beliefs. That, it might be suggested, shows that justification and evidence do in fact have a place in religion. Wittgenstein makes a number of points in response to that objection. In the first place, he thinks, the mere fact that someone *says* that they hold their religious beliefs on the basis of evidence does not show that they do (see LC: 60); those who seek to defend religious beliefs by producing evidence for their truth might have misconstrued the character of their own and other people's belief. Relatedly, though it is true that philosophers and theologians offer proofs of the existence of God, it is not on the basis of those proofs that anyone actually believes in God. Nor, Wittgenstein suggests, *could* anyone come to believe in God on the basis of such proofs:

> A proof of God's existence ought really to be something by means of which one could convince oneself that God exists. But I think that what believers who have furnished such proofs have wanted to do is to give their 'belief' an intellectual analysis and foundation, although they themselves could never have come to believe as a result of such proofs.
>
> (CV: 85 [revised edition: 97])

Wittgenstein agrees that people argue about religious beliefs, and that they give reasons for believing one thing or another. But, he says, in religious controversies 'reasons look entirely different from normal reasons' (LC: 56). What counts as a reason for holding a religious belief is different from what counts as a reason for holding an ordinary, factual belief. So the fact that there is a legitimate sense in which people can give reasons for their religious beliefs does not show that religious beliefs can be supported or criticized by the standards of justification that are appropriate to other beliefs. Similarly, Wittgenstein agrees that people sometimes come to accept religious beliefs as the result of *experiences*. But again, he thinks, that does not show that religious beliefs are based on evidence. For the experiences that lead people to religious belief are not sensory perceptions: experiences that reveal God to us in the kind of way that our visual experiences reveal the material objects around us. The sorts of experiences that lead people to believe in God are, for example, experiences of suffering or despair. And those experiences do not bring people to religious belief by providing *evidence* for the existence of God; they function in an essentially non-rational way.

> Life can educate one to a belief in God. And experiences too are what bring this about; but I don't mean visions and other forms of sense experience which show us the 'existence of this being', but, e.g., sufferings of various sorts. These neither show us God in the way a sense impression shows us an object, nor do they give rise to conjectures about him. Experiences, thoughts, – life can force this concept on us.
>
> (CV: 86 [revised edition: 97])

Religion and relativism. The idea that religious belief is 'something like a passionate commitment to a system of reference' has an important implication for the common-sense thought that religious beliefs, like any other beliefs, may be true or false, correct or incorrect. Wittgenstein often compares a system of concepts to a system of measurement. There are many different systems and units for the measurement of length or distance. Now one system of measurement can be simpler or more natural to use than another; it can be more convenient for a given purpose; and so on. But, Wittgenstein insists, it would be a mistake to think that one of these systems is right and the others are wrong; they are simply different systems. And, he thinks, the same goes for systems of concepts. One set of concepts can be simpler or more natural to use than another; it can be more convenient or more memorable; and so on. But a system of concepts cannot itself be right or wrong, true or false. And if religious belief is a commitment to using a particular system of concepts, then the same will apply to religious beliefs too. If one person believes in the Last Judgement and another does not, they will employ very different sets of concepts: one will conceive all actions in terms of reward, punishment, and retribution; the other will not. But, on Wittgenstein's view, it will make no sense to say that one of these people is right and the other wrong; that one set of concepts is correct and the other incorrect. The two people will simply have different 'world-pictures' or 'forms of life'. And world-pictures or forms of life cannot themselves be correct or incorrect.

Supporters of Wittgenstein have defended that idea. They have defended the idea that religious belief has its own standards of reason and argument, internal to the religious world-picture. And they have defended the idea that it is, therefore, a mistake to criticize religious beliefs for failing to meet the standards of rationality that are drawn from other world-pictures: for example, the standards internal to the scientific world-picture. Critics have responded that, if world-pictures or forms of life are answerable only to their own internal standards of evidence and reasoning, we will be left with a radical relativism in which any set of beliefs, however ridiculous, will be insulated from criticism and counted as legitimate, provided only that it is adequate by its own standards (see e.g. Nielsen 1967). (This is a version of the criticism we have already seen in connection with On Certainty: that Wittgenstein's position about justification and world-pictures, specifically his idea that justification can only take place within a system of belief, leads to a pernicious relativism (see Chapter 7 section 4 above).)

Wittgenstein is right that beliefs should not be judged by inappropriate standards: standards they do not and need not attempt to meet. We should not assess the justification of an aesthetic judgement, for example, by the standards appropriate to the justification of a scientific theory; we should not judge the strength of an inductive argument by the standards of deductive proof; and so on. But in the case of religious belief, what *are* the appropriate standards of justification and criticism?

If religion were a completely self-contained 'language-game' – an isolated compartment of our lives, cut off from non-religious beliefs and forms of reasoning – then it might be right to hold that religious beliefs are immune from being criticized by the standards of evidence and justification we apply elsewhere. It would certainly be possible for people to engage in a kind of religious practice that was completely self-contained in this way: a practice that involved ceremonies and rituals, that employed certain forms of words, and so on, but that had nothing to do with any other activities or beliefs. But, Wittgenstein's critic will say, religion as it actually exists is not completely cut off from all non-religious beliefs and forms of reasoning in that way. For one thing, religion involves beliefs about the nature of reality, and about the causes and consequences of various events. And those beliefs are not completely isolated and self-contained; they are factual beliefs about the world, which are susceptible of truth and falsity in the same way as any other beliefs. For another thing, if religious beliefs are supposed to be true, they are answerable to the same standards of coherence and rationality as other beliefs. If the Christian doctrine of the Trinity is logically incoherent, for instance, we cannot simply shrug our shoulders and say that religious belief does not aspire to meet the standards of rationality we apply elsewhere; we must acknowledge that the doctrine cannot be true.

What should we conclude? If religious beliefs are supposed to be true in the same sense as other beliefs, they cannot be judged by a distinctive set of standards that are internal to the religious world-picture to which they belong; they are answerable to the same standards of truth and rationality that we apply elsewhere. On the other hand, if religion is a self-contained practice, with no implications for our other beliefs – if, in particular, religious utterances and beliefs are not supposed to be literally true – then religion is not answerable to the standards of truth and rationality that are appropriate to non-religious beliefs. The question, then, is whether or not religious beliefs are supposed to be literally true: true in just the same way as other beliefs. It does seem possible for there to be a religious practice that is insulated from normal standards of truth and rationality, because the beliefs involved do not aspire to literal truth. Such a practice would fit Wittgenstein's characterization of religion and religious belief. And, as we said above, perhaps Wittgenstein's account is true of the religious beliefs of some sophisticated contemporary believers. But, as before, his account seems much less plausible as a description of the religious beliefs of most ordinary religious believers.

2. ANTHROPOLOGY

Like his views about religious belief, Wittgenstein's views about anthropology – in particular, his views about explanation in anthropology, and about the understanding of ritual and ceremonial actions – have had an important impact outside philosophy. His writings on anthropology, like his comments on religious belief, are brief and were not intended for publication. But they express a powerful series of intuitions – articulated in a critique of Sir James George Frazer's monumental study of magic and religion, *The Golden Bough*. Wittgenstein's response to Frazer's book – contained in his 'Remarks on Frazer's *Golden Bough*' – occupies a significant place in scholarly discussion of Frazer (it is described as 'seminal' by the editor of a recent edition of Frazer's work (Frazer 1994: xlv)). It has helped to inspire an approach to anthropological explanation – and to explanation in the social sciences more generally – that goes beyond mere criticism of Frazer. And it connects in various illuminating ways to other strands in Wittgenstein's philosophy.

The Golden Bough was first published in 1890; the 12-volume third edition was completed in 1915. In it, Frazer describes the rituals and ceremonies of a wide range of early and pre-industrial societies throughout the world. He sees magic, religion, and science as different systems for understanding and manipulating the natural world. And he advances the simple, general thesis that the development of human thought 'has on the whole been from magic through religion to science' (Frazer 1994: 804). As human beings become more knowledgeable and sophisticated, he thinks, 'magic is gradually superseded by religion', which in turn 'is displaced by science' (Frazer 1994: 805). Frazer's work was widely read and discussed in the years between the two world wars; it had a deep influence on the literature and intellectual life of its time.

Wittgenstein's friend Maurice Drury, reports that, in 1931:

> Wittgenstein told me he had long wanted to read Frazer's The Golden Bough and asked me to get hold of a copy out of the Union library and read it out loud to him. I got the first volume of the full edition and we continued to read from it for some weeks.
>
> (Drury 1984: 134)

During that time, Wittgenstein wrote comments on Frazer, some of which were later incorporated in a typescript he assembled in 1938, now published as part I of Wittgenstein's 'Remarks on Frazer's Golden Bough'. Part II of those 'Remarks' comprises a series of 'pencil notes on scraps of paper' that Wittgenstein made for himself while reading an abridged edition of Frazer's book some years later. As well as these written comments, there are records of remarks about Frazer from Wittgenstein's lectures in 1933 (see Moore 1954–55: 106–7; and WLC ii: 33–4). None of these remarks was intended for publication; they are nothing like a finished work. Nonetheless, a number of themes emerge very clearly. And there is good reason to think that the main themes in Wittgenstein's critique of Frazer would have survived any revision or reformulation.

Wittgenstein is particularly critical of three features of Frazer's work. First, there is the essentialism that informs Frazer's discussion: the fact that Frazer aims to give a uniform explanation of different ceremonies or practices. Second, there is Frazer's instrumentalism: his idea that people engage in magic and rituals in order to bring about certain effects. Third, there is Frazer's idea that we can explain a ritual or ceremony by tracing it back to its historical origins: so that, for example, a ceremony in which people burn an effigy is explained by showing that it is descended from an earlier practice in which real people were burnt (see WLC ii: 33). We can take these points in turn.

i. Wittgenstein's critique of Frazer: against essentialism and instrumentalism

Frazer asks, 'What is the meaning of [the sacrificial rites of the ancient Celts]? Why were men and animals burnt to death at these festivals?' (Frazer 1994: 748). In answering that question, he first advances a theory about the purpose of 'modern' European fire festivals: festivals celebrated in various places in Europe as late as the seventeenth and eighteenth centuries. Then he connects the ancient Celtic practice to these modern festivals:

> If we are right in interpreting the modern European fire-festivals as attempts to break the power of witchcraft by burning or banning the witches and warlocks, it seems to follow that we must explain the human sacrifices of the [ancient] Celts in the same manner; that is, we must suppose that the men whom the Druids burnt . . . were condemned to death on the ground that they were witches or wizards, and that the mode of execution by fire was chosen because . . . burning is deemed the surest way of getting rid of these noxious and dangerous beings.
>
> (Frazer 1994: 748)

He comments explicitly on the merits of explaining the modern festivals and the ancient Celtic sacrifices in the same way:

> One advantage of explaining the ancient Celtic sacrifices in this way is that it introduces, as it were, a harmony and consistency into the treatment which Europe has meted out to witches from the earliest times down to about two centuries ago.
>
> (ibid.)

Wittgenstein's first objection to these views of Frazer's is that it is a mistake to assume that there is one underlying feature or motive common even to all the modern fire festivals Frazer describes – let alone a feature that is also common to the practices of the ancient Celts: a motive for engaging in such festivals that can be found in every case. Of course, he acknowledges, there are similarities between the fire festivals found at different times and places. But: 'Besides these similarities, what seems to me to be most striking is the dissimilarity of all these rites. It is a multiplicity of faces with common features which continually emerges here and there' (RFGB: 143).

Wittgenstein makes essentially the same point in his lectures, in connection with a different example. Moore reports him as saying:

> That it was a mistake to suppose that there was only one 'reason' in the sense of 'motive', which led people to perform a particular action – to suppose that there was 'one motive, which was the motive'. He gave as an instance of this sort of mistake Frazer's statement, in speaking of Magic, that when primitive people stab an effigy of a particular person, they believe that they have hurt the person in question. He said that primitive people do not always entertain this 'false scientific belief', though in some cases they may: that they may have quite different reasons for stabbing the effigy. But he said that the tendency to suppose that there is 'one motive which is the motive' was 'enormously strong', giving as an instance that there are theories of play each of which gives only one answer to the question 'Why do children play?'
>
> (Moore 1954–55: 106)

The same erroneous tendency, Wittgenstein thinks, 'comes out in such questions as, Why do people hunt?, Why do they build high buildings?' (WLC ii: 33): questions that assume that people have a single reason for doing such things.

Wittgenstein's second objection to Frazer develops naturally from this first point. Frazer explains magical and ceremonial practices in terms of their supposed utility: people stab effigies, he thinks, because they believe that doing so will cause injury to the person whom the effigy resembles; they perform rain-making ceremonies because they believe that doing so will bring about rain; they light fires and burn effigies in order to drive out witches; and so on. Wittgenstein does not deny that people may *sometimes* engage in magic and ritual because they believe that it will have such effects. But, he claims, it is not true that that is *generally* the reason why people engage in such practices. He offers a number of considerations in favour of that claim.

In the first place, he thinks, we should compare the primitive or ritual actions of other peoples with actions that we perform ourselves:

> Burning in effigy. Kissing the picture of one's beloved. That is obviously not based on the belief that it will have some specific effect on the object which the picture represents. It aims at satisfaction and achieves it. Or rather: it aims at nothing at all; we just behave this way and then we feel satisfied.
>
> (RFGB: 123)

We do not kiss someone's picture in the belief that it will affect the person whom the picture represents. Nor is our action grounded in any other beliefs. It is simply a way of acting that comes naturally to us. By the same token, Wittgenstein argues, there is no reason to assume that the people who stab or burn an effigy believe that their action will have an effect on the person the effigy represents. Like our action of kissing a picture, their action may simply be something that they find it natural or appropriate to do in that kind of situation.

Second, Wittgenstein argues that, if people really believed that they could affect a thing by acting on a representation of that thing, one would expect them to act on that belief quite generally. So we would, for example, expect them to think that repairing a model hut would have effects on the real hut that the model represents; or that carving a model arrow would have effects on a real arrow. But people do not think that: 'The same savage, who stabs the picture of his enemy apparently in order to kill him, really builds his hut out of wood and carves his arrow skilfully and not in effigy' (RFGB: 125). The fact that the man builds his hut and carves his arrow in the ordinary way, Wittgenstein suggests, shows that his beliefs about cause and effect are not generally false. So it is reasonable to think that the man also knows perfectly well that stabbing a picture will not cause injury to the person it represents, and thus that stabbing the picture is not something done for its supposed utility.

Third, Wittgenstein thinks, Frazer's own account itself suggests that some of the practices he describes are not undertaken out of false causal beliefs:

> I read, among many similar examples, of a Rain-King in Africa to
> whom the people pray for rain when the rainy period comes. But
> surely that means that they do not really believe that he can make it
> rain, otherwise they would do it in the dry periods of the year in which
> the land is a 'parched and arid desert'.
>
> (RFGB: 137)

So the action of praying to the Rain-King should be conceived in some
non-instrumental way. Perhaps it is a celebration of impending rain,
for example; or an anxious expression of the expectation of rain.

Wittgenstein is plainly right that people sometimes engage in rituals
and ceremonies without believing that their actions have any instrumental value. In many cases, as he says, performing ritual or ceremonial
actions is an end in itself; something we do for its own sake. That is true
of many of our own ritual or ceremonial actions. We ourselves do not
lay flowers on a grave because we think that the dead person will enjoy
the scent, or because we think that she will need them in an afterlife, or
for any other instrumental reason: giving flowers is simply the thing to
do when someone has died; it is an expression of our grief and sympathy. However, it is one thing to say that those who perform rituals
and ceremonies *need not* suppose that their actions have any instrumental value. It is another thing to say that the participants in this or that
actual ceremony *do not* believe that their actions have an instrumental
value. And Wittgenstein might well have underestimated the extent to
which some of the practices he mentions *are*, or were, supposed by the
participants to have such a value. For example, he implies that the fact
that people only pray to the Rain-King when rain is anyway expected
shows that they do not really believe that he has the power to make
rain. But the continuation of Frazer's account casts doubt on that idea:
'If no shower falls, the people assemble and demand that the king shall
give them rain; and if the sky still continues cloudless, they rip up his
belly, in which he is believed to keep the storms' (Frazer 1994: 78).
That suggests that the people really do believe that the Rain-King could
have brought rain, and that their action in killing him will increase the
chance of rain. It is of course an empirical question whether any actual
ritual or ceremony is believed by the participants to have an instrumental value. But it is plausible that Wittgenstein underestimates the extent
to which the participants in many rituals and ceremonies have, in fact,
approached them in that way.

ii. Wittgenstein's critique of Frazer: causal explanation and surveyable representation

Wittgenstein's third main criticism of Frazer's discussions of ritual and ceremony in *The Golden Bough* is that Frazer wrongly thinks that the meaning or significance of a practice can be explained by tracing it back to its historical origins. Moore reports Wittgenstein as saying:

> that it was a mistake to suppose that why, e.g. the account of the Beltane Festival 'impresses us so much' is because it has 'developed from a festival in which a real man was burnt'. He accused Frazer of thinking that this was the reason. He said that our puzzlement as to why it impresses us is not diminished by giving the causes from which the festival arose, but is diminished by finding other similar festivals: to find these may make it seem 'natural', whereas to give the cause from which it arose cannot do this.
>
> (Moore 1954–55: 106–7)

To understand Wittgenstein's point, we need to know what the Beltane festival was; how Frazer explains it; why Wittgenstein objects to Frazer's explanation; and how he himself thinks the festival should be understood.

Frazer writes:

> In the central Highlands of Scotland bonfires, known as the Beltane fires, were formerly kindled with great ceremony on the first of May, and the traces of human sacrifices at them were particularly clear and unequivocal. The custom of lighting the bonfires lasted in various places far into the eighteenth century . . .
>
> (Frazer 1994: 716)

He quotes a description from the late 1700s:

> After kindling the bonfire with the tein-eigin [need-fire] the company prepared their victuals . . . . Towards the close of the entertainment, the person who officiated as master of the feast produced a large cake baked with eggs and scalloped round the edge, called am bon-nach beal-tine – i.e. the Beltane cake. It was divided into a number of pieces, and distributed in great form to the company. There was one particular piece which whoever got was called cailleach beal-tine – i.e.

the Beltane carline, a term of great reproach. Upon his being known, part of the company laid hold of him and made a show of putting him into the fire; but the majority interposing, he was rescued. And in some places they laid him flat on the ground, making as if they would quarter him. Afterwards, he was pelted with egg-shells and retained the odious appellation during the whole year. And while the feast was fresh in people's memory, they affected to speak of the cailleach beal-tine as dead.

(Frazer 1994: 718)

Frazer comments that, in this festival, 'the pretence of burning people is . . . carried so far that it seems reasonable to regard it as a mitigated survival of an older custom of actually burning them' (Frazer 1994: 744). 'Human sacrifices by fire are known, on unquestionable evidence, to have been systematically practised by the Celts' (ibid.: 745) in ancient times. And the Beltane fires, says Frazer, exhibit 'unequivocal traces' (ibid.: 745) of those human sacrifices.

Wittgenstein raises two kinds of question about the Beltane festival. First, what is the festival *about*; what is it *to do* with? Like Frazer, he thinks it has to do with human sacrifice. But, he asks, what is it about the festival that makes it true that it has to do with human sacrifice? Second, why does the festival impress us in the way it does; what makes it seem so terrible or sinister?

According to Wittgenstein, Frazer's idea is that what makes it the case that the eighteenth-century festival has to do with human sacrifice is that it developed from an ancient custom of actually sacrificing people. Similarly, according to Wittgenstein, Frazer thinks that it is the fact that the modern festival had that origin that gives it its terrible or sinister quality. It is not in fact obvious from Frazer's text that he does think what Wittgenstein represents him as thinking; but since our interest is in Wittgenstein rather than Frazer, we can leave the accuracy of Wittgenstein's reading aside and focus on Wittgenstein's reasons for rejecting what he takes to be Frazer's view.

Wittgenstein asks:

Does the sinister, as we may call it, attach to the practice of the Beltane Fire Festival itself, as it was carried on one hundred years ago, or is the Festival sinister only if the hypothesis of its origin turns out to be true?

(RFGB: 143–5)

His answer is unequivocal: the sinister character of the festival is not dependent on its causal origin: 'I believe it is clearly the inner nature of the modern practice which itself seems sinister to us' (RFGB: 145). And it is neither necessary nor sufficient for having that 'inner nature', he thinks, that a practice should be derived from an earlier practice in which people were actually sacrificed. On the one hand:

> even if both the prehistoric origin of the practice and its derivation from an earlier practice are proven historically, it is nevertheless possible that the practice has nothing whatever sinister about it today, that nothing of the prehistoric horror remains attached to it. Perhaps today it is engaged in only by children who compete in baking cakes and decorating them with knobs.
>
> (RFGB: 145)

On the other hand, where a modern practice *does* have something sinister about it, 'the deep, the sinister, do[es] not depend on the history of the practice having been like this at all; nor on the fact that it was perhaps probably like this' (RFGB: 147), but rather on the features that now give it the appearance of being concerned with human sacrifice. That is a matter of the words and actions the practice now involves, the spirit in which the participants enter into it, their character and intentions, and so on (see RFGB: 145). And those aspects of the festival could be as they are whether or not the festival is actually derived from a historic practice of human sacrifice.

In arguing that the significance of a practice is a matter of its 'inner nature' rather than its causal origin, Wittgenstein is applying to this case a general principle that he applies in other contexts too: that a thing's meaning or significance is not determined by its causal origins or its causal relations to other things. We saw another application of that principle in Wittgenstein's objection to Russell's causal theory of intentionality (see Chapter 5 section 1.i above). It is neither necessary nor sufficient for my desire's being a desire *for an apple*, he argues, that getting an apple would remove my feeling of discomfort. Rather, being a desire *for an apple* is an intrinsic feature of the desire itself. Similarly, in a discussion of aesthetics, Wittgenstein considers such questions as 'Why is this beautiful?', 'What is wrong with this melody?', 'Why will this bass not do?' (see WLC ii: 34–9; Moore 1954–55: 103–7). Those questions, he argues, are not to be answered by giving causal explanations: what makes something beautiful, for instance, is not that it causes pleasure; and what makes a melody wrong is not that it causes a feeling of dissatisfaction. To 'remove the aesthetic puzzle one feels when asked what makes a thing beautiful' (WLC ii: 38) we need an account, not of a thing's causal origins or the effects that it produces, but of the reasons why it is beautiful. He makes parallel points in many other contexts.

If the character and significance of a practice are not to be explained by tracing its causal history, how *should* they be explained? In Wittgenstein's view, explaining a practice involves seeing connections between it and other things: connections between this practice and other practices that are already familiar, for example; or between this practice and things we do ourselves. To understand a practice in that way, Wittgenstein says, involves achieving a 'perspicuous' or 'surveyable' representation of the facts:

> The concept of perspicuous representation is of fundamental importance for us. It denotes the form of our representation, the way we see things . . .
>   This perspicuous representation brings about the understanding which consists precisely in the fact that we 'see the connections'. Hence the importance of finding connecting links.
>
> (RFGB: 133)

(That passage, written in 1931, is reproduced almost word-for-word in *Philosophical Investigations* §122 (quoted above in Chapter 4 section 1). 'Perspicuous representation' and 'surveyable representation' (which is the phrase used in the English translation of *Philosophical Investigations*) are alternative renderings of the same German expression.) One way to understand the Beltane festival, for example, is to connect it to 'the familiar facts of human sacrifice' (RFGB: 145): to see the practice 'along the lines' of human sacrifice. And seeing it in that way has nothing to do with any hypothesis about the causal origin of the festival. Similarly, we might come to understand the Beltane festival by finding other festivals that we already understand and seeing the Beltane festival as similar in various respects to them (see Moore 1954–55: 107). Or again, we can come to understand an unfamiliar practice, Wittgenstein thinks, by seeing connections between it and things that we ourselves do. We have already seen one example: Wittgenstein's juxtaposition of the practice of burning people in effigy and our own habit of kissing the picture of one's beloved, which gets us to appreciate why people might see a point in burning effigies without thinking that there is any instrumental value in doing so. Similarly, he says, suppose we want to understand a practice in which people beat an inanimate object with sticks. We should reflect on our own behaviour:

> When I am furious about something, I sometimes beat the ground or a tree with my walking stick. But I certainly do not believe that the ground is to blame or that my beating can help anything. 'I am venting my anger.' And all rites are of this kind. Such actions may be called Instinct-actions . . . .
> Once such a phenomenon is brought into connection with an instinct which I myself possess, this is precisely the explanation wished for; that is, the explanation which resolves the particular difficulty.
> (RFGB: 137–9)

We explain the alien or unfamiliar practice by seeing it in the light of a natural instinct that we have ourselves.

The idea that philosophical understanding of a phenomenon is achieved by gaining a 'perspicuous representation' or 'surveyable representation' of the facts, a representation that displays connections between the phenomenon in question and others in a way that reveals the nature of the puzzling phenomenon, is a central theme in Wittgenstein's later philosophy. And he first articulated that idea in 1931, in connection with Frazer and explanation in anthropology. He went on to see a much more general application for the idea of perspicuous or surveyable representation. As we saw in Chapter 4, a fundamental feature in the transition from the *Tractatus* to Wittgenstein's later work was a change in his conception of the proper methodology for philosophy. The *Tractatus* envisaged a programme of logical analysis that would reveal the clear, unambiguous structure of elementary propositions that lies hidden beneath the misleading structure of ordinary language. In the later philosophy, clarity is to be achieved, not by penetrating to the hidden essence of phenomena, but by achieving a surveyable representation of facts that already lie open to view. Wittgenstein's remarks on *The Golden Bough* provide an early illustration and application of his notion of surveyable representation.

SUMMARY

Wittgenstein was not a conventionally religious man. He had no sympathy with organized religion, and no interest in the idea of God as creator of the universe. But his powerful sense of duty, his sense of his own guilt, unworthiness, and failings of character, and his desire for redemption, gave him an affinity with certain religious ideas.

In the *Notebooks* and *Tractatus*, Wittgenstein treats 'God' as a term for the meaning of life – the meaning of the world. The meaning of life, he says there, is something that we cannot put into words, but that shows itself in the existence of the world. So believing in God is not a matter of having any factual beliefs; it is a matter of seeing that life has a meaning. In his later philosophy, Wittgenstein retains the idea that religious beliefs are not factual beliefs; and, he says, they cannot be justified or criticized by appeal to evidence. A religious belief is 'something like a passionate commitment to a system of reference': to have religious beliefs is to conceive of the world and oneself in terms of a distinctively religious set of concepts, and to live one's life in a religious way. So the difference between the religious believer and the non-believer is not a difference about any matters of fact; it is a difference in the way they conceive themselves and the world, and in the way they lead their lives. Critics of Wittgenstein's account argue that even if religious beliefs are not *simply* factual beliefs, they do have a factual component, and are true or false in the same way as any other belief. They argue that religious beliefs are susceptible of justification and criticism by reference to evidence. And they object that the idea that world-pictures or systems of reference, including religious world-pictures, cannot themselves be true or false leads to an unacceptable relativism.

Wittgenstein's discussion of Frazer's *Golden Bough* makes three main criticisms of Frazer's explanations of rituals and ceremonies. Wittgenstein rejects Frazer's essentialist assumption that practices in different times and places will have the same basic character and will be explicable in the same way. He objects to Frazer's instrumentalist assumption that people always engage in rituals and ceremonies as a means to achieving a desired end – proposing instead that much ceremonial behaviour is performed as an end in itself. And he rejects the idea that the meaning or significance of a practice is to be explained by tracing it back to its historical origins. We explain a practice by achieving a perspicuous or surveyable representation of the facts, he thinks; not by determining its causal origin.

FURTHER READING

The *Tractatus*'s remarks on God come at 6.372 and 6.432. A slightly fuller expression of Wittgenstein's early view of God and religion is contained in Wittgenstein's *Notebooks 1914–16*, 72–9.

For Wittgenstein's later views on religion and religious belief, see:

'Lectures on Religious Belief' in Wittgenstein's *Lectures and Conversations on Aesthetics, Psychology and Religious Belief*.
Culture and Value. (Remarks on God, religion, Christianity, etc. appear throughout this volume, interspersed with comments on a range of other topics. The index helps to identify relevant passages.)

Some brief but significant comments about religion are contained in:

'A Lecture on Ethics', in Wittgenstein, *Philosophical Occasions*.

Wittgenstein's written remarks on Frazer can be found in:

'Remarks on Frazer's *Golden Bough*', in Wittgenstein, *Philosophical Occasions*.

For a one-volume abridgement of *The Golden Bough*, which contains the passages on which Wittgenstein commented, see:

Frazer, J. (1994) *The Golden Bough: A Study in Magic and Religion*, new abridged edition, ed. R. Fraser, Oxford: Oxford University Press.

There are discussions of Wittgenstein's own relation to religion in both the main biographies:

McGuinness, B. (1988) *Wittgenstein: A Life –Young Ludwig 1889–1921*, London: Duckworth; reprinted by Penguin Books, Harmondsworth, 1990.
Monk, R. (1990) *Wittgenstein: The Duty of Genius*, London: Jonathan Cape.

There are interesting comments on Wittgenstein and religion in a number of memoirs, including:

Drury, M. O'C. (1981) 'Some Notes on Conversations with Wittgenstein' and 'Conversations with Wittgenstein', in R. Rhees (ed.) *Ludwig Wittgenstein: Personal Recollections*, Oxford: Blackwell.
Engelmann, P. (1967) *Letters from Ludwig Wittgenstein with a Memoir*, ed. B. McGuinness, trans. L. Furtmüller, Oxford: Blackwell, pp. 70–81.
Malcolm, N. (1984) *Ludwig Wittgenstein: A Memoir*, 2nd edition, Oxford: Oxford University Press, pp. 58–60, 82–3.
von Wright, G. H. (1955) 'Ludwig Wittgenstein: A Biographical Sketch', *Philosophical Review* 64: 527–45; reprinted in Malcolm, *Ludwig Wittgenstein: A Memoir*, pp. 17–18.

For a sympathetic introduction to Wittgenstein's philosophy of religion, see:

Clack, B. (1999) *An Introduction to Wittgenstein's Philosophy of Religion*, Edinburgh: Edinburgh University Press.

Kai Nielsen is an influential critic of Wittgenstein's discussion of religious belief. He published a critique of Wittgensteinian philosophy of religion in the mid-1960s:

Nielsen, K. (1967) 'Wittgensteinian Fideism', *Philosophy*, 42: 191–209.

A more recent paper is:

Nielsen, K. (2001) 'Wittgenstein and Wittgensteinians on Religion', in R. Arrington and M. Addis (eds) *Wittgenstein and Philosophy of Religion*, London: Routledge.

D. Z. Phillips has used Wittgensteinian ideas enthusiastically in his extensive writings on philosophy of religion. A representative example is:

Phillips, D. Z. (1981) 'Belief, Change, and Forms of Life: The Confusions of Externalism and Internalism', in F. Crosson (ed.), *The Autonomy of Religious Belief*, Notre Dame: University of Notre Dame Press.

A good collection, containing a selection of papers that offer differing assessments of Wittgenstein's ideas, is:

Arrington, R. and Addis, M. (eds) (2001) *Wittgenstein and Philosophy of Religion*, London: Routledge.

The secondary literature on Wittgenstein's discussion of Frazer is less extensive than that on most other aspects of Wittgenstein's work. The following is a good sample:

Bouveresse, J. (2007) 'Wittgenstein's Critique of Frazer', *Ratio*, 20: 357–376.

Cioffi, F. (1981) 'Wittgenstein and the Fire-festivals', in Block, I. *Perspectives on the Philosophy of Wittgenstein*, Oxford: Blackwell.

Clack, B. (2001) 'Wittgenstein and Magic', in R. Arrington and M. Addis (eds) *Wittgenstein and Philosophy of Religion*, London: Routledge.

Hacker, P. M. S. (2001) 'Developmental Hypotheses and Perspicuous Representations: Wittgenstein on Frazer's *Golden Bough*', in Hacker, *Wittgenstein: Connections & Controversies*, Oxford: Oxford University Press.

Johnston, P. (1989) *Wittgenstein and Moral Philosophy*, London: Routledge, pp. 26–38.

Nine

Legacy and influence

Wittgenstein was a great philosopher; and the *Tractatus* and *Philosophical Investigations* have central places in the history of twentieth-century philosophy. But there is deep disagreement both about the interpretation of Wittgenstein's work and about the relevance or importance of his ideas for contemporary philosophy.

Many philosophers see a fundamental tension between Wittgenstein's later philosophy and contemporary Anglo-American philosophy. Contemporary philosophy, on this view, is systematic and constructive; it treats philosophical problems as genuine problems, to be solved by producing correct philosophical theories. Wittgenstein's philosophy, on the other hand, is diagnostic and therapeutic; it conceives philosophical problems not as genuine problems but as signs of intellectual confusion, to be dissolved by revealing how those confusions arise and how they can be avoided. So, it is said, a genuinely Wittgensteinian discussion of a philosophical problem will be quite different from the kinds of discussion found in mainstream contemporary philosophy.

Among those who see the relation between Wittgenstein's work and mainstream contemporary philosophy in this way, there are contrasting views about the merits of his ideas. On one side there are supporters of Wittgenstein, who lament the lack of influence his ideas have had on the style and content of current work. On the other side, there are many philosophers who are unimpressed by Wittgenstein's later philosophy and reject its key ideas; if we are looking for the right answers to philosophical questions, they think, Wittgenstein's later work is a bad guide.

My own view is that both these attitudes exaggerate the distance between Wittgenstein's later work and the questions and debates that occupy contemporary philosophers, and that they assess Wittgenstein's contribution in an unnecessarily all-or-nothing way. Wittgenstein has many ideas that are insightful and profound. His work is a rich source of acute insights about language, mind, and knowledge; his critical arguments are always worth taking seriously, and are sometimes decisive; and his positive suggestions are often fruitful. But, like any philosopher, he is not always right. He sometimes takes a genuinely illuminating intuition and pushes it to an unwarranted conclusion; as for example when he moves from the insight that we are not observers of our own beliefs – that we do not find out what we believe on the basis of evidence – to the conclusion that our relation to our own beliefs is not one of knowledge at all. Sometimes his views seem unconvincing; as, for instance, in some of what he says about religious belief. Sometimes it is hard to be clear about exactly what he thought: in some cases, because he was himself unclear what to think. So we should approach Wittgenstein as we would approach any other philosopher. Where Wittgenstein's ideas seem promising, we should see how they can be applied and developed, even if that leads in directions that he himself would not have approved. Where his arguments seem unsuccessful or his conclusions implausible, we should try to understand why he said what he did; but we need not follow him wherever he goes. Above all, if we want to learn from Wittgenstein we should not treat his work as if it existed in isolation; we must consider whether he has good replies to criticisms of what he says, whether his arguments are effective against the best and most convincing versions of the positions he rejects, and so on.

Approached in this spirit, Wittgenstein's work certainly has a continuing relevance for contemporary philosophy. But Wittgenstein is one philosopher among many: part of a philosophical tradition that has continued to develop since his death. It would be wrong to regard him as having a unique position in philosophy, or to credit him with devising an entirely new approach that reveals 'traditional philosophy' to be mistaken or even incoherent.

Wittgenstein's influence on twentieth-century philosophy was immense. It began with his early interactions with Russell; it accelerated with the publication of the *Tractatus*; took a new turn after 1929 through his lectures, conversations, and typescripts; and continued to develop after his death, with the publication first of *Philosophical Investigations* and then of many other writings. This chapter is not the place to review that history (for a comprehensive review, by an author whose sympathies are very much with Wittgenstein, see Hacker 1996). Instead, as a way of illustrating the continuing relevance of Wittgenstein's later philosophy,

I shall highlight some of its key themes and their relation to contemporary philosophical thought. By way of a preliminary, I comment first on the contemporary status of the *Tractatus*.

1. THE *TRACTATUS* AND CONTEMPORARY PHILOSOPHY

The *Tractatus* is a work of supreme elegance and economy, whose ideas combine a captivating simplicity with a profundity and comprehensiveness that becomes more striking the more one studies the book. Its historical influence was profound. But few if any contemporary readers accept its vision of language, logic, and reality. It is for the most part seen rather as a powerful statement of a particular historical position: a position developed in response to problems with which Russell and Frege were wrestling, which offers a novel and ingenious solution to those problems, but which is not, in the end, sustainable.

The *Tractatus*'s account of language is driven by the idea that the meaning of a proposition is a matter of its truth conditions: the sense of a proposition is 'how things stand if it is true' (TLP: 4.022). The idea that meaning is to be understood in terms of truth conditions remains a central commitment of most mainstream philosophy of language. And the *Tractatus*, along with Frege's work, is often cited as a particularly clear and explicit statement of the view. But Wittgenstein's particular way of working out the view – his idea that an elementary proposition represents the particular state of affairs it does by being a picture of that state of affairs – has little if any influence in current work. One reason for that is that Wittgenstein's account is too abstract and sketchy to be much help as an account of the meanings of ordinary propositions. Another reason is that there are significant disanalogies between pictorial representation and propositional representation which undermine the idea that a proposition represents a state of affairs in the very same way that a picture does: for an ordinary picture represents numerous different states of affairs simultaneously; but a proposition represents only one (see Dummett 1981: 35–8). Furthermore, few contemporary philosophers share the *Tractatus*'s conviction that we cannot use language to describe the logical features of language; the features in virtue of which language represents the world. In his Preface to the *Tractatus*, Russell suggested the following possibility:

> that every language has, as Mr Wittgenstein says, a structure
> concerning which, *in the language*, nothing can be said, but that there

may be another language dealing with the structure of the first language, and having itself a new structure, and that to this hierarchy of languages there may be no limit.

(TLP: xxii)

As Russell goes on to say, the *Tractatus* rejected the idea that there could be such a hierarchy of languages. But it is accepted as a piece of uncontroversial orthodoxy today. Finally, contemporary philosophers of language regard the *Tractatus*'s theory of meaning as giving too limited or restricted an account of language: for one thing, it gives no account of the meanings of whole classes of propositions that are clearly meaningful, but which the *Tractatus* regards as nonsensical pseudo-propositions; for another thing, it says nothing at all about any aspect of linguistic meaning other than truth-conditional content.

Similarly, it is a central claim of the *Tractatus* that every proposition is a truth-function of elementary propositions, that all logical relations between propositions result from the way in which complex propositions are built up from elementary propositions, and thus that the only kind of necessity is truth-functional necessity. But none of these ideas has many contemporary supporters. It is not at all plausible that every proposition can be analysed truth-functionally, in terms of a stock of basic, contingent elementary propositions each of which is logically independent of all the others. (It is hard to see how ascriptions of beliefs could be analysed that way, for example, or statements about causation.) Nor is it at all plausible that all logical relations between propositions are analysable truth-functionally – as Wittgenstein himself came to see when he recognized that the logical incompatibility between propositions ascribing different colours to the same point is basic and unanalysable. And it is correspondingly wrong to think that all necessity and possibility can be analysed truth-functionally.

So, though there are many in contemporary philosophy who admire the *Tractatus*, there are few if any who agree with its author that it contains, 'on all essential points, the final solution of the problems' of philosophy (TLP: 4).

2. WITTGENSTEIN'S LATER WORK AND CONTEMPORARY PHILOSOPHY

In previous chapters we have discussed a series of central topics in Wittgenstein's post-*Tractatus* writings: the relation of meaning and use; intentionality; rule-following; sensations and sensation language; the philosophy of psychology; knowledge and certainty; religion and anthropology. In the light of those discussions, we can reflect on some central intellectual themes that run through his later work. That is a good way of drawing his discussions of different topics together. It is also helpful in assessing Wittgenstein's relation to contemporary philosophy. For many of the most significant elements in Wittgenstein's treatment of philosophical problems still have a central place in contemporary discussions.

i. Anti-reductionism

'Everything is what it is and not another thing.' Wittgenstein quoted 'that marvellous motto' with approval in a 1938 lecture (LC: 27). The same motto appeared in his notebooks more than 20 years earlier (NB: 84). It comes from Bishop Butler (see Butler 1914: Preface §39), and was used by G. E. Moore as the epigraph to his book, *Principia Ethica* (Moore 1903). And it is a perfect expression of Wittgenstein's anti-reductionism: his opposition to all attempts to analyse or explain one concept, or one phenomenon, in terms of another. This anti-reductionism is a central theme throughout Wittgenstein's later work. He insists, for example, that there can be no illuminating analysis of the concept *game*: no non-circular set of conditions that are necessary and sufficient for something's being a game. He says that it is impossible to explain in any other terms what it is to follow a rule correctly: to follow a rule correctly is to do what the rule requires; but that such-and-such *is* what the rule requires is a basic, unanalysable truth; it cannot be explained in any other terms. He holds that facts about the meanings of words cannot be reduced to facts about use, characterized in purely physical or behavioural terms. He says that the phenomenon of seeing an aspect is *sui generis* (unique), and cannot be reduced to some combination of experience and thought. And so on.

Like Wittgenstein, many contemporary philosophers reject reductionism. They maintain, for example, that we cannot analyse the concepts of knowledge, truth, meaning, goodness, beauty, and so forth in terms that do not presuppose the concepts to be analysed; they hold that the mental cannot be reduced to the physical, that ethical facts cannot be reduced to non-ethical facts, and so on. But the lure of reductionism in philosophy remains powerful. Some philosophers hold that the ordinary notions of meaning, thought, and so on can be reductively explained in other terms: terms that they take to be more basic and more scientifically respectable. Others accept that the ordinary notions cannot be reduced to anything more basic or scientific, but argue, for that reason, that the ordinary notions should be abandoned and replaced by others that can be explained in more basic terms.

So the anti-reductionism that runs through Wittgenstein's philosophy informs much current philosophy, too. But it is by no means universally accepted.

ii. Anti-scientism

In a passage written in 1930, Wittgenstein contrasts his way of thinking with the scientific way of thinking:

> It is all one to me whether or not the typical western scientist understands or appreciates my work, since he will not in any case understand the spirit in which I write. Our civilization is characterized by the word 'progress'. Progress is its form rather than making progress being one of its features. Typically it constructs. It is occupied with building an ever more complicated structure. And even clarity is sought only as a means to this end, not as an end in itself. For me on the contrary clarity, perspicuity are valuable in themselves.
>
> I am not interested in constructing a building, as much as in having a perspicuous view of the foundations of possible buildings.
>
> So I am not aiming at the same target as the scientists and my way of thinking is different from theirs.
>
> (CV: 7 [revised edition: 9])

Wittgenstein does not claim that there is nothing to be learned by applying scientific method. Nor does he reject the findings of science itself. But he is hostile to the tendency he finds in modern culture to think that science has a monopoly on the truth; that only science has anything to teach us: 'People nowadays think that scientists exist to instruct them, poets, musicians etc. to give them pleasure. The idea that these have something to teach them − that does not occur to them' (CV: 36 [revised edition: 42]). In particular, Wittgenstein is hostile to the idea that philosophy is, or should be, conducted in the same way as science. And he laments philosophy's 'preoccupation with the method of science':

> I mean the method of reducing the explanation of natural phenomena to the smallest possible number of primitive natural laws; and, in

mathematics, of unifying the treatment of different topics by using a generalization. Philosophers constantly see the method of science before their eyes, and are irresistibly tempted to ask and answer questions in the way science does. This tendency is the real source of metaphysics, and leads the philosopher into complete darkness. I want to say here that it can never be our job to reduce anything to anything, or to explain anything. Philosophy really *is* 'purely descriptive'. (Think of such questions as 'Are there sense data?' and ask: What method is there of determining this? Introspection?).

(BB: 18)

The contrast Wittgenstein sees between science and philosophy has many aspects. Science, he thinks, is *essentialist*; it looks for features that are common to different things of the same kind. It has a *craving for generality*; it explains things by subsuming the particular case under general laws. It is characteristically *reductionist*; it seeks to explain things in terms of 'the smallest possible number of primitive natural laws'. Philosophy, Wittgenstein thinks, must resist all those tendencies. For the understanding it seeks is fundamentally different in kind from the understanding sought by science. When a philosopher asks whether it is possible for someone who has spent their entire life in total isolation to follow a rule, she is not asking a scientific question: whether such a thing is physically or psychologically possible; whether it could ever happen. She is asking a conceptual question: whether anything that such an individual did would *count* as following a rule. Similarly, when the philosopher asks how it is possible to grasp the whole meaning of a word at a stroke, or in a flash, she is not asking how people manage to do it: what causal processes make it possible. She wants an account of what it is to grasp the meaning of a word that shows why there is no mystery in the fact that grasping the whole meaning of the word is something that can happen in a flash.

The anti-scientism of Wittgenstein's philosophy runs through all the discussions we have seen. One instance is his insistence that there need be no feature that is common to all the things that fall under a general term. Another is his rejection of the causal theories of intentionality proposed by Russell and by Ogden and Richards, which were explicitly motivated by the aim of showing how the 'mysterious' relation between a thought and its object could be explained in scientifically respectable terms. And opposition to scientism pervades Wittgenstein's critique of Frazer's *Golden Bough*, the central thrust of which is that Frazer pursues the study of anthropology as though it were a science (offering causal explanations, for example, and aiming to explain practices of very different sorts by appeal to a small set of general principles of human behaviour). Furthermore, Wittgenstein objects, Frazer treats magic and religion as though they were themselves a form of science – a set of beliefs about the causal structure of the world, and a set of practices designed to bring about desired results. For Wittgenstein, by contrast, understanding a practice is a matter not of determining its causal origin but of seeing the point it has for its participants. And people's reasons for engaging in magic and religion are not generally instrumental reasons.

How does Wittgenstein's anti-scientism compare with current views in philosophy? There remains a deep divide between those who conceive philosophy as aiming for an entirely different kind of understanding from science and those who conceive it as being continuous with science. And there remains deep disagreement about the extent to which we should allow our conception of the nature and extent of reality to be dictated by science. On one side, there are philosophers who hold that there is no more to reality than is revealed by science. On this view, the only genuine features of reality are features that are either directly studied by science or can be systematically mapped onto things that are studied by science. On this view, for instance, the truth about human psychology is a matter of what neuroscience tells us about the functioning of the brain. So if the properties in terms of which we ordinarily understand one another – belief, intention, and so forth – turn out not to map onto the properties discovered by neuroscience, it will follow that human beings do not really have those properties: it might be useful or convenient in everyday life to talk about beliefs, intentions, and so on; but such talk will not be literally true. On the other side of this divide, there are philosophers who, like Wittgenstein, see no reason to restrict what is real to what is revealed by science. It is an obvious truth, they think, that human beings do have beliefs and intentions. And that truth does not require any justification or vindication from neuroscience. So if it turns out that belief and intention have no systematic relation to any of the properties that figure in neuroscience, that will not show that human beings do not really have beliefs or intentions. It will simply show that the descriptive and explanatory purposes of our common-sense psychological talk are very different from those of neuroscience. The dispute between these two approaches remains a live issue in contemporary philosophy: one of the fundamental dividing lines between different schools of philosophical thought.

iii. Anti-intellectualism

It is a recurrent theme of Wittgenstein's later philosophy that our language and beliefs are grounded in natural, pre-linguistic behaviour. 'The origin and primitive form of the language game is a reaction; only from this can more complicated forms develop. Language – I want to say – is a refinement. "In the beginning was the deed"' (CE: 395). So wrote Wittgenstein in 1937. (The final sentence, quoted from Goethe's play, *Faust*, is repeated in *On Certainty* (OC: 402).) That basic idea is applied at many points in Wittgenstein's philosophy. We can list some examples.

Wittgenstein criticizes Augustine for offering an over-intellectualized account of language-acquisition, on which the child starts off with a set of concepts, and learns language by consciously matching up people's words with the concepts he already has. The truth, Wittgenstein thinks, is that the process of learning a first language is not an intellectual one at all; it is a non-rational process of training or conditioning.

Our ability to learn and follow rules, Wittgenstein thinks, depends on our natural, pre-linguistic tendency to respond to training in the same way as others. We all find it natural, for example, to respond to the usual training in counting by continuing the number series in the same way. If we did not, it would be impossible for us to learn and follow mathematical rules. And the process of applying a familiar rule, he insists, is fundamentally a matter of action, not thought: when we apply a familiar rule, we do not engage in any intellectual activity; we do not have reasons for following the rule as we do; we act blindly, without reasons.

In a similar way, Wittgenstein thinks, the whole structure of knowledge and belief is grounded not in thought or reasoning but in action. The end of giving grounds 'is not an ungrounded presupposition: it is an ungrounded *way of acting*' (OC: 110, emphasis added). Our certainty about Moorean propositions is 'something that lies beyond being justified or unjustified'; it is 'something animal' (OC: 359).

A final example comes from Wittgenstein's discussion of the concept of pain. Self-ascriptions of pain, he suggests, are a taught addition to our natural, pre-linguistic expressions of pain. And ascriptions of pain to others are a taught addition to the natural, pre-linguistic reactions of sympathy and concern with which we respond to others' expressions of pain.

Contemporary philosophy is thoroughly in sympathy with Wittgenstein's insistence that thought and language have their basis in primitive, pre-linguistic behaviour; with his opposition to rationalistic, intellectualized models of thought and language; and with his stress on the continuities between the conscious, linguistic behaviour of adults and the pre-linguistic, pre-conceptual behaviour of infants and non-human animals. These interests are often pursued in a somewhat different spirit from Wittgenstein's. In particular, many modern philosophers are less concerned than Wittgenstein to preserve a sharp distinction between empirical, psychological enquiry and conceptual, philosophical enquiry. For Wittgenstein, the point of drawing attention to the essentially non-rational nature of the early stages of a child's acquisition of language is not to stimulate an investigation of the details of the process by which human children actually acquire their first language. From the point of view of philosophy, he thinks, those details do not matter. All that matters is the general point that it is possible to acquire language in a way that does not presuppose the possession of a rich set of concepts. And in order to make that general point, he thinks, it is enough to remind us of the way in which children pick up their first language, by a process of imitation and training; we need no more detail than that. Similarly, the point of Wittgenstein's suggestion that we learn the expression 'I am in pain' by being taught to use it in place of our natural, pre-linguistic expressions of pain, is not to stimulate a detailed empirical investigation of the process by which people actually acquire the concept of pain. It is simply to show how the concept could be acquired in a way that does not essentially depend on an internal ostensive definition. And so on. Many modern philosophers take a less rigid view of what should figure in a philosophical account, and are happy to incorporate the results of empirical psychological enquiry in their philosophical discussions. But, however it is pursued, Wittgenstein's stress on the non-rational basis of thought and language is a real insight. And the same insight is central to much contemporary work in philosophy of mind and psychology.

iv. Anti-mentalism

Closely related to Wittgenstein's anti-intellectualism is his anti-mentalism: his opposition to views on which the properties of thought and language are explained in terms of the properties of inner mental states; and his stress on the role of action and practice in understanding the properties of thought, language, and experience. Thus, we saw, he argues against the mentalist view that the meaning of a word is a matter of the images with which it is associated in people's minds. Instead, he thinks, a word's meaning is a matter of its 'whole use in the language': the circumstances that justify its use, the point or purpose of using it, and so on. Similarly, he argues against the mentalist view that the content of an intention, say, is determined by what comes before the mind of the thinker at the time of the intention. The fact that I intend to play a game of chess, for example, is not determined just by what comes before my mind at the time; it depends also on my background abilities – including my mastery of the rules of chess – and on the actual existence of a social practice of playing chess: 'An intention is embedded in a setting, in human customs and institutions. If the technique of the game of chess did not exist, I could not intend to play a game of chess' (PI §337). And Wittgenstein opposes the mentalist view of conscious experience itself. What individuates a sensation, he thinks – what makes it the kind of sensation it is – is not an intrinsic, purely introspective feature of the sensation: something completely independent of external circumstances and the subject's behaviour. It is 'tied up with' the sensation's behavioural expression, and the circumstances in which it is experienced.

Few philosophers nowadays take seriously the idea that the meanings of words should be explained by reference to mental images. There are many, however, who argue, against Wittgenstein, that the meanings of words should be explained by reference to the contents of thoughts; the intentionality of thought, they think, is more basic than the intentionality of language, and can be used to explain it. But there remain prominent modern advocates of the Wittgensteinian view that linguistic meaning is on a par with mental representation; on their view, having beliefs, intentions, and so on, and having a language are mutually interdependent (see e.g. Davidson 1982; McDowell 1994; Brandom 2000).

Some of the issues involved in Wittgenstein's rejection of a mentalist view of thought have returned to philosophical attention in recent debates between *individualism* (or internalism) and *anti-individualism* (or externalism) in philosophy of mind. For individualists, the contents of a person's thoughts depend only on factors intrinsic to the subject: her conscious experiences, her physical make-up, and her behavioural dispositions. So if two individuals are exactly alike in all those respects, the contents of their thoughts will be exactly alike, too. Anti-individualists, by contrast, hold that the contents of thoughts are in part constituted by factors external to the subject: by the physical and social environment in which she is situated. So two people who are alike in all individualistic respects will not necessarily have exactly similar thoughts; if they are located in very different physical and/or social environments, their thoughts will be correspondingly different. Wittgenstein's account of the dependence of intentional states on the existence of social practices of various kinds (for instance, the dependence of the intention to play chess on the existence of a practice of chess-playing) puts him very clearly on the anti-individualist side of this debate. And some arguments deployed by modern anti-individualists are strikingly similar to Wittgenstein's. (A popular style of argument in anti-individualist writings is to describe imaginary subjects who are just like us in all individualistic respects, but are situated in very different contexts, and to appeal to the intuition that the contents of their thoughts would be very different from the contents of our own. Wittgenstein argues in exactly that way (for two examples, see RFM: 336; PI §200).) Surprisingly few participants in the modern debate have commented on the parallels with Wittgenstein. But they are certainly there to be drawn.

Wittgenstein's anti-mentalist conception of sensation has parallels in some modern views of consciousness and experience. Many participants in the contemporary debate about consciousness hold views that are diametrically opposed to Wittgenstein's: they take it for granted that the intrinsic character of a sensation is entirely independent of any relation to external circumstances or behaviour; that it is perfectly possible for the intrinsic quality of two people's sensations of red to be completely different, even if the two people are exactly alike in all physical and behavioural respects; and so on. But other views on those questions are close to Wittgenstein's. Some writers argue, like Wittgenstein, that we can make no sense of the idea of absolutely undetectable differences between the character of different people's sensations (see e.g. Dennett 1991). And there are influential advocates of the view that the character of a person's perceptual experience is essentially tied to the nature of her behavioural dispositions (so hearing a sound as coming from *over there*, for example, is partly constituted by the disposition to turn and look in that direction) (see e.g. Noë 2004). Broadly Wittgensteinian views of consciousness and experience like these remain serious contenders in current philosophy.

3. WITTGENSTEIN'S CONCEPTION OF PHILOSOPHY

We have reviewed a number of key themes that run through Wittgenstein's later work. And we have seen how these same themes can be found at various points in contemporary debates, where ideas that play a central role in Wittgenstein's work are still discussed as serious contributions to philosophical enquiry. Wittgenstein himself, however, would probably not have welcomed the way in which his ideas are used and developed in current work. In part, that is a matter of his distaste for professional philosophy, which he regarded as in general dishonest: driven by vanity and ambition rather than a genuine search for truth. He certainly disliked the effects of his own teaching:

> he believed that his influence as a teacher was largely harmful. He was disgusted and pained by what he observed of the half-understanding of his philosophical ideas, or a tendency towards a shallow cleverness in his students. He felt himself to be a failure as a teacher . . . . He once concluded a year's lectures with this sentence: 'The only seed that I am likely to sow is a certain jargon'.
>
> (Malcolm 1984: 53)

But another, and more serious, reason why Wittgenstein would object to the contemporary use of his ideas is that most current philosophers do not embrace his conception of the nature and source of philosophical problems, and the way they should be addressed. So even if ideas like Wittgenstein's play a part in current philosophical debates, the spirit in which they are used, he would object, is very different from the spirit in which he put them forward.

For the later Wittgenstein, as we saw in Chapter 4 section 1, philosophical problems characteristically arise when we misunderstand the 'grammar' of our language. Such misunderstandings are 'brought about, among other things, by certain analogies between the forms of expression in different regions of our language' (PI §90). So philosophical problems are to be solved:

> through an insight into the workings of our language, and that in such a way that these workings are recognized – *despite* an urge to

misunderstand them. The problems are solved, not by coming up with
new discoveries, but by assembling what we have long been familiar
with.

(PI §109)

Philosophy, on this conception, is therapeutic. It works by identifying the conceptual confusions that give rise to particular philosophical
problems. And once we avoid those confusions, we see that the philosophical problems we started with were not genuine problems at all.

Many scholars of Wittgenstein's work have embraced his view of the
character of philosophical problems. But beyond that community, few
contemporary philosophers share Wittgenstein's conception of the
source and nature of philosophical problems. No doubt some philosophical questions are prompted by misunderstandings and mistaken
assumptions. But it is hard to believe that *all* philosophical problems
are produced in that way; or that *all* philosophical problems can be
dissolved by showing that they rest on conceptual confusions. When
philosophers of language ask what the connection is between a proper
name and the person it names, for instance – what has to be true
for a given word to function as a name of a particular person – that
looks like a genuine question; it does not seem to depend on false
assumptions; and it is perfectly reasonable to think that it has a correct
answer. Similarly, when philosophers of mind ask what the difference
is between a person's relation to her own beliefs and her relation to
other people's beliefs, they are raising a perfectly good question: it does
not depend on conceptual confusion; and it is reasonable to think that
it has a right answer. (In this case, indeed, Wittgenstein's comments on
the distinctive character of one's relation to one's own beliefs are an
important contribution to giving the right answer.) The same goes for
very many other philosophical questions. So, though many contemporary philosophers agree that Wittgenstein's work contains real insights,
the majority choose to develop those insights within positive philosophical theories of their own, rather than pursuing Wittgenstein's
own official methodology.

Furthermore, many have questioned whether Wittgenstein's own
treatment of philosophical problems really is merely therapeutic. Is his
work *purely* descriptive; and how far does he succeed in eschewing *all*
positive theoretical claims? His positive views may not take the form
of what he would call 'theories': they are not reductive; they are not

systematic; they do not offer causal explanations. But they are often controversial. And they are far from obviously correct. For example, Wittgenstein sees links between the meaning of a proposition and the ways it could be verified, and between its meaning and the point or purpose of using it, which are controversial and eminently contestable; they are rejected by many philosophers of language. His views about the dependence of intentional states on a subject's participation in social practices are, again, controversial; they are rejected by individualists in the philosophy of mind. And his argument against the possibility of a private sensation language depends on an opposition to Platonism about standards of similarity and standards of correctness that is controversial and is, again, rejected by many philosophers. To say that Wittgenstein's views are controversial is not, of course, to say that they are wrong. But it does cast doubt on the extent to which his philosophy succeeds in avoiding all positive theorising.

Wittgenstein's work has not, then, brought about the radical revision in philosophy for which he hoped. Many of his views about particular issues, however, remain influential in philosophical debates. And his work is rightly read not just for its historical interest but also for its enduring insights.

SUMMARY

Wittgenstein was a great philosopher, whose work had a profound effect on twentieth-century philosophy. But views about the contemporary relevance of his ideas are sharply polarised.

Many contemporary philosophers accept the Tractarian view that meaning is to be explained in terms of truth-conditions. But the Tractarian ideas that a proposition is literally a picture of reality, and that all propositions are truth-functions of elementary propositions, have been generally abandoned.

A number of important themes run through Wittgenstein's later philosophy: anti-reductionism; anti-scientism; anti-intellectualism, and the idea that thought and language are grounded in natural, prelinguistic behaviour; anti-mentalism, and a stress on action and practice in understanding the properties of thought, language, and experience. Those themes remain central to much contemporary philosophy: sometimes under the influence of Wittgenstein's work; sometimes in ways that have developed independently of Wittgenstein. Wittgenstein would dislike the way these ideas are generally employed in current debates. For few contemporary philosophers embrace his conception of the source and nature of philosophical problems, or his therapeutic approach to their solution. But even if Wittgenstein himself would disapprove of the way they are currently used, his ideas continue to make a serious contribution at many points in contemporary philosophy.

FURTHER READING

For a comprehensive study of the influence of Wittgenstein's work on twentieth-century philosophy, and of the relations between his ideas and those of other philosophers, from an author who is very sympathetic to Wittgenstein, see:

Hacker, P. M. S. (1996) *Wittgenstein's Place in Twentieth-Century Analytic Philosophy*, Oxford: Blackwell.

There are helpful discussions of Wittgenstein's later conception of philosophy in:

Hacker, P. M. S. (1986) *Insight and Illusion: Themes in the Philosophy of Wittgenstein*, Revised Edition, Oxford: Oxford University Press, chapter 6.
McGinn, M. (1997) *Wittgenstein and the* Philosophical Investigations, London: Routledge, chapter 1.

For a more critical treatment of Wittgenstein's later methodology, see:

Dummett, M. (1977) 'Can Analytical Philosophy be Systematic, and Ought it to Be?' in Dummett, M. (1978) *Truth and Other Enigmas*, London: Duckworth.

Two recent collections, both assembled to mark the fiftieth anniversary of Wittgenstein's death in 1953, offer assessments of Wittgenstein's philosophical legacy, and illustrate the ways in which Wittgenstein's ideas are pursued in contemporary debates:

Kölbel, M. and Weiss, B. (eds) (2004) *Wittgenstein's Lasting Significance*, London: Routledge.
Zamuner, E. and Levy, D. (eds) (2009) *Wittgenstein's Enduring Arguments*, London: Routledge.

anti-essentialism The view that kinds or categories do not in general have essential properties: properties, or sets of properties, that are common to every member of the kind, and in virtue of which a thing belongs to that kind. For the anti-essentialist, there need be nothing in common to all the things that belong to a particular kind or category – other than their membership of that kind. Anti-essentialism is an important theme in *Philosophical Investigations*, where Wittgenstein argues, in opposition to the *Tractatus*, that there is no such thing as the essence of language, or the essence of a proposition. A famous illustration of the anti-essentialism of *Philosophical Investigations* is Wittgenstein's contention that there is no property that is essential to something's being a game: no property common to all and only the things that count as games. (See also: **family resemblance**.)

anti-individualism In philosophy of mind, the doctrine that a person's mental properties depend not just on her intrinsic properties – the properties she would share with any molecule-for-molecule replica: such as physical constitution, conscious phenomenology, and behavioural dispositions – but also on her physical and social environment.

anti-intellectualism Opposition to the tendency to over-emphasize the role of reasoning and conscious thought in our lives, and to represent behaviour that is really instinctive or non-rational as flowing from a process of rational contemplation. Anti-intellectualism is a pervasive theme in Wittgenstein's later philosophy, figuring prominently in his discussions of rule-following, of the acquisition and retention of belief, of the acquisition and use of language, of religious belief, of ritual and ceremonial behaviour, and so on. An important aspect of Wittgenstein's anti-intellectualism is his stress on the idea that language and thought are grounded in natural, pre-linguistic behaviour.

anti-mentalism   Opposition to **mentalism**. Wittgenstein's anti-mentalism goes hand in hand with his stress on the role of action and practice in understanding the properties of thought, language, and experience.

anti-realism about rules   See **constructivism about rules**.

anti-reductionism   Opposition to **reductionism**. Wittgenstein's anti-reductionism is a pervasive theme in his later philosophy. It runs through his discussions of meaning, intentionality, rule-following, and much else. He holds, for example, that facts about meaning cannot be explained in terms that do not presuppose meaning. And that normative facts about what counts as following a given rule correctly cannot be reduced to non-normative facts about what people agree in doing when they try to apply that rule. Anti-reductionism is nicely expressed by the motto 'everything is what it is and not another thing'.

anti-scientism   Opposition to **scientism**. Wittgenstein's anti-scientism is directed in particular at what he sees as the tendency of philosophers to apply the assumptions and methods of science to philosophical enquiry.

Cartesian view of sensations   The view that the identity conditions of sensations are purely introspective, and wholly independent of any links to external circumstances or behaviour; so it is possible 'that one section of mankind [has] one visual impression of red, and another section another' (PI §272). That view of sensations is naturally associated with the idea that sensation words get their meanings by introspective attachment to one's own sensations; so, for instance, each person knows what the word 'pain' means only from her own case. And there is a natural association, too, with the view that each person knows the nature of her own sensations with certainty, but no one can know the nature of anyone else's. Wittgenstein argues in *Philosophical Investigations* against each element of the Cartesian view.

complex proposition   In the *Tractatus*, a proposition that is made up of two or more simpler propositions.

constructivism about rules (also called anti-realism about rules)   The view that the standard of correctness for applying a rule is constructed from what we actually accept as correct when we apply that rule. For the constructivist, what counts as the correct continuation of a mathematical series at a given point is determined by what we actually accept as correct when we reach that point and continue the series. And what counts as a correct application of a descriptive word in a particular case is determined by what we actually accept as correct when we consider that case.

deflationism; quietism The philosophical stance of taking phenomena at face value, accepting that they have the features we all ordinarily take them to have, and rejecting any attempt to explain those features by appeal to a philosophical theory. Wittgenstein's later philosophy is generally deflationary or quietist in character. Some commentators argue that the *Tractatus*, too, takes a deflationary attitude to metaphysical questions.

deflationism about rules The deflationist about rules thinks that what counts as applying a rule correctly is to be taken at face value. And she holds that facts about rules and standards of correctness are basic and irreducible; they cannot be explained by appeal to any philosophical theory. Thus, the deflationist rejects the constructivist view of rules: what counts as the correct continuation of the series '+ 2' at a given point, she says, is not a matter of what we judge to be correct when we reach that point; it is a matter simply of what it is to add 2 at that point. And the deflationist rejects the Platonist's claim that there is just one way of continuing a series that is absolutely correct: absolutely simpler or more natural than any other.

elementary proposition In the *Tractatus*, an elementary proposition is the simplest kind of proposition. Elementary propositions consist of names. And they are logically independent; from the truth or falsity of one elementary proposition, nothing follows about the truth or falsity of any other elementary proposition.

empirical reality For idealists, empirical reality is reality as it appears to us: reality as it is shaped or conditioned by our concepts. It is contrasted with noumenal reality: reality as it is in itself.

essentialism The view that kinds or categories are associated with sets of essential properties, and that a thing belongs to a given kind in virtue of its possession of those essential properties. In this spirit, the *Tractatus* advances claims about, for example, the essence of a proposition, the essence of all description, and the essence of the world.

fact In the *Tractatus*, a fact is the existence of states of affairs. (Wittgenstein sometimes uses a different formulation, saying that a fact is an existing state of affairs.)

family resemblance The phrase Wittgenstein uses in *Philosophical Investigations* to characterize the relations between different instances of a category or kind whose members have no one property or set of properties in common. For example, Wittgenstein says that games form a family; the members of that family are related by 'a complex network of similarities overlapping and criss-crossing'. He calls these similarities 'family resemblances' (PI §67). In the literature, a 'family-resemblance concept' is one that picks out a category or kind of this sort: one whose instances have no one property or set of properties in common but are related in this way by family resemblances.

Gestalt Psychology A school of early-twentieth-century psychology developed by Max Wertheimer, Wolfgang Köhler, and others in opposition to **Introspectionism**. The Gestalt psychologists rejected the Introspectionist doctrine that visual experience presents us with nothing but a mosaic of shapes and colours; they held that the organization of experience into objects and patterns is itself a genuinely sensory phenomenon.

idealism The doctrine that reality is in some way conditioned by, or dependent on, our minds. Extreme versions of idealism hold that reality is entirely composed of mental phenomena: minds, and the experiences and thoughts they contain. Less extreme versions allow that there is a physical world, but hold that the form of physical reality – for example, its organization into objects – is dependent on our concepts or language.

individualism In philosophy of mind, the doctrine that a person's mental properties are determined exclusively by her intrinsic properties – the properties she would share with any molecule-for-molecule replica: such as physical make-up, conscious phenomenology, and behavioural dispositions.

intentionality The property, possessed by thought and language, of representing objects and states of affairs. Sometimes called the 'aboutness' or 'representational character' of thought and language.

Introspectionism A school of psychology developed in the late nineteenth-century by Wilhelm Wundt and others. The Introspectionists held that visual experience comprises no more than a mosaic of shapes and colours. We do not *see* the individual objects around us as objects; rather, we *take* or *interpret* this or that region of the visual field as the representation of an object. Similarly, we do not *see* a puzzle picture – the duck-rabbit figure, for example – now in one way, now in another: what changes is just the way we interpret our experience; the character of the visual experience itself remains the same throughout.

logical atomism   The label given by Russell to the view of language and reality he held at the time when he worked closely with Wittgenstein. That label is often applied to the *Tractatus* as well. Logical atomism holds that the nature of reality can be revealed by a process of logical analysis. Reality is ultimately composed of atoms, combined in various ways. But these atoms are the 'logical atoms' that are revealed by logical analysis, not the physical atoms revealed by science.

logical constants   The expressions 'and', 'not', 'or', and 'if . . . then . . . .' It is a key doctrine of the *Tractatus* that the logical constants do not stand for objects: 'My fundamental idea', says Wittgenstein, 'is that the "logical constants" are not representatives; that there can be no representatives of the *logic* of facts' (TLP: 4.0312). The logical constants tell us how propositions are combined together in complex propositions; but they do not themselves represent any element of reality.

mentalism   The view that the properties of language and thought are to be explained by appeal to the features of inner mental states. Mentalism about language explains the meanings of words by appeal to the contents of thoughts. Mentalism about thought explains the contents of thoughts by appeal to what comes before the mind of the thinker when she has those thoughts.

Moorean proposition   A term for propositions of the kind highlighted by G. E. Moore in 'A Defence of Common Sense': propositions such as 'The earth has existed for millions of years' or 'I have two hands'. Wittgenstein says in *On Certainty* that such propositions 'play a peculiar logical role' in our system of empirical propositions. They are not believed on the basis of evidence but are parts of the 'inherited background' of our enquiries; they are like 'hinges' on which our doubts turn.

noumenal reality   Reality as it is in itself. Contrasted by idealists with empirical reality: reality as it appears to us.

object   In the *Tractatus*, an object is a basic component of a state of affairs. Objects are simple: they cannot be broken down into smaller components. And they are common to all imaginable or describable worlds – and therefore, Wittgenstein thinks, to all possible worlds. Commentators disagree about the metaphysical status of Tractarian objects. Some hold that Wittgenstein takes a realist view of objects:

the division of reality into Tractarian objects is a feature of reality as it is in itself. Others interpret the *Tractatus* as a form of idealism: the division of reality into objects is an artefact of the system of language or thought we use to represent reality. A third interpretation holds that Wittgenstein takes a deflationary view of objects, rejecting both realism and idealism.

perspicuous representation   See **surveyable representation**.

picture theory   The theory of representation advanced in the *Tractatus*. A proposition, according to the *Tractatus*, is a picture of reality; it represents a state of affairs in exactly the same way as an ordinary picture. A proposition, on this view, is composed of names that are correlated with objects. The fact that the names are arranged in the particular way they are represents that the objects they stand for are arranged in the same way.

Platonism about rules   The view that the standards of correctness associated with linguistic and mathematical rules are dictated by the nature of reality. For the Platonist, there is an absolute, objective standard of what it is to continue a given mathematical series *correctly*, or what it is to go on using a particular descriptive word *in the same way as before*. And those standards are determined not by us but by reality itself.

pragmatism   The view that the meaning of a proposition is to be explained in terms of the point or function of asserting it: what it is used to achieve, or the practical consequences of asserting it. For the pragmatist, understanding a proposition is a matter of grasping its consequences or function: using it to bring about those consequences, and reacting in the right way to others' use of the proposition.

private language argument   Wittgenstein's argument, in *Philosophical Investigations* §§243–315, that there could not be a **private sensation language**. A central element in the argument is the claim that it would be impossible for the putative private linguist to establish a genuine standard of correctness for the use of his private sensation words.

private sensation language   A language that someone uses to talk about his 'inner experiences', using words that 'refer to what only the speaker can know – to his immediate private sensations' (PI §243). A speaker's private sensation language is supposed to be intelligible only to the speaker himself; no one else can understand it, for no one else can know what its words refer to. Wittgenstein argues in *Philosophical Investigations* that there could be no such language.

problem of other minds The *epistemic* problem of other minds focuses on the question: how do we *know* that other people have thoughts and experiences? The *conceptual* problem of other minds raises a prior question: how do we even *make sense of* the thought that other people have thoughts and experiences?

quietism See **deflationism**.

realism The doctrine that the general structural features of the world are determined by the nature of reality and do not depend in any way on our minds or language.

reductionism The philosophical approach of explaining phenomena of one kind in terms of phenomena of another kind, at a lower level. A reductionist about mental phenomena, for instance, might aim to reduce mental states to brain states or behavioural dispositions. A reductionist about meaning might aim to reduce facts about the meanings of words to facts about the use of words that can be stated without presupposing anything about their meanings.

referentialism The view that linguistic meaning is to be accounted for in terms of the reference of words and the truth or falsity of propositions. The *Tractatus* takes a fundamentally referentialist view of language. The repudiation of referentialism is a major theme of the early sections of *Philosophical Investigations*, which stress 'the diversity of kinds of word and sentence'.

relativism The view that the truth of a proposition, or its justification, is relative to a 'world-picture' or 'system of belief'. On this view, a proposition can be true in one system of belief but false in a different system of belief; it is never true or false *simpliciter* – true or false without qualification. Similarly, considerations that in one system of belief count as good reasons for believing a particular proposition might not count as good reasons within a different system of belief.

scientism The tendency to regard science as the only valid form of enquiry, scientific reasoning as the only genuine form of reasoning, and scientific explanation as the model for all genuine explanation.

seeing an aspect Wittgenstein's term for the phenomenon of seeing something *as such-and-such*. Examples include seeing one face *as similar to another*; seeing the duck-rabbit figure *as a picture of a duck*; seeing an illustration *as a picture of a glass cube*.

state of affairs   In the *Tractatus*, a state of affairs is a possible combination or configuration of objects.

surveyable representation   In his later work, Wittgenstein holds that philosophy aims for the kind of clarity that is produced by achieving a 'surveyable representation' (in some translations: a 'perspicuous representation') of the phenomena in question. Achieving a surveyable representation involves arranging familiar facts in a way that makes them 'surveyable'. It 'produces precisely that kind of understanding which consists in "seeing connections"': seeing relations between this phenomenon and others in such a way that what was previously puzzling becomes intelligible.

tautology   In the *Tractatus*, a complex proposition that is true for every combination of truth and falsity of its component propositions. Examples include the propositions 'p or not-p' and 'if (p and (if p then q)) then q'. The *Tractatus* holds that tautologies say nothing; they have no sense. But they are not nonsensical; they are a legitimate part of the symbolism. According to the *Tractatus*, all logical propositions are tautologies.

truth-conditional conception of meaning   The view that the meaning of a proposition is a matter of what has to be the case for it to be true. Understanding a proposition, on this view, involves knowing what must be the case if it is true.

truth-conditions   The conditions that have to obtain in order for a proposition to be true.

truth-function   A complex proposition that is composed of simpler propositions in such a way that the truth or falsity of the whole proposition is determined by the truth or falsity of the propositions that make it up.

verificationism   The view that the meaning of a proposition is to be explained in terms of the evidence that would establish its truth, or (in a more modest version) in terms of the evidence that would justify its assertion. Understanding a proposition, for the verificationist, involves knowing what would establish its truth, or what would justify asserting it.

world   In the *Tractatus*, the world is 'all that is the case'. It is 'the totality of facts, not of things'.

world-picture   The overall view of the world that, according to Wittgenstein in *On Certainty*, is 'the inherited background against which [we] distinguish between true and false' (OC: 94) and forms 'the substratum of all [our] enquiring and asserting' (OC: 162). Our world-picture in part comprises propositions that capture the general character we take the world to have – propositions that we accept as a matter of course in all our investigations: for example, that the earth has existed for millions of years, or that human beings do not grow on trees. It also involves our conception of reason and justification, our conception of what is intelligible and what stands in need of explanation, and our conception of what counts as a good explanation. Thus, for example, it is part of our world-picture that general truths can be established by observation of particular cases, and that scientific investigation gives better grounds for belief than do the pronouncements of an oracle.

Bibliography

WORKS BY OR ORIGINATING FROM WITTGENSTEIN

BB   *The Blue and Brown Books*, 2nd edition, Oxford: Blackwell, 1969.

BT   *The Big Typescript*, eds. and trans. C. Luckhardt and M. Aue, Oxford: Blackwell, 2005.

CE   'Cause and Effect: Intuitive Awareness', in Wittgenstein, *Philosophical Occasions*.

CV   *Culture and Value*, 2nd edition, ed. G. H. von Wright and H. Nyman, trans. P. Winch, Oxford: Blackwell, 1978; revised 2nd edition, ed. A. Pichler, trans. P. Winch, Oxford: Blackwell, 1998. (Quotations in the text are from the 1978 translation. But page references to both editions are supplied.)

LC   *Lectures and Conversations on Aesthetics, Psychology and Religious Belief*, ed. C. Barrett, Oxford: Blackwell, 1966.

LE   'A Lecture on Ethics', in Wittgenstein, *Philosophical Occasions*.

LFM   *Wittgenstein's Lectures on the Foundations of Mathematics, Cambridge, 1939*, ed. C. Diamond, Chicago: Chicago University Press, 1989.

LW i   *Last Writings on the Philosophy of Psychology* Volume I, eds. G. H. von Wright and H. Nyman, trans. C. Luckhardt and M. Aue, Oxford: Blackwell, 1982.

LW ii   *Last Writings on the Philosophy of Psychology* Volume II, eds. G. H. von Wright and H. Nyman, trans. C. Luckhardt and M. Aue, Oxford: Blackwell, 1992.

NB   *Notebooks 1914–1916*, 2nd edition, eds. G. H. von Wright and G. E. M. Anscombe, trans. G. E. M. Anscombe, Oxford: Blackwell, 1979.

NL   'Notes on Logic', in Wittgenstein, *Notebooks 1914–16*.

OC   *On Certainty*, eds. G. E. M. Anscombe and G. H. von Wright, trans. D. Paul and G. E. M. Anscombe, Oxford: Blackwell, 1969.

PG   *Philosophical Grammar*, ed. R. Rhees, trans. A. Kenny, Oxford: Blackwell, 1974.

PI   *Philosophical Investigations*, 4th edition, eds. P. M. S. Hacker and J. Schulte, trans. G. E. M. Anscombe, P. M. S. Hacker, and J. Schulte, Oxford: Blackwell, 2009.

PO   *Philosophical Occasions 1912–1951*, eds. J. Klagge and A. Nordmann, Indianapolis: Hackett Publishing Company, 1993.

PR   *Philosophical Remarks*, ed. R. Rhees, trans. R. Hargreaves and R. White, Oxford: Blackwell, 1975.

RC   *Remarks on Colour*, ed. G. E. M. Anscombe, trans. L. McAlister and M. Schättle, Oxford: Blackwell, 1977.

RFGB   'Remarks on Frazer's Golden Bough', in Wittgenstein, *Philosophical Occasions*.

RFM   *Remarks on the Foundations of Mathematics*, 3rd edition, eds. G. H. von Wright,

R. Rhees, and G. E. M. Anscombe, trans. G. E. M. Anscombe, Oxford: Blackwell, 1978.

RLF   'Some Remarks on Logical Form', *Proceedings of the Aristotelian Society Supplementary Volume*, 9: 162–71, 1929; reprinted in Wittgenstein, *Philosophical Occasions*.

RPP i   *Remarks on the Philosophy of Psychology* Volume I, eds. G. E. M. Anscombe and G. H. von Wright, trans. G. E. M. Anscombe, Oxford: Blackwell, 1980.

RPP ii   *Remarks on the Philosophy of Psychology* Volume II, eds. G. H. von Wright and H. Nyman, trans. C. Luckhardt and M. Aue, Oxford: Blackwell, 1980.

TLP   *Tractatus Logico-Philosophicus*, trans. D. Pears and B. McGuinness, 2nd edition, London: Routledge, 1971.

WIC   *Wittgenstein in Cambridge: Letters and Documents 1911–1951*, ed. B. McGuinness, Oxford: Blackwell, 2008.

WLC i   *Wittgenstein's Lectures: Cambridge, 1930–32*, ed. D. Lee, Oxford: Blackwell, 1980.

WLC ii   *Wittgenstein's Lectures: Cambridge, 1932–35*, ed. A. Ambrose, Oxford: Blackwell, 1979.

WVC   *Ludwig Wittgenstein and the Vienna Circle: Conversations recorded by Friedrich Waismann*, ed. B. McGuinness, trans. J. Schulte and B. McGuinness, Oxford: Blackwell, 1979.

Z   *Zettel*, 2nd edition, eds. G. E. M. Anscombe and G. H. von Wright, trans. G. E. M. Anscombe, Oxford: Blackwell, 1981.

The CD-ROM containing all of Wittgenstein's manuscript and typescript writings in the language in which they were written (mostly German, but sometimes English) is: *Wittgenstein's Nachlass: The Bergen Electronic Edition*, Oxford: Oxford University Press, 2000.

OTHER WORKS

Anscombe, G. E. M. (1959) *An Introduction to Wittgenstein's Tractatus*, London: Hutchinson University Library.

Arrington, R. (2001) '"Theology as Grammar": Wittgenstein and Some Critics', in Arrington and Addis 2001.

Arrington, R. and Addis, M. (eds) (2001) *Wittgenstein and Philosophy of Religion*, London: Routledge.

Augustine (1961) *Confessions*, trans. R. S. Pine-Coffin, Harmondsworth: Penguin Books.

Baker, G. P. and Hacker, P. M. S. (1984) *Scepticism, Rules and Language*, Oxford: Blackwell.

Baker, G. P. and Hacker, P. M. S. (2009) *Wittgenstein: Rules, Grammar and Necessity*, 2nd edition, extensively revised by P. M. S. Hacker, Oxford: Wiley-Blackwell.

Black, M. (1964) *A Companion to Wittgenstein's Tractatus*, Cambridge: Cambridge University Press.

Blackburn, S. (1984) *Spreading the Word: Groundings in the Philosophy of Language*, Oxford: Oxford University Press.

Block, I. (ed.) (1981) *Perspectives on the Philosophy of Wittgenstein*, Oxford: Blackwell.

Bloor, D. (1997) *Wittgenstein: Rules and Institutions*, London: Routledge.

Bouveresse, J. (2007) 'Wittgenstein's Critique of Frazer', *Ratio*, 20: 357–76.

Brandom, R. (2000) *Articulating Reasons: An Introduction to Inferentialism*, Cambridge, MA: Harvard University Press.

Budd, M. (1989) *Wittgenstein's Philosophy of Psychology*, London: Routledge.

Butler, J. (1914) *Fifteen Sermons Preached at the Rolls Chapel*; and *A dissertation Upon the Nature of Virtue*, with introduction, analyses and notes by W. R. Matthews, London: Bell.

Canfield, J. (1996) 'The Community View', *Philosophical Review*, 469–88.

Clack, B. (1999) *An Introduction to Wittgenstein's Philosophy of Religion*, Edinburgh: Edinburgh University Press.

Clack, B. (2001) 'Wittgenstein and Magic', in Arrington and Addis 2001.

Conant, J. (1989) 'Must We Show What We Cannot Say?', in R. Fleming and M. Payne (eds) *The Senses of Stanley Cavell*, Lewisberg, PA: Bucknell University Press.

Coope, C., Geach, P., Potts, T., and White, R. (1971) *A Wittgenstein Workbook*, Oxford: Blackwell.

Craig, E. (1990) *Knowledge and the State of Nature*, Oxford: Oxford University Press.

Crary, A. and Read, R. (eds) (2000) *The New Wittgenstein*, London: Routledge.

Davidson, D. (1982) 'Rational Animals', *Dialectica*, 36, 317–27.

Davidson, D. (1988) 'The Myth of the Subjective', in Davidson, *Subjective, Intersubjective, Objective*, Oxford: Oxford University Press, 2001.

Day, W. and Krebs, V. (eds) (2010) *Seeing Wittgenstein Anew*, Cambridge: Cambridge University Press.

Dennett, D. (1991) *Consciousness Explained*, Boston, MA: Little, Brown.

Diamond, C. (1991a) 'Throwing Away the Ladder: How to Read the *Tractatus*', in Diamond, *The Realistic Spirit*, Cambridge, MA: MIT Press.

Diamond, C. (1991b) 'Ethics, Imagination and the Method of Wittgenstein's *Tractatus*', in R. Heinrich and H. Vetter (eds) *Wiener Riehe: Themen der Philosophie*, Vienna: Oldenbourg; reprinted in Crary and Read 2000.

Drury, M. O'C. (1981) 'Some Notes on Conversations with Wittgenstein' and 'Conversations with Wittgenstein', in R. Rhees (ed.) 1991.

Dummett, M. (1959) 'Wittgenstein's Philosophy of Mathematics', *Philosophical Review* 68: 324–48; reprinted in Dummett 1978.

Dummett, M. (1977) 'Can Analytical Philosophy be Systematic, and Ought it to Be?' in Dummett 1978.

Dummett, M. (1978) *Truth and Other Enigmas*, London: Duckworth.

Dummett, M. (1981) 'Wittgenstein and Frege', in Block 1981.

Dummett, M. (1993) 'Wittgenstein on Necessity: Some Reflections', in Dummett, *The Seas of Language*, Oxford: Oxford University Press.

Dummett, M. (1994) 'Reply to Pears', in B. McGuinness and G. Oliveri (eds) *The Philosophy of Michael Dummett*, Dordrecht: Kluwer.

Engelmann, P. (1967) *Letters from Ludwig Wittgenstein with a Memoir*, ed. B. McGuinness, trans. L. Furtmüller, Oxford: Blackwell.

Finkelstein, D. (2003) *Expression and the Inner*, Cambridge, MA: Harvard University Press.

Fogelin, R. (1996) 'Wittgenstein's Critique of Philosophy', in H. Sluga and D. Stern 1996.

Frazer, J. (1994) *The Golden Bough: A Study in Magic and Religion*, new abridged edition, ed. R. Fraser, Oxford: Oxford University Press. (Third edition first published in 12 volumes, London: Macmillan, 1906–15.)

Frege, G. (1964) *The Basic Laws of Arithmetic*, ed. and trans. M. Furth, Los Angeles: University of California Press.

Hacker, P. M. S. (1986) *Insight and Illusion: Themes in the Philosophy of Wittgenstein*, Revised Edition, Oxford: Oxford University Press.

Hacker, P. M. S. (1993) *Wittgenstein: Meaning and Mind: Part II Exegesis*, Oxford: Blackwell.

Hacker, P. M. S. (1996) *Wittgenstein's Place in Twentieth-Century Analytic Philosophy*, Oxford: Blackwell.

Hacker, P. M. S. (2000) 'Was He Trying to Whistle It?', in Crary and Read 2000.

Hurka, T. (2006) 'Games and the Good', *Proceedings of the Aristotelian Society, Supplementary Volume*, 80: 217–35.

Ishiguro, H. (1969) 'Use and Reference of Names', in P. Winch (ed) *Studies in the Philosophy of Wittgenstein*, London: Routledge.

James, W. (1890) *The Principles of Psychology*, Cambridge, MA: Harvard University Press, 1983.

Janik, A. and Toulmin, S. (1973) *Wittgenstein's Vienna*, London: Weidenfeld and Nicolson.

Johnston, P. (1989) *Wittgenstein and Moral Philosophy*, London: Routledge.

Kenny, A. (1981) 'Wittgenstein's Early Philosophy of Mind', in Block 1981.

Kober, M. (1996) 'Certainties of a World-Picture: The Epistemological Investigations of *On Certainty*', in Sluga and Stern 1996.

Koffka, K. (1935) *Principles of Gestalt Psychology*, London: Kegan Paul, Trench, Trübner & Co.

Köhler, W. (1947) *Gestalt Psychology*, New York: Liveright Publishing Company.

Kölbel, M. and Weiss, B. (eds) (2004) *Wittgenstein's Lasting Significance*, London: Routledge.

Kripke, S. (1982) *Wittgenstein on Rules and Private Language*, Oxford: Blackwell.

Kusch, M. (2006) *A Sceptical Guide to Meaning and Rules*, Chesham, Bucks: Acumen.

Lewis, D. (1983) 'New Work for a Theory of Universals', *Australasian Journal of Philosophy*, 61: 343–77.

Lewis, D. (1984) 'Putnam's Paradox', *Australasian Journal of Philosophy*, 62: 221–36.

McDowell, J. (1984) 'Wittgenstein on Following a Rule', *Synthese* 58: 325–63; reprinted in McDowell 1998, and in A. Miller and C. Wright (eds) *Rule-Following and Meaning*, Chesham: Acumen, 2002.

McDowell, J. (1992) 'Meaning and Intentionality in Wittgenstein's Later Philosophy', in P. French, T. Uehling, and H. Wettstein (eds) *Midwest Studies in Philosophy XVII: The Wittgenstein Legacy*, Notre Dame: University of Notre Dame Press; reprinted in McDowell 1998.

McDowell, J. (1994) *Mind and World*, Cambridge, MA: Harvard University Press.

McDowell, J. (1998) *Mind, Value and Reality*, Cambridge, MA: Harvard University Press.

McGinn, C. (1984) *Wittgenstein on Meaning: An Interpretation and Evaluation*, Oxford: Blackwell.

McGinn, M. (1989) *Sense and Certainty*, Oxford: Blackwell.

McGinn, M. (1997) *Wittgenstein and the Philosophical Investigations*, London: Routledge.

McGinn, M. (2006) *Elucidating the* Tractatus, Oxford: Oxford University Press.

McGuinness, B. (1981) 'The So-Called Realism of the *Tractatus*', in Block 1981; reprinted as 'The Supposed Realism of the *Tractatus*', in B. McGuinness, *Approaches to Wittgenstein*, London: Routledge, 2002.

McGuinness, B. (1988) *Wittgenstein: A Life – Young Ludwig 1889–1921*, London: Duckworth; reprinted by Penguin Books, Harmondsworth, 1990.

McManus, D. (ed.) (2004) *Wittgenstein and Scepticism*, London: Routledge.

Malcolm, N. (1984) *LudwigWittgenstein:A Memoir*, 2nd edition, Oxford: Oxford University Press.

Malcolm, N. (1986) *Nothing is Hidden*, Oxford: Blackwell.

Malcolm, N. (1993) *Wittgenstein:A Religious Point ofView?*, London: Routledge.

Monk, R. (1990) *Wittgenstein:The Duty of Genius*, London: Jonathan Cape.

Moore, G. E. (1903) *Principia Ethica*, Cambridge: Cambridge University Press.

Moore, G. E. (1925) 'A Defence of Common Sense', in J. Muirhead (ed.) *Contemporary British Philosophy* (Second Series), London: George Allen & Unwin; reprinted in Moore 1993.

Moore, G. E. (1939) 'Proof of an External World', in *Proceedings of the British Academy* 25: 273–300; reprinted in Moore 1993.

Moore, G. E. (1954–55) 'Wittgenstein's Lectures in 1930–33', Mind, 63: 1–15, 289–315, and Mind, 64: 1–27, 264; reprinted in Wittgenstein, *Philosophical Occasions*.

Moore, G. E. (1993) *SelectedWritings*, ed.T. Baldwin, London: Routledge.

Morris, M. (2008) *Wittgenstein and the Tractatus Logico-Philosophicus*, London: Routledge.

Mounce, H. (1981) *An Introduction toWittgenstein's Tractatus*, Oxford: Blackwell.

Moyal-Sharrock, D. (2004) *UnderstandingWittgenstein's On Certainty*, Basingstoke: Palgrave Macmillan.

Moyal-Sharrock, D. and Brenner, W. (eds) (2005) *Readings ofWittgenstein's On Certainty*, Basingstoke: Palgrave Macmillan.

Mulhall, S. (2001) 'Seeing Aspects', in H.-J. Glock (ed.) *Wittgenstein: A Critical Reader*, Oxford: Blackwell.

Mulhall, S. (2007) *Wittgenstein's Private Language:Grammar, Nonsense,and Imagination in Philosophical Investigations* §§243–315, Oxford: Oxford University Press.

Nielsen, K. (1967) 'Wittgensteinian Fideism', Philosophy, 42: 191–209.

Nielsen, K. (2001) 'Wittgenstein and Wittgensteinians on Religion', in Arrington and Addis 2001.

Noë, A. (2004) *Action in Perception*, Cambridge, MA: MIT Press.

Ogden, C. K. and Richards, I. A. (1923) *The Meaning of Meaning*, London: Routledge & Kegan Paul.

Passmore, J. (1966) *A HundredYears of Philosophy*, London: Duckworth.

Pears, D. (1987) *The False Prison: A Study of the Development ofWittgenstein's Philosophy*, vol. 1, Oxford: Oxford University Press.

Pears, D. (1988) *The False Prison: A Study of the Development ofWittgenstein's Philosophy*, vol. 2, Oxford: Oxford University Press.

Phillips, D. Z. (1981) 'Belief, Change, and Forms of Life:The Confusions of Externalism and Internalism', in F. Crosson (ed.) *The Autonomy of Religious Belief*, Notre Dame: University of Notre Dame Press.

Proops, I. (2001) 'The New Wittgenstein: A Critique', European Journal of Philosophy, 9: 375–404.

Proops, I. (2004) 'Wittgenstein on the Substance of the World', European Journal of Philosophy, 12: 106–26.

Quine, W.V. (1960) *Word and Object*, Cambridge, MA: MIT Press.

Rhees, R. (ed.) (1981) *LudwigWittgenstein: Personal Recollections*, Oxford: Blackwell.

Ricketts, T. (1996) 'Pictures, Logic, and the Limits of Sense in Wittgenstein's *Tractatus*', in Sluga and Stern 1996.

Russell, B. (1903) *The Principles of Mathematics*, London: Allen & Unwin.

Russell, B. (1910) 'On the Nature of Truth and Falsehood', in Russell's *Philosophical Essays*, London: Routledge, 1994.

Russell, B. (1912) *The Problems of Philosophy*, Oxford: Oxford University Press, 1976.

Russell, B. (1913) *Theory of Knowledge: The 1913 Manuscript*, London: Routledge, 1984.

Russell, B. (1914) 'The Relation of Sense-Data to Physics', reprinted in Russell, *Mysticism and Logic*, London: Routledge, 1989.

Russell, B. (1918) 'The Philosophy of Logical Atomism', reprinted in Russell, *Logic and Knowledge: Essays 1901–1950*, London: Allen & Unwin, 1956.

Russell, B. (1921) *The Analysis of Mind*, London: Allen & Unwin.

Russell, B. (1922) 'Introduction', in Wittgenstein *Tractatus Logico-Philosophicus*.

Russell, B. (1959) *My Philosophical Development*, London: Allen & Unwin.

Sheffer, H. (1913) 'A Set of Five Independent Postulates for Boolean Algebras, with Application to Logical Constants', *Transactions of the American Mathematical Society*, 14: 481–8.

Sluga, H. and Stern, D. (eds) (1996) *The Cambridge Companion to Wittgenstein*, Cambridge: Cambridge University Press.

Stern, D. (2004) *Wittgenstein's Philosophical Investigations: An Introduction*, Cambridge: Cambridge University Press.

Stern, D. (2010) 'Another Strand in the Private Language Argument', in A. Ahmed (ed.) *Wittgenstein's Philosophical Investigations: A Critical Guide*, Cambridge: Cambridge University Press.

Stroud, B. (2001) 'Private Objects, Physical Objects, and Ostension', in D. Charles and W. Child (eds) *Wittgensteinian Themes: Essays in Honour of David Pears*, Oxford: Oxford University Press; also available in Stroud, B., *Meaning, Understanding, and Practice*, Oxford: Oxford University Press, 2000.

Suits, B. (1978) *The Grasshopper: Games, Life and Utopia*, Toronto: University of Toronto Press.

Sullivan, P. (2004) 'What is the *Tractatus* about?', in M. Kölbel and B. Weiss (eds) *Wittgenstein's Lasting Significance*, London: Routledge.

Thomas, K. (1978) *Religion and the Decline of Magic*, Harmondsworth: Penguin.

von Wright, G. H. (1955) 'Ludwig Wittgenstein: A Biographical Sketch', *Philosophical Review* 64: 527–45; reprinted in Malcolm 1984.

von Wright, G. H. (1993) 'The Wittgenstein Papers', in Wittgenstein, *Philosophical Occasions*.

Wertheimer, M. (1944) 'Gestalt Theory', *Social Research* 11: 78–99.

White, R. (2006) *Wittgenstein's Tractatus Logico-Philosophicus: A Reader's Guide*, London: Continuum.

Williams, M. (2004) 'Wittgenstein's Refutation of Idealism', in D. McManus (ed.) *Wittgenstein and Scepticism*.

Williamson, T. (2000) *Knowledge and Its Limits*, Oxford: Oxford University Press.

Wittgenstein, H. (1981) 'My Brother Ludwig', in Rhees 1981.

Wright, C. (1980) *Wittgenstein on the Foundations of Mathematics*, London: Duckworth.

Wright, C. (2004) 'Wittgensteinian Certainties', in McManus 2004.

Wundt, W. (1907) *Outlines of Psychology*, Leipzig: Engelmann.

Zamuner, E. and Levy, D. (eds) (2009) *Wittgenstein's Enduring Arguments*, London: Routledge.